"Eddie Robinson was the most underrated and best clutch hitter I ever played against."

—Ted Williams, Hall of Fame outfielder for the Boston Red Sox

"What can you say about Eddie? Good baseball man and a pretty good left-handed hitter in his day. He was one of our first basemen in the '50s and fit in real good."

—Yogi Berra, Hall of Fame catcher for the New York Yankees

"Eddie Robinson was general manager when I was asked to manage the Orioles' 1960 Winter Instructional League team. He took me under his wing and showed me just by being himself how a Major Leaguer should act. When I later became the Orioles' manager, all the things I learned from him were invaluable to my future successes."

—Earl Weaver, Hall of Fame manager for the Baltimore Orioles

"Eddie Robinson and I worked together for about six years when I was a managing partner of the Texas Rangers baseball team. Eddie is The Big Easy—easy smile, easy to have fun, easy to be a great friend. He had a keen eye for talent and the ability to spot a player's strengths and his weaknesses."

—Brad Corbett, former owner of the Texas Rangers

"Eddie Robinson gave me an opportunity to work with him as assistant farm director for the Colt 45s. It was on-the-job training, and I thank him for taking a chance and believing in me."

—Pat Gillick, former general manager of the Toronto Blue Jays, the Baltimore Orioles, the Seattle Mariners, and the Philadelphia Phillies

"Eddie Robinson was a fine ballplayer. He had a remarkably long, fascinating, and colorful career as a baseball scout and front-office man for many big league teams. I know of no book that gives as much insight into the front-office machinations in baseball organizations. [Eddie Robinson's] autobiography will interest people inside baseball who remember Eddie, and many others will enjoy reading about the experiences of men who've been in the game."

—Charles C. Alexander, author of *Ty Cobb*

T0366493

# Lucky Me

Eddie Robinson with the Baltimore Orioles in 1946, the year he beat out Jackie Robinson and Bobby Brown to win the International League Most Valuable Player Award.

# Lucky Me

## MY SIXTY-FIVE YEARS IN BASEBALL

*Eddie Robinson*
*with C. Paul Rogers III*

Foreword by Tom Grieve
Introduction by Bobby Brown

UNIVERSITY OF NEBRASKA PRESS
*Lincoln and London*

© 2011 by Eddie Robinson and C. Paul Rogers III
Foreword © 2011 by Tom Grieve
Introduction © 2011 by Bobby Brown
Afterword © 2015 by C. Paul Rogers III

All rights reserved
Manufactured in the United States of America

First Nebraska paperback printing: 2015

Library of Congress Cataloging-in-Publication Data
Robinson, Eddie, 1920–
Lucky me: my sixty-five years in baseball / Eddie Robinson, with C. Paul Rogers III;
foreword by Tom Grieve; introduction by Bobby Brown.
pages   cm
Includes index.
ISBN 978-0-8032-7411-2 (paper: alk. paper)
1. Robinson, Eddie, 1920– 2. Baseball players—United States—Biography.
3. Baseball managers—United States—Biography. 4. Major League Baseball (Organization)—History—20th century. 5. Major League Baseball
(Organization)—History—21st century. I. Rogers, C. Paul. II. Title.
GV865.R587R6 2015
796.357092—dc23
[B]
2015019114

*To Bette, a big-leaguer in every way.*

**EDDIE ROBINSON**


*For the special women in my life: Julie;
mother Leigh; and daughters Heather, Jillian,
and Ruthie. None of them care a whit
about baseball but they all support my passion
for the game and its history.*

**C. PAUL ROGERS III**

# CONTENTS

Foreword by Tom Grieve | ix
Author's Preface | xiii
Introduction by Bobby Brown | xv

**Chapter 1** *Paris, Texas, Roots* .................................................................... 1
**Chapter 2** *Breaking into Pro Ball* ................................................................ 7
**Chapter 3** *Making Progress* ........................................................................ 13
**Chapter 4** *A Taste of the Big Time and a World War II Detour* ................ 21
**Chapter 5** *International League MVP* ........................................................ 35
**Chapter 6** *Big League Rookie* .................................................................... 41
**Chapter 7** *A Magical Year in Cleveland* .................................................... 51
**Chapter 8** *An All-Star Year in Washington* .............................................. 71
**Chapter 9** *With the Pale Hose* .................................................................... 79
**Chapter 10** *A Year in Purgatory, er, Philadelphia* .................................... 93
**Chapter 11** *From the Outhouse to the Penthouse* .................................... 103
**Chapter 12** *Fun and Games with the Yankees* .......................................... 117
**Chapter 13** *Playing Out the String* .......................................................... 123
**Chapter 14** *Coaching with Paul Richards and the Orioles* ...................... 129
**Chapter 15** *The Move to Houston and the Start of the Expansion Colt .45s* ... 143
**Chapter 16** *On to Kansas City and Charlie Finley* .................................... 157
**Chapter 17** *Back to the National League with the Atlanta Braves* .......... 163
**Chapter 18** *Fun and Games with Ted Turner* ............................................ 183
**Chapter 19** *Home to Texas* ........................................................................ 189
**Chapter 20** *The Eddie Chiles Era* .............................................................. 203
**Chapter 21** *Working for George* ................................................................ 215
**Chapter 22** *Team Consultant—The Last Stage* ........................................ 219

Retrospective | 225
Afterword | 229
Acknowledgments | 233
Index | 235

# FOREWORD

What do a surprising draft pick, one of the biggest trades ever—eleven players involved at a baseball winter meeting—and a silver bullet have in common? Each played a part in my relationship with Eddie Robinson, one that has endured now for more than four decades. I can only hope it has been as rewarding for Eddie as it has been for me.

Our relationship started in 1966. I was an eighteen-year-old kid about to graduate from Pittsfield (Mass.) High School when I got a call from Eddie Robinson, who was with the Kansas City A's. He wanted to fly to Pittsfield with the A's major league batting practice pitcher, Cot Deal, to watch me hit before the amateur draft in June.

Like most kids who grew up in the sixties and followed baseball, I collected baseball cards. I knew who Eddie Robinson was, knew he had played for the New York Yankees, my favorite team. Having him come to my hometown to see me hit was a big deal. I'd been scouted by other teams at games I'd played, but none had shown this kind of interest.

I'd been offered a baseball scholarship from the University of Michigan, but I was thinking about going to Dartmouth, where I could play baseball and Ivy League football. What I really hoped was that I would get drafted and be offered enough money to sign but if that didn't happen, I was prepared to go to college. Either way would be great.

The day Eddie Robinson came to Pittsfield was like a hitter's dream. Cot Deal threw every pitch down the middle of the plate. I was so pumped up, I think the first fifteen or so pitches I hit were pulled foul down the left-field line.

From behind the batting cage Eddie told me, "You're swinging fine, just relax and hit the ball back through the middle." From that point it was probably the best batting practice session I'd ever had.

The Mets had the No. 1 pick and everyone expected them to take Arizona State University outfielder Reggie Jackson. The A's had the second pick.

After I took my cuts off Deal, I remember Eddie saying to me, "Don't let anyone change your swing." He told me there was a chance the A's would select me with their pick.

Plans changed though. Pretty much everyone in baseball was shocked when the Mets passed on Reggie, taking California high school catcher Steve Chilcott instead. When Reggie fell into their laps, the A's selected him with their second pick.

Four picks later the Washington Senators called my name, and the rest, as they say, is history.

It took ten years, but eventually I wound up playing for Eddie anyway. We renewed our relationship in 1976 when he became general manager of the Texas Rangers early that season. I'd moved to Texas when the Senators relocated there from Washington in 1972, and '76 turned out to be a pretty good year for me. But after being injured and playing only seventy-nine games in 1977 I was one of six Rangers players included by Robinson and owner Brad Corbett in a confusing, eleven-player, four-team trade with the Mets, Pirates, and Braves that brought Jon Matlack and Al Oliver, among others, back to the Rangers.

The end of my relationship with Eddie Robinson? Hardly. After I was released by the St. Louis Cardinals in May of 1979, one of the first calls I got was from Eddie, who asked me to sign a free agent deal with Texas and report to Tucson to play for the Rangers' Triple A club there. After a mediocre season in Tucson, I returned home to Texas at the end of August. I needed some time to contemplate my future, and I wasn't sure it would be on the ball field.

When the phone rang one day in late September, I suppose I shouldn't have been surprised to hear Eddie's voice once again. He had called to invite me to join him and owner Brad Corbett in the owners' suite for the final game of the 1979 major league season. As we watched the game together, they presented me with an opportunity to start a new career in the Rangers' front office. It wasn't something I needed to take a long time to think about. I quickly accepted the offer.

Interestingly, I wasn't the only "free agent" Brad and Eddie were wooing that day. Also sitting with us that Sunday afternoon was Clayton Moore, better known as the "Lone Ranger." Corbett offered Moore $5,000 per appearance to represent the team and ride his famed white horse Silver (or his stand-in) for six dates during the 1980 season. It didn't take a lot of calculating for me to realize that Clayton Moore would be making ten grand more than I would for about a week's work while I'd be in the office every day. Then again, I didn't ride a white horse or twirl six-shooters with both hands either.

"The Lone Ranger" left the game early to catch his flight that day, but as we were departing a few innings later, we noticed his signature calling card on the counter—a single silver bullet.

My first job in baseball off the playing field was as director of group sales and then assistant farm and scouting director of the Rangers while Eddie continued to serve as the team's general manager. I admired him then, as I do now. He was thorough in his deliberations, extremely well organized, and a baseball innovator, which was amply demonstrated in 1982 when he hired sabermetrician Craig Wright, when most teams had no idea what a sabermetrician was.

With Eddie Robinson, I would touch all the bases in baseball. He scouted me, traded me, signed me as a free agent, and gave me my first job in the baseball front office. From a relationship standpoint, that goes down on my personal scorecard as a grand slam.

*Tom Grieve, former Texas Rangers general manager*
*and current Rangers broadcaster*

## AUTHOR'S PREFACE

I've thought about writing a book about my career in baseball for the past twenty years or so, starting when I was working for George Steinbrenner and the New York Yankees in the 1980s. I even had a title all picked out: *And Now I Work for George.* I'd been closely associated with and in the employ of so many colorful baseball personalities, like Bill Veeck, Paul Richards, Judge Roy Hofheinz, Charlie Finley, Ted Turner, Brad Corbett, and Eddie Chiles, during my career that it seemed only fitting I should end up working for Steinbrenner, one of baseball's most controversial characters.

I kept delaying writing my memoirs, however, and finally decided that my time had passed and that my story wouldn't generate much interest anymore. But friends both inside and out of baseball kept encouraging me to tell the story of my sixty-five years in the game. It is true that I've witnessed firsthand all the changes in our great game (not all the changes are great, however) and had the opportunity to play with or work for many of the legends of baseball. The enthusiasm of my friends rekindled my own and then I met Paul Rogers, my collaborator on this book, who loves the stories and oral history of baseball, and all the pieces of the puzzle seemed to fall into place.

I began playing professional baseball in 1939 and officially retired from my last baseball job in 2004. It almost goes without saying that I owe all of my good fortune to our National Pastime. Baseball got me far from my east Texas hometown of Paris during the Great Depression, was responsible for my happening to be on a train when I met my future wife Bette, my lifetime partner, and enabled me to comfortably raise a great family and have many wonderful experiences. I was lucky enough to play on a World

Championship team, managed to make four American League All-Star teams, played for seven of the eight American League teams, including two seasons with the New York Yankees, and then was able to transition to coaching, scouting, and the front office for my second career in baseball.

I didn't travel this path alone. All along the way I was helped by or mentored by men who took an interest in me. Some of these folks are not well known, such as Charlie Osborne and Pop Nobles from Paris, Texas, while others, such as Bill Veeck, Paul Richards, and Ted Turner, are famous, at least in baseball circles. Although what follows is my story, it's also a tribute to those men who paved the way for me.

# INTRODUCTION

ddie Robinson spent sixty-five years in professional baseball. He has been a minor league player, a major league player, a coach, a farm director, a general manager, a scout, and a consultant. During the past sixty-four years I have at times been an opponent and a teammate but, most importantly, at all times Eddie has been my good and special friend.

Eddie's playing career began prior to World War II, but was interrupted by three years in the U.S. Navy, and resumed postwar during the forties and fifties. It was during this latter period that he became one of the elite power hitters in the American League. He is one of the few hitters to hit a home run completely out of Chicago's Comiskey Park. As gigantic as that home run was, it was dwarfed by a home run he hit for Baltimore against my 1946 Newark team in the International League. Baltimore at that time was playing in a football stadium with a very short left field and a high fence, and a right field that had no fence and seemed about a quarter of a mile long. Eddie hit a home run about sixty feet over the head of our right fielder, Hal Douglas, that shot about two hundred feet beyond him. The ball rolled all the way to the steps of a temporary clubhouse in deep, deep right field. Eddie at best was a below average runner, but he had circled the bases and was sitting in his dugout by the time Douglas had retrieved the ball.

Eddie played on seven of the eight American League clubs. He played on good teams, mediocre teams, and bad teams. He participated in All-Star and World Series games. He played for many managers—some very good, some good, some fair, and some who struggled. He played for some managers who could and did communicate, some who remained quiet, some who were colorful and outgoing, and some he didn't appreciate.

He played and worked for a variety of owners. Some were public figures, unpredictable, often bombastic, and always in the papers (Ted Turner in Atlanta, George Steinbrenner with the Yankees, and Charlie Finley, Kansas City). Some were quiet, respectful, and remained behind the scenes (Connie Mack—Philadelphia and Clark Griffith—Washington). Some were steady, soft spoken, considerate, and wise, who left baseball matters to their baseball people (Dan Topping and Del Webb—Yankees, Walter O. Briggs and John Fetzer—Detroit, and Carl Pohlad—Minnesota). Some were lovable, fun loving, smart, and very supportive (Bill Veeck—Cleveland and Brad Corbett—Texas Rangers).

He has witnessed and in some instances participated in the important events that erupted in baseball over the past forty years. Eddie observed the birth of the players union and watched it become the most powerful entity in baseball. He endured all of the player strikes, witnessed the advent of free agency, the maturation of the TV monster, the entrance and proliferation of player agents, the escalation of player salaries and ticket prices, the cancellation of a World Series, the temporary halt of a World Series because of an earthquake (San Francisco, 1989), the sad era of the hard drugs contamination (1980s cocaine, heroin, amphetamines), and the steroid scandals.

Eddie has seen and experienced it all. He describes it vividly and accurately, sometimes with humor, sometimes with sadness, and occasionally with anger. He tells stories, relates anecdotes, and provides opinions.

This book is the remarkable tale of a small-town east Texas boy who at a tender age was introduced to the game of baseball and then never left it. Eddie's life in baseball is a real American success story. Read it—you will enjoy it.

*Bobby Brown, former New York Yankees third baseman,*
*cardiologist, and retired president of the American League*

# Lucky Me

*Chapter 1*
## PARIS, TEXAS, ROOTS

W hen I was a youngster, getting a contract to play professional baseball was beyond my imagination. There's no way I ever could have envisioned myself as general manager of a major league club, and giving advice to owners. My high school didn't even field a baseball team when I was a kid growing up. That was during the Depression. Times were so bad people didn't have money to spend on clothes or movies. Whatever we had went toward necessities. If we got a new baseball, we played with it until the cover came off. Then we taped it up and played with it some more.

I was born on December 15, 1920, in Paris, a small farming town of fifteen thousand in northeast Texas, a few miles south of the Red River and the Oklahoma state line. My folks were Hazel and Ed Robinson, who were loving parents. Since I was an only child I received a lot of attention during my early years. My father owned a prosperous auto repair business, and my mother was a homemaker, spending her days gardening, taking care of the house, and looking after me.

We lived peacefully until 1929 when the Great Depression hit. Times got tough very quickly. My father started drinking heavily and soon lost his business. About two years later, when I was twelve, my parents separated and divorced. My mother and I moved in with my grandmother and my mother's brother, Uncle Herbert. It was a struggle financially. The four of us worked at various jobs to make enough money to survive. I picked cotton every summer for a half cent a pound. The most I ever picked in one day was one hundred pounds; I made all of fifty cents that day. I also collected Coca-Cola bottles and turned them in for the one-cent deposit. That meant I could pay my way into a movie once in a while and could get a fifteen-cent haircut when I needed one.

My favorite Western star was Tom Mix, with his horse Tony. I also liked Gene Autry and Roy Rogers. The family's favorite radio show was Major Edward Bowes's "Amateur Hour" on Sunday night. I still remember the phone number to call in to vote—Murrayhill 8-9933. We also enjoyed "The Shadow," "Little Orphan Annie," "The Secret Three," and "Jack Armstrong, the All-American Boy." Every afternoon I'd stop whatever game I was playing, come inside, and lie down in front of the radio to listen to my favorite shows. I wanted to be a Western movie star when I grew up.

For fun my best friend Pee Wee Griffin and I hunted rabbits for meat for our families' dinner. We called the rabbits "Hoover Hogs" since Herbert Hoover was president and many people thought he'd brought on the Depression. One Christmas all Santa brought me was a box of .22 shells so that I could shoot more rabbits. My grandmother had to borrow five dollars from the local bootlegger so we could have Christmas dinner that year.

During the school year I attended the First Ward Elementary School. I liked school and made good grades. The first time I ever thought about playing baseball was in grammar school when I was about eleven years old. During recess we played softball, and I soon became one of the better players. I was the catcher and discovered I was a good hitter. My claim to fame was that I was the only kid who could hit the ball over the right field fence. From the beginning I threw right-handed but always hit from the left side. I don't know why; I guess I was just more comfortable that way.

At the end of grammar school in 1931 my school had an assembly to honor the seventh graders who were graduating and going on to high school. The teachers read their predictions of what they thought each student would become. When they came to me they said I'd play baseball for the New York Yankees. I guess those Paris, Texas, grammar school teachers were pretty perceptive.

There was a park near my home where folks played baseball, tennis, croquet, and volleyball. We called the baseball field the Thirty-second Street diamond. It had a large wire backstop, dirt infield, and a nice grass outfield but no fences. We had to drag, rake, and wet down the infield before every game. When the game began each infielder had to smooth the ground in front of his position as well as he could with his spiked baseball shoes, but bad bounces were common.

Growing up, I was fortunate to have Charlie Osborne as a neighbor. Since we had no high school baseball, Charlie put together a team so that his son Charlie Jr. and the rest of us would have a team to play on. Charlie Osborne became the first significant man in my life because he started me on the road to becoming a professional baseball player. Charlie's players were all between fourteen and twenty years old and played teams from neighboring towns. We became fondly known as Charlie Osborne's Cubs.

At first, I wasn't old enough to play on Charlie's team, but I worked out with them, and I was pretty good. So as some of the fellows left the team, some of us younger players moved in. I played first base. I didn't have a strong arm, but I was a pretty good hitter.

We played on Sundays and practiced during the week. Small towns in those days all had a baseball team. We played in the towns around Paris, or other town teams came in and played us. We didn't have uniforms. We just played in our overalls or tattered trousers. We were lucky to have equipment. In fact, we used to take up a collection at the games on Sunday to help buy balls and bats. If we broke a bat, we would nail it together and use it some more.

When the Cubs' original first baseman moved away from Paris, I became the new first sacker at the ripe old age of fourteen. For six dollars, which was a small fortune, I'd bought a new Bill Doak glove to play the outfield. I was paying it off at fifty cents a week. I couldn't afford a first baseman's mitt too, so I just played first base with my fielder's glove.

The Cubs held their own with the nearby towns, winning more games than we lost. I became the best hitter on the team and began to dream of playing professional baseball after I'd graduated from college. My parents had instilled in me the need to get a college education to succeed in life. My cousin George Robinson was attending the University of Texas in Austin and seemed to be having a good time, so I thought I might want to go there, too.

I enjoyed all sports as a kid and played football and basketball and participated in the field part of track and field for the Paris High Wildcats. I played center for the football team and made all-district. I was a decent basketball player and won medals in the discus and javelin in track. But baseball was always my favorite and best sport.

During my high school years my family continued to struggle to make ends meet. My uncle Louis Robinson owned the Northeast Texas Motor Freight Line, a prosperous business with big six-wheeler trucks that hauled freight from Paris to Dallas and Texarkana. When I turned sixteen, I started working for his freight line, loading trucks beginning at 5 a.m. and delivering produce and pharmaceuticals to local grocery and drug stores before 8 a.m. For the remainder of my high school days, my schedule never changed. A taxi would pick me up at my house at 4:45 a.m. For ten cents, the taxi drove me to the freight line where I worked until 8 a.m. Then I went to school all day and after school practiced whatever sport was in season. I'd be home for dinner and then manage to see my steady girlfriend, June Rowland, almost every night. I made six dollars a week at the freight line, which included working all day Saturday. It was a tough schedule, but thanks to the boundless energy of youth I managed to handle it.

I played for Charlie's Cubs in 1935 and 1936, my freshman and sophomore years of high school. Paris also had a semipro team called the Coca-Cola Bottlers. The Bottlers played once a week against tougher competition than the Cubs. The Coca-Cola Company sponsored the team, which wore fancy red satin uniforms. The Bottlers had no shortage of bats and balls and played their home games at a former professional field with a wooden grandstand, outfield fences, and a much better playing field. The Bottlers were managed by Pop Nobles, who owned a domino parlor and confectionery store in town.

I hated like the devil to leave Charlie Osborne. But Pop Nobles told me I'd have a much better chance of being seen by a professional scout if I played for the Bottlers. Pop didn't know much about managing a team, but he was able to recruit good players. The Bottlers went to the state semipro tournament every year, and that tournament drew a number of major league scouts.

When I went over to the Bottlers, I was a sixteen-year-old kid playing ball with grown men. I faced some pitchers who'd played pro ball, but I was still able to hit pretty well. That experience whetted my appetite. From that time on, I set my sights on becoming a professional baseball player. I couldn't wait from one Sunday to the next to play the game.

**Extra Inning**

My high school football coach was Emmitt Wishard. He was succeeded as coach the following year, 1939, by Raymond Berry, who went on to coach at Paris High School for twenty-five years, becoming an East Texas legend in the process. Raymond Berry's son, Raymond Jr., played for his father at Paris High, but didn't start until his senior year. He then played receiver at SMU, catching thirty-three passes and one touchdown pass in three years. The Baltimore Colts drafted Raymond Jr. in the twentieth round, and he developed into a perennial all-pro receiver in the late 1950s and early 1960s. He was elected in 1973 to the Professional Football Hall of Fame in Canton, Ohio, and became a successful NFL coach with the New England Patriots, leading them to Super Bowl XX. When Raymond Jr. played for the Colts, he frequented the Baltimore restaurant I owned during that time, along with other Colts such as Johnny Unitas, Lenny Moore, Gino Marchetti, Jim Parker, Alan Ameche, Art Donovan, and Big Daddy Lipscomb. I guess all roads lead from Paris, Texas.

*Chapter 2*
## BREAKING INTO PRO BALL

P op Nobles was right about my getting noticed because we went to the state semi-pro tournament in Waco in 1937, my first year with the Bottlers. I hit well down there and was approached by Clyde "Deerfoot" Milan. He wanted to sign me to a professional contract with the Washington Senators organization. Milan was born and raised in Clarksville, Texas, about twenty miles east of Paris. He'd been a fine major league player for the Senators and had once held the American League stolen-base record. He now was a coach for the Senators.

In those days you didn't have to wait until you were out of high school to sign a professional contract. If I signed, however, I would lose my last year of eligibility for football, basketball, and track. I was a good student and decided to wait to sign until I graduated.

I continued to play for the Bottlers in 1938 when I was a senior, and we again made the state tournament in Waco. We didn't win but were voted the best-dressed team because of our fancy red satin uniforms. I made the All-tournament team, and Clyde Milan still wanted to sign me, as did Bully McClain, a scout for the Knoxville, Tennessee, Smokies of the Southern Association. Back then, a minor league club had scouts who would sign a player to its minor league team and then hope to sell the player to a major league club if he performed well. Bully liked me and Red Beville, our best pitcher. He took us over to Little Rock, Arkansas, where Knoxville was playing, and let us work out in front of the manager, Neal Caldwell. Before the game in Little Rock, they let me hit and Red pitch. I hit the ball well, but then they asked me to take infield practice. I always had a scatter arm, and I showed it at an inopportune time. The opposing pitcher just happened to be walking along the stands behind home plate toward his dugout when I threw a ball over the catcher's head. It hit the pitcher on the leg and hurt him badly enough that he was unable to pitch that night. Caldwell got me out of there in a hurry. But the club told me I had some ability and that they'd think about signing me.

The Boston Red Sox offered to pay my tuition to the University of Texas to play baseball. Billy Disch, the UT baseball coach, invited me down to Austin to work out. The UT baseball field in those days was memorable because of a limestone cliff in center field that was in the field of play. I must have impressed Uncle Billy because he offered me a four-year scholarship. Then, when I graduated, I would sign to play for the Red Sox organization since they were footing the bill for my education. I would've loved to have gotten a college education. But times were still tough because of the Depression, and I was the principal breadwinner in our family because my parents were divorced. My mother and I talked it over and decided I should sign with a professional baseball organization. I figured in four years of pro baseball, if I was as good as I thought, I could be in the big leagues or close to it instead of starting in the minor leagues after college.

So I signed with the Knoxville Smokies and received a $300 bonus. I bought my mother a washing machine with part of it and paid off several debts I had around town. I owed about $15 to a couple of restaurants that had given me credit, and I was paying a dollar a week for a wristwatch I'd bought for my girlfriend for Christmas. Uncle Louis told me to make a list of what I owed in town and he'd go around and pay everyone. So that's what I did. I made a list, gave it to Uncle Louis along with the money to cover what I owed, and left town with all my debts paid. I left Paris for spring training in 1939, headed for Valdosta, Georgia, with six dollars and a bus ticket in my pocket.

Before I left I asked Pop Nobles to arrange for me to meet Jack Russell, a Paris native who was a veteran pitcher for the Chicago Cubs. I thought Jack might be able to give me some advice before I started my professional career. We met in Pop Nobles's confectionery store, and I asked him if there was anything he could tell me that would help me. He said, "There sure is. Don't ever save money on your stomach. Always eat at the best restaurants you can afford and don't try to pocket your meal money."

That was the last thing I expected him to say. I thought he'd tell me I had to learn to hit the curveball or something. But I took his advice to heart and to this day still eat at the best restaurants in town.

In those days, Class A or A1 clubs, such as Knoxville, had farm teams. They'd develop players and then sell them to the big leagues. The Knoxville Smokies had a working agreement with Valdosta, Georgia, which had a new ballpark and its first professional baseball team. I had a feeling that if I didn't make the Smokies, I'd play for the Valdosta Trojans of the Georgia-Florida League.

Neal Caldwell, the manager of the Smokies, held a clubhouse meeting on the first day of spring training, and I was eager to get on the field and show what I could do. Neal was talking, and I was standing there pounding my glove without being aware of it. I guess I was making a lot of noise because, all of a sudden, he stopped, looked at me, and said, "Robinson, quit pounding that damn glove until we get out on the field." Well, that shook me up, but I figured at least he knew my name.

At the end of spring training, Caldwell called me in to tell me that I wasn't going to make their team, but they were going to option me to Valdosta. He said, "We think you're a great prospect. In fact, we think you're as good a fielder as Zeke Bonura right now." I knew Zeke Bonura was a major leaguer, and so that comment made me feel like I was as good as a big leaguer. The thing I didn't know was that Zeke Bonura was the worst fielder in the world. I later found out that when you mentioned Zeke Bonura's fielding, everyone would laugh.

When the Knoxville Smokies broke camp, I was left in Valdosta with several other players who'd been optioned to the Trojans. Bill Morrell, an ex-pitcher for the Washington Senators and the New York Giants, was our manager. Our long bus rides were entertaining because Bill drove the bus to all of our games with his wife sitting in the seat next to him, invariably telling him how to drive. Bill was a good-looking guy with gray hair and light blue eyes, but his wife always told him what to do, and we thought he was henpecked.

Valdosta was a sleepy south Georgia town. Many beautiful old homes and huge trees covered with Spanish moss helped make it a charming place. The Georgia-Florida League, however, was a Class D league, the lowest of the low. There were eight teams in the league, and we made all our trips in a Bluebird School bus. The only towns we spent the night in were Tallahassee, Florida, and Albany and Cordele, Georgia. We returned home after the games from the other four cities. We received fifty cents meal money each day, and we didn't have any coaches or trainers. It was tough, but I was happy to be playing professional baseball.

I soon learned about the wear and tear of playing every day. Although not serious, one of the most painful and aggravating problems I had came from sliding. In those days we wore sliding pads under our baseball pants to protect our hips from sliding burns we called strawberries. The pads were large pieces of cloth, but they didn't seem to help much. The dirt on the base paths was packed hard, and when we slid into a base the friction between the wool uniform and the packed dirt would burn the skin right off our hips.

During the season I managed to get strawberries on both hips, making it very painful to slide. Since we played every day, it was tough to get the strawberries to heal. A friend told me that it would help to put cigarette wrappers on the strawberries until the burns healed. Then I could peel the wrappers off. I put wrappers on both hips, and they seemed to be healing nicely until a doctor told me the wrappers were likely to give me a bad infection. So I ripped the wrappers off and continued to suffer from the raw, burning strawberries for weeks.

I was happy to be with the Trojans, but I wasn't hitting or fielding very well. I wasn't making much contact at the plate and was having trouble catching throws at first base. I'm sure I was almost released. Morrell told me one morning that another first baseman was coming in, but they were going to give me one more chance. I said, "Thanks, I'll try to hit better." He said, "It's not your hitting that's bothering me, it's your fielding." I was hitting less than .200, so you can imagine what a bad fielder I was. Zeke Bonura was a good fielder compared to me. Then I asked Morrell what I needed to do to get better, and he said I had to learn to catch balls thrown in the dirt.

In the low minor leagues, infielders were wild. First basemen were needed who could catch any kind of throw. So the next day my roommate, Eddie Lukon, and I went out and put the batting cage behind first base to stop the balls I missed. He stood over at shortstop and threw me ball after ball in the dirt until I learned to catch them. After I worked out there for two or three days in a row, I became proficient at catching wild throws. I could almost catch them with my eyes closed.

As the season progressed, my batting average began to come up, and I hit a few home runs. There was a steeplejack who came to every game, and when I hit a home run he'd pass his hat and take up a collection for me. He'd bring me the money, and I'd put it in a towel until after the game. Then I'd go to my girlfriend's home and we'd count it. Fans would put pieces of paper in the hat saying they would bake me a pie, or give me a free dancing lesson, or free gasoline, all kinds of goodies. Although I only hit seven home runs that first year, we drew big crowds almost every night, so by the end of the season I had almost $400 in my bank account just from hitting home runs.

As a side note to my first year, our catcher, Joe Berry, scheduled his wedding at home plate before one of our games. After two rainouts he was finally able to get married on the third night. His marriage drew a sellout crowd.

After my slow start, I managed to raise my batting average to .249 by the end of the season. We had a pretty good year as a team, finishing in second place with a 73–63 record, eight and a half games behind the Albany Cardinals, who were managed by Johnny Keane, later manager of the Cardinals and Yankees in the big leagues.

We finished the year in Albany, Georgia, and Bill Morrell called a meeting to evaluate each player's progress and ability. When he came to me he said, "Robinson, you may as well go back to Paris and open an ice cream parlor because I don't think you'll ever make a big league ballplayer." That evaluation made me more determined than ever to become a good player.

## Extra Inning

Albany, Georgia, was famous for its red-light district. One night after a game some of us were shooting the bull in our hotel room when one of the guys suggested that we call a house in the district and have one of the girls sent to us. We thought that was a good idea and pretty soon a woman showed up at our door. We were all awestruck to have a prostitute in the room and were just talking to her when we heard a knock on the door. We asked, "Who is it?" Our manager Bill Morrell answered, so we quickly shuffled the woman into the closet. Bill came in and chatted with us about nothing in particular for about ten minutes and then left. We weren't sure whether he knew anything was going on or not so we quickly sent the woman on her way. I never did find out if Morrell was jerking us around or if his visit was just an innocent one.

*Chapter 3*

## MAKING PROGRESS

After my first pro season ended, I bought a train ticket back to Paris. With the money I'd saved, I decided I'd go first class and not take the bus home. During the winter of 1939 I attended classes at Paris Junior College, as I had the previous year before reporting to my first spring training. Since I was a professional baseball player I wasn't eligible to play football for the Paris Junior College Dragons, but many of my friends did. In fact, my best friend Pee Wee Griffin was captain of the team, and I attended all the games.

Another dear friend of mine, George Stephens, was a running back on the team. We'd played football together in high school. George was valedictorian of our class and editor of the high school annual. We looked up to him because he was so bright. Late in the season George was injured in a game and taken to the hospital. None of us thought it was serious, but it turned out he'd ruptured his spleen. He died two days later. I was a pallbearer at his funeral. That tragedy cast a dark shadow over us for the rest of the winter.

Although none of us knew it, George had a creed, which he called "A Game Guy's Prayer," that was found in his room after he passed away. The *Paris News*, our local paper, ran a story about George's creed and printed it. It begins, "Dear God: Help me to be a sport in this little game of life. . . . I only ask for the stuff to give You 100 percent of what I've got," and ends, "When in the falling dusk I get the final bell . . . I'd just like to know that You feel I've been a good game guy." As far as anyone knows, George wrote this himself. It had great impact on all of us who knew him well. George lived his creed, although I still have trouble understanding why he was taken from us so soon.

I cut George's prayer out of the newspaper and carried it with me for years. In the early days when I was struggling in the minors and in my first two years in the big leagues, I referred to it many times. It always seemed to put things in perspective for me.

In early 1940 I received a notice in the mail that my contract had been acquired by Baltimore of the International League. That news upset me, because if I had to play in Class D again, I wanted to go back to Valdosta. I knew the Orioles had a farm team in Thomasville, Georgia, in the same league. That was the last place I wanted to play, even though the ballpark there had a short right-field fence.

I'd just about resigned myself to going to Thomasville when I got a notice from Baltimore saying my contract was being assigned to Valdosta. I couldn't figure out why, but I was delighted to be going back to Valdosta for my second year, even with a cut in salary. I had made $150 a month my first year with Valdosta. When the club sent me a contract for my second year, it was for $100 a month. I'd had such a miserable year, I just took the $50 cut, signed the contract, and returned it.

That season, 1940, gave me more confidence that I could be a good professional player. I had a great year. I made the All-Star team, and for the season hit .323 with 21 triples and 105 runs batted in. I wasn't very fast even then, but the league had big ballparks with lots of room between the outfielders. If you hit the ball in the gap you could run all day, and that's what I did quite often. Even so, I only finished second in the league in triples. Casey Kimbrell of the Tallahassee Capitols hit 22 to beat me.

Four guys from those Valdosta teams eventually made it to the big leagues, which was unusual for the low minors. Eddie Lukon made the Cincinnati Reds as an outfielder for three years, mostly after the war. Lou Rochelli appeared in five games for the Brooklyn Dodgers at the height of the war in 1944, and after the war Eddie Kazak played quite a bit of third base for about five years for the St. Louis Cardinals and made the National League All-Star team—not bad for a podunk little Class D ballclub.

After the season I took the train home to visit my mother, but then returned to Valdosta, where I spent the winter working as a flagman on the Florida Coastline Railroad. Having grown up in the Depression, I was very conscious of the need for a job to fall back on, and I knew that railroad work would be steady.

I showed a lot of improvement in 1940, but the big leagues still seemed far away. I was still in Class D. There was Class C, Class B, Class A, Class A1, and Class AA above me. It seemed like an impossibility that I'd get to the big leagues. I'd come into professional baseball in 1939 full of confidence that I'd set the baseball world on fire, but after that first lousy season, my sights were lowered substantially. I now figured if I could get to the Southern League and play in Atlanta or Nashville or one of those big cities, that would be great. I'd given up the idea of a college education in order to play professional baseball, and I was determined to continue chasing my dream of playing in the major leagues.

After my great year in Valdosta, Baltimore recalled me and gave me a contract for $200 a month for 1941—double my salary from the year before. I went to spring training with the Orioles in Haines City, Florida. I was thrilled to be in spring training with a Double-A (then the highest minor league classification) ballclub for the first time and was excited to be playing with some of the players I'd read about in the paper. The manager of the Orioles was Tommy Thomas, one of the best managers I ever had, who would remain a friend throughout my years in baseball.

That spring was the first time I saw my boyhood hero, Hank Greenberg, in person. It was only a fleeting glance but I remember it like it was yesterday. Hank had become my hero when I was in high school in Paris. I scoured the sports pages religiously in those days and followed Greenberg, the slugging first baseman of the Detroit Tigers. I read how Greenberg, early in his career, had trouble hitting the curveball. That was something I could relate to. Greenberg had solved his problem by hiring semipro pitchers and catchers to pitch extra batting practice to him when no one else was around. They'd throw him curveball after curveball, until he finally began to make consistent, solid contact. Greenberg's diligence made a great impression on me.

That spring we traveled from Haines City over to Lakeland, where the Tigers trained, for an exhibition game. We were warming up to play some minor leaguers from the Tigers organization when Greenberg drove up in a Cadillac convertible about half a block long. He was 6'4" and was dressed in an expensive sport coat. He was an imposing figure, and when he got out of the car, I thought to myself, "Now, that is a big league ballplayer."

I finally got to meet Greenberg in 1947 when I was a rookie in the big leagues with the Cleveland Indians. Bill Veeck, the Indians' owner, brought Greenberg in as farm director the year after Hank retired as an active player. I found Hank to be a stand-up guy whom everyone admired and respected. My boyhood hero didn't disappoint.

• • •

I played well as our exhibition games started, getting many hits and improving at first base, and I thought I might make the Orioles. The sportswriters thought so, too, because they wrote that this young first baseman from Texas was one of the bright spots of camp. As we broke camp and headed north, I was still the first baseman and felt like I'd made the club.

When we arrived in Baltimore to start the season, word came that Boston was optioning Al Flair, a first baseman of some note, to Baltimore. They called him "Broadway" Al Flair because he was such a spiffy dresser. He came in with "Broadway Al Flair" printed on his bats, and everybody knew he was going to be the first baseman for the Orioles. Although having Flair join the Orioles was bad news for me, I didn't let it get me down. I still had visions of becoming a big leaguer.

I was sent to the Elmira, New York, Pioneers of the Class A Eastern League, jumping over the Class C and B leagues, which I thought was quite an accomplishment. I had a good year in Elmira, batting .295 in 491 at bats. Sal Maglie was one of my teammates in Elmira, but he had not yet developed the terrific curveball he later became famous for. He still won twenty games and led the league with 270 innings pitched.

A feisty little guy named Ray Brubaker was the manager. He ran a good ball game but didn't do a lot of teaching. In fact, none of my minor league managers did much teaching. We were, more or less, expected to learn on our own.

Early Wynn, who went on to win three hundred big league games, pitched for the Springfield Nationals that year. In one game, I smashed a line drive back at him that hit him flush in the stomach. The ball dropped at his feet, and Early picked it up and threw me out at first as if it didn't bother him in the least. He never even rubbed his stomach. He carried a little extra padding even then, and I guess it must have helped to absorb the shock.

We finished the 1941 regular season in third place but made the four-team playoffs for the Governor's Cup. We played the pennant-winning Wilkes-Barre Barons in the first round and faced Red Embree, a highly touted prospect in the Cleveland Indians organization. Embree threw a great curveball and good fastball, and after nine innings we were tied 0–0 and had yet to get a hit. Ray Brubaker had started Clarence Pickerel, who wasn't one of our top pitchers, probably to save our aces for the games Embree wouldn't pitch. But Pickerel matched Embree inning after inning. Jess Pike hit a home run off Embree in the tenth inning to win the game for us 1–0. It was the only hit we got all day.

We went on to sweep the favored Barons and then defeated the Williamsport Grays four games to three, beating a pretty good knuckleball pitcher named Roger Wolff in the seventh game, when Willie Duke hit a home run to win it for us. Wolff later was a fine major league pitcher for the Washington Senators and Philadelphia Athletics; he became well known for holding Ted Williams hitless near the end of 1941, the season Ted hit .406.

We got a hero's welcome for winning the Governor's Cup and were big shots around Elmira. As our reward, we each got a cut of the gate receipts, which totaled about $60 each. That almost paid for my Hartman trunk, which I needed badly. Buying a Hartman trunk was a milestone. You could hang all your clothes in it, and it had drawers so that when you were traveling by train you could pack all your belongings in it. All the major league players had Hartman trunks, so I was elated when I was able to buy my first one.

I spent the winter of 1941 and spring of 1942 back in Valdosta, working for the Moody Field fire department. Ellis Clary, who played for the Washington Senators and was the local hero, also worked for the fire department in the off season and helped me get the job. We drilled day after day learning to fight fires but didn't have an actual fire for several weeks. The fire department had only two fire trucks. When we finally did have a fire, I piled on one of the trucks, but it never left the station, since it was only a one-alarm fire and only one truck responded. Both trucks were called on our second call, to a fire in the army barracks. We punched a hole in the ceiling, put a ladder up, and they sent me on the ladder up through the ceiling to see where the fire was in the attic. While I was on the ladder, I snagged my pants on a nail, tearing a hole in the best pair of pants I owned. We had so few fires, we didn't wear our firefighting clothes most of the time. That was the highlight of my firefighting career.

One of my best buddies on the Valdosta Trojans had been Pat Patterson from Pulaski, Tennessee. Pat had enlisted in the Army and was in the infantry, but happened to be visiting me in Valdosta on December 7, 1941. We were having lunch in the Roosevelt Restaurant when a news flash came over the radio that the Japanese had bombed Pearl Harbor. We talked about the horrors of war, and Pat told me he was assigned to a dangerous anti-tank unit.

Afterwards we corresponded regularly. His unit was part of the invasion of Italy at the Anzio beachhead. I received two or three letters from him from Anzio. I later learned that, as our boys were breaking out of the beachhead and beginning to move up through Italy, Pat had been killed. I'd lost a great friend much too soon.

The 1941 winter baseball meetings were being held in Jacksonville, Florida, in early December, so Ellis Clary and I drove down to the meetings. I was in awe when we got to Jacksonville and saw all those major leaguers at the meetings. Ellis knew Clyde McCullough, who was a catcher with the Chicago Cubs. Clyde had been a late season call-up to the Cubs in 1940 and was slated to make the club in 1941. He told us how he'd negotiated a $5,000 raise for himself. That sounded like $100,000 to me. Since I'd just played for $200 a month, I couldn't believe anyone could get a $5,000 raise playing professional baseball.

Once when Clary was playing for Washington, a fan in Griffith Stadium was riding him hard. Ellis, being a hothead, climbed up in the stands to confront the fan. Cooler heads prevailed, but the next day he received a telegram from Morris Frank, a well-known after-dinner speaker from Houston. Morris and Ellis were longtime friends, so Morris wired Ellis "to stay out of the stands because at your age you're going to be there soon enough anyway."

After jumping from Class D to Class A, I could hardly wait for the 1942 spring training to begin. I was slated to be with Baltimore, and if I had a good year, I thought I'd be in the major leagues soon. Just before I left Valdosta for spring training in Hollywood, Florida, I happened to watch some kids playing baseball on a playground. They knew I was a professional baseball player and asked me if I'd like to hit, so I picked up a bat to take a few swings. The kids were expecting me to hit some long drives, but I couldn't make solid contact. I was embarrassed, and I finally just laid the bat down and walked away. I couldn't figure out why I couldn't hit. I suppose I was trying to hit the ball too hard and too far, but the kids had a good laugh out of it. That experience made me even more eager to get to spring training and take some batting practice, so I could see if something had happened to louse up my swing. Once I arrived in spring training, a few turns in the hitting cage got my timing back, and to my relief I began stroking the ball as I always did.

## Extra Inning

In those days, many ballplayers chewed tobacco. One day, Bill Morrell, my manager at Valdosta, said, "Eddie, I want you to start chewing tobacco and get mean." I never got mean, but I did start chewing tobacco and, unfortunately, still do to this day. When I was with Elmira, Clarence Pickerel, who had defeated Red Embree in the first game of the playoffs, was a big tobacco chewer. One day he was pitching a game in Elmira and a batter smashed a line drive right back at him. It hit him in the chest and caused him to swallow his cud of tobacco. He got so sick he had to leave the ball game—one of the hazards of chewing tobacco and playing baseball.

*Chapter 4*
## A TASTE OF THE BIG TIME AND A WORLD WAR II DETOUR

O ne of the first people I met after arriving at spring training in Hollywood, Florida, in 1942 was Bob Lemon. Bob had played third base for Wilkes-Barre the year before, so I knew him as an opposing player. We became instant buddies and room-mates and remained good friends until Bob passed away in 2000. Bob hit twenty-one home runs for us that year in Baltimore and could have been a fine major league third baseman, but Cleveland had one of the best in baseball in Ken Keltner. Bob knew he couldn't replace Keltner anytime soon, so while Bob was in the U.S. Navy during World War II he tried pitching and was successful. When Bob came out of the Navy he continued to pitch, and the rest is history. It's hard for me to realize Bob became one of the great pitchers of all time. But maybe Kenny Keltner is the reason Bob is in the Hall of Fame with 207 wins and a .618 winning percentage. When we won the pennant in Cleveland in 1948, Bob pitched twenty-seven complete games while posting twenty victories. That's unheard of today when six good innings is called a quality start. Lemon would have laughed at that notion.

The International League was a train league, meaning all travel was by train. It was a good feeling to be away from the bus leagues. The Eastern League had been a killer with long bus trips between each city. The Pullman cars on the trains had upper and lower berths. If you were a regular player you got a lower berth in the middle of the car away from the noisy rattle of the wheels. The pitchers slept in the upper berths, and the substitutes slept over the wheels.

Before spring training ended, I learned Cleveland wanted to option another first baseman, Larry Barton, to Baltimore. Barton had been the most valuable player of the

Eastern League with Wilkes-Barre the year before and had led the league in home runs with seventeen. I thought here we go again, because if the Indians sent Barton down, it was going to be a battle to see which of us would play first base for Baltimore. But Tommy Thomas, our manager, came to me during spring training and advised me that he had told Cleveland he didn't want Barton. Tommy said, "I think you can help us as much as Barton, and I told Cleveland I was going to keep you as our first baseman, so you don't have to worry about it. You just go out and play your game and you'll be our first baseman." Well, that was great news and a strong vote of confidence, which I appreciated. I knew if I had a good year in Baltimore, Cleveland might purchase my contract and I would play in the major leagues.

The International League was loaded with good players like Ewell Blackwell, Max Surkont, Red Barrett, Hank Majeski, and Gene Moore. It was a long, tough year. I battled through a couple of slumps and wound up hitting .306 with 27 home runs (one behind league-leader Les Burge of Montreal) and 104 runs batted in. We finished 75–77 in fifth place, just out of the playoffs.

I managed to get into one altercation during the 1942 season. Max Macon was pitching for the Montreal Royals and was covering first base on a ground ball I'd hit to the first baseman. He put his foot on the middle of the bag and I stepped on it crossing first. After the play, I walked back to see if I'd cut him with my spikes, and Max slugged me while I was down on one knee inspecting his shoe that I'd stepped on. We went after each other until our teammates separated us. Then my roommate George "Stopper" Staller went after Max, and it took several minutes to restore order and resume the game. I later found out Macon was generally thought to be a disagreeable guy, as I'd learned firsthand.

The Cleveland Indians and Baltimore had a working agreement that allowed the Indians to purchase two ballplayers from the Orioles for $10,000 apiece. Right after our 1942 season ended, Tommy Thomas called me into his office and told me Ted Sepkowski, our second baseman, and I had been sold to the Cleveland Indians for $10,000 each. Not only that, Tommy told me he was going to give me 10 percent of my sales price since I'd had such a great year for the club. There was nothing that obligated him to do so, but he handed me a check for $1,000. It was a huge amount of money at the time that I really appreciated.

Getting sold to the Indians was a glorious day in my baseball career. Ted and I arrived in Cleveland the next day and checked into the Tudor Arms Hotel, where many of the Cleveland players were staying. The Indians were playing a game in old League Park, and reporting to the clubhouse for the first time was for me an awesome experience. Lou Boudreau, the manager, welcomed us and introduced us to the players. It took awhile for it to all soak in.

A few days later, I got into my first major league game in Cleveland Municipal Stadium against the Philadelphia Athletics. I'll never forget Lou Boudreau, who at twenty-five was only about two and a half years older than I was, telling me to get up there and pinch-hit against Luman Harris. It was a night game without many people in the stands, maybe five or six thousand, but I was shaking when I went up to the plate. I took a couple of fastballs, but then Luman changed up on me. I swung and popped up to the second baseman, Pete Suder. It was still a thrill just to get my name in a box score in a big league ball game. Ironically, Luman Harris later became a very good friend of mine. He was a coach when I was in Chicago, and we worked together in Houston and Atlanta.

Later at League Park I got my first base hit, a line drive to right field on a curveball, against Ray Scarborough of the Washington Senators. Ray later became my roommate in Chicago. I ended up getting into eight games in 1942, six as a pinch hitter. I drew two walks in addition to my lone base hit, in eight official at bats.

You can imagine how thrilled I was, after a meager beginning, and in only my fourth year of professional baseball, to be in the big leagues. I was sitting on the bench and associating with guys like Ken Keltner, Jeff Heath, Jim Bagby, Mel Harder, and Roy Weatherly, whom I'd read about and looked up to as a kid. Just to be on the team with them and have them call me by my first name was astounding. I knew I didn't have great tools for baseball. I couldn't run very fast. I wasn't a great fielder, and my arm wasn't strong enough to play any position but first base. The main reason I was in the big leagues was because I wouldn't give up and I could hit with power. I was making the most of the tools I had. All of a sudden, those past four years seemed very short, and it looked like my mother and I had made the right decision. Instead of just starting out in professional baseball after finishing college, I was already a big league player.

The nation's war effort continued to gather momentum during the winter after the 1942 season. Fighting a war wasn't what I had in mind after finally making the big leagues. But I knew I'd have to go into the service, and I wasn't alone. Many major league players soon went into the military. My teammates and buddies like Bob Lemon, Jim Hegan, Gene Woodling, and Ted Sepkowski went into the service about the same time.

I was first classified 3A, because I was the sole support of my mother. But when the war picked up, many men were reclassified 1A. As soon as I was reclassified, I thought I'd better enlist. I didn't want to be drafted into the Army and thought the Navy would better suit me.

During the 1942 season, Alfred Gwynne Vanderbilt, a good friend of our manager Tommy Thomas and a multi-millionaire who owned a horse ranch just outside Baltimore in Green Spring Valley, used to come down and sit on the bench with us. Alfred and I became good friends during the season. He was a Navy warrant officer, and he told me if I got reclassified, he'd get me into the Navy's new Athletic Specialist program. Gene Tunney, the former world heavyweight champion, was in charge of the program and was a friend of Alfred's. As a result, Alfred arranged a meeting for me with Tunney in Tunney's Washington office. Alfred told me to bring my scrapbooks and anything else that would prove I was proficient in athletics. Tunney glanced over my scrapbooks and visited with me for quite a while. Then he told me he'd accept me into the Navy as a Chief Athletic Specialist. He asked if I wanted to report in October or December and I chose December.

Tunney told me to report to the Naval Training Station in Norfolk, Virginia, on December 15, 1942, my twenty-second birthday. I was put into a squad of sixty top athletes from all over the United States. I bunked with football players, baseball players, wrestlers, tennis players, and high school and college football coaches. One athlete who became a good friend was Aaron Rosenberg, a former All-American football player from the University of Southern California, who later became a Hollywood movie producer. In fact, he produced one of my favorite westerns, *Winchester '73*, one of the most popular films of its time, starring Jimmy Stewart. I also palled around with Homer Peel, a fellow Texan, who was a successful minor league manager after playing the outfield for the Cardinals, Phillies, and Giants for five years. Homer was reputed to be one of the best curveball hitters of his time but couldn't hit the fastball, the opposite of many guys who have trouble with the curve but can sit on the fastball.

One odd duck in our unit was Gus Gustafson, who was a world champion wrestler. Gus was sloppy in his dress and personal hygiene, which are important in the military.

He seemed to be sick a lot and wouldn't shave. He ended up as an outcast because he'd get the whole unit in trouble.

Part of our basic training involved swimming, since this was the Navy and you were expected to be a good swimmer. The base had a pool that was smaller than Olympic size. I didn't know how to swim and was placed in the non-swimmers class with about twenty-four other sailors, most of whom had played baseball or other summer sports and had never learned to swim. I was in that class for six weeks, and at the end of it only two of us were left: Frank Scott, who was later traveling secretary for the Yankees and one of the first player agents, and me. We had to be able to swim across the pool and back to graduate from the class. I could dive in and make it across but couldn't make it back.

Finally, when our squad was ready to graduate from basic training, they told Frank and me they were going to pass us, but to make sure we had a life preserver with us when we were at sea because we wouldn't be able to save ourselves if our ship went down.

During that six-week training, I heard about a chief warrant officer named Gary Bodie, who was manager of the Norfolk Training Station baseball team. The training station had fielded a pretty good team the year before, and Bodie was trying to assemble the best baseball team in the Navy. I thought I might have a chance to stay in Norfolk and play baseball if Bodie knew about me, so I made it a point to hang around the gym so I could meet him. Eventually I did meet him and he checked my record. I think Bodie had already heard a little about me because he indicated that I might be stationed at Norfolk to play on the team. I wanted to play baseball while I was in the service, because if I could play with major league caliber players, I knew it would help me when I was discharged and returned to professional baseball.

The commanding officer of the Norfolk Training Station was Captain H. A. McClure. He was a career-line officer and was tough. He followed Navy regulations right down the line, except that he was a fanatic about sports and professional athletes. He wanted the Naval Training Station to have the best baseball and basketball teams in the Navy. In the Navy you usually have to go through channels to talk with a superior officer. But Captain McClure thought Bodie, who was the basketball coach as well as the baseball manager, knew everything there was to know about both sports. As a result, Bodie had a direct pipeline to the captain. Any time Bodie would find a ballplayer he wanted on his team, he'd just call Captain McClure, who would have orders cut to keep the athlete in Norfolk. That must have been what happened to me, because when they read our orders on graduation day, I was to be stationed at Norfolk. I was pleased to be a member of the training station ballclub, but I knew I had to play well because Bodie had a reputation for shipping players out to sea if they didn't play up to his expectations.

Since Bodie was a hero worshiper and would get any good baseball player he heard about ordered to Norfolk, we came up with two teams mostly comprised of major leaguers. One day he came to Freddie Hutchinson, who was also a big league ballplayer, and me and told us he'd heard about a pitcher in destroyer escort boat training in Norfolk named Johnny Vander Meers. Bodie asked us if we thought we should get him for our ball team. He apparently had never heard of Johnny. So Freddie told him that Johnny *Vander Meer* had pitched back-to-back no-hitters for the Cincinnati Reds and that, yes, he could help us. Sure enough the next day Johnny was on our team.

We had six different sets of uniforms in Norfolk, all different colors. We had the best gloves and all the bats we wanted. We had what amounted to a major league operation. In fact, it was better than what the major league clubs had at the time because they couldn't get good equipment. We had it.

Bodie even managed to get the Washington Senators' groundskeeper to come down to Norfolk to make our infield major league caliber. Our dugout bench was padded with tilted backs and armrests so that we had individual seats and could recline with our feet up on the edge of the dugout. Captain McClure and the chaplain would put a sheet over their seats so they could sit in the dugout in their dress white Navy uniforms and not get them dirty.

The only thing we didn't have was a bell to signal when to start and stop pre-game infield, batting practice, and so forth. Bodie wanted a bell in the worst way, but there weren't any bells being made because all of the metal was being used for tanks and weaponry. Finally, however, Bodie was able to secure a big school bell. It was electric; you just pushed a button and it would ring. Bodie was so pleased with it that he mounted it right on the edge of the dugout.

One day Freddie Hutchinson was pitching a game and getting pretty well knocked around. When it came Freddie's turn to bat, he hit his head on the bell as he started out of the dugout. He was already angry because of the way the game was going, and when he hit his head it made him so mad he took his bat and beat the bell against the dugout wall. It flew into a thousand pieces while Bodie just sat there with his mouth open. That was the end of the bell, and we never got another one. Bodie was so mad at Freddie he suspended him for two games.

We didn't have wooden outfield fences either. We had a canvas fence that was held up by ropes and metal poles. We had some pretty good left-handed hitters, and we could hit with some power. The wind blew in from right field so they put the right field fence at 330 feet, so that our left-handed hitters could reach it. When the left-handers would go into a slump, Bodie would have a work crew go out there and move the fence in so we could reach it. The fence would still say 330 feet but would actually be about 315 or 320 feet from home plate. When we came out of our slump and started hitting again, he'd have the fence moved back. Bodie would do everything he could to get the advantage and win.

One day Bodie gathered us all in the clubhouse, told us he just found out there were some vacancies at the Anacostia Naval Air Station in Washington, D.C., and asked who'd like to be transferred. Anacostia was a very desirable assignment, so about five or six players, including Walt Masterson and Jimmy Gleason, held up their hands and said they'd like to go to Anacostia. Nothing happened for a couple of days. Then suddenly all of the players who'd raised their hands received orders to go to the South Pacific. Masterson was assigned to a submarine, and Gleason got orders to a ship in the South Pacific. It turned out that there weren't any vacancies at Anacostia: Bodie just wanted to find out who really wanted to stay in Norfolk and was dedicated to his ballclub. So we had to really be careful. If Bodie got down on someone, he would immediately have that person shipped out. If that's not pressure, I don't know what is—hit the ball or you're off to the South Pacific on a submarine or warship.

Even though we were in the Navy and our major league baseball careers were on hold during World War II, we were fortunate to play baseball. We played all of the Navy and Army teams around the area. We played against the North Carolina Preflight School in Chapel Hill. They had a good team with players like Johnny Pesky and Ted Williams. We played the Norfolk Naval Air Station two or three times a week and had some great games. They were comprised of players Bodie didn't think were good enough to play for his outfit. He wasn't much of a judge of talent, because the Naval Station included Pee Wee Reese, Hugh Casey, Eddie Shokes, Herman Franks (their manager), and a host of other fine players.

We had a good team also with Vinnie Smith at catcher, me at first base, Benny McCoy at second, Phil Rizzuto at shortstop, Jeff Cross at third, and Dom DiMaggio, Don Padgett, and Mel Preibisch in the outfield. Our pitching staff consisted of mostly big leaguers, including Johnny Rigney, Charlie Wagner, Maxie Wilson, Hank Fernster, Tom Early, Freddie Hutchinson, Tommy Byrne, and Johnny Vander Meer.

Captain McClure's driver always parked the captain's car by the side of our dugout. At the end of the game, he'd drive the captain wherever he wanted to go next. One time Dom DiMaggio and Fred Hutchinson ran into each other chasing a fly ball in the outfield. Freddie got up and looked okay, but Dom remained down and looked like he might be hurt. The captain jumped off the bench, got into his car, and had his driver take him out to the outfield to check on Dom. Fortunately, DiMaggio was okay except for a cut on his head caused by his glasses. Captain McClure got back into his car, his driver drove him back to the dugout, and the game continued.

Phil Rizzuto was a great little guy who was very well liked. Perhaps because of his small stature, he bore the brunt of a lot of pranks. While he was in Norfolk he was to be married to his fiancée, Cora. The day before the wedding the team was showering after the game when Hank Fernster, a couple of other guys, and I grabbed Phil and held him down while we painted his private parts with a violet colored solution we knew wouldn't wash off. We didn't act in very good taste, but poor Phil had some explaining to do to Cora on their wedding night.

After the 1942 baseball season, I worked in the Katz Jewelry Store in Baltimore to make ends meet while waiting to report for induction. There I met Elayne Elder, a pretty young woman who came into the store as a customer one morning. We struck up a conversation and began dating. We got married on Valentine's Day, 1943, in Norfolk, Virginia, right after my basic training. I was a big enough guy that none of my buddies tried anything funny on me as they had with Rizzuto. Nine months later our daughter Robby Ann was born, to be followed by our son William E. Robinson III, whom we called Robby, in 1948.

Elayne had a brother, Eddie Elder, who had been an outstanding football player at Gettysburg College. Early in World War II he entered the army as a lieutenant and quickly rose to the rank of captain. He saw a lot of action with the First Army Division in Africa and then in several major campaigns in the European theater. While Eddie was in Africa he was captured by Rommel's troops, but managed to escape and rejoin his unit. He was awarded two Bronze Stars and the Silver Star for valor.

Eddie's troops loved him. He probably would have risen above captain but for a single incident. During one campaign he got into an argument with his superior over an order that he thought would put his men at unusual risk. Eddie ended up decking his superior. The army didn't court-martial Eddie, but he was never promoted beyond the rank of captain.

I liked Eddie a lot. He once gave me a .25 automatic hand gun that he'd taken from a captured German officer. I treasure it and have it to this day. Unfortunately, however, the war haunted Eddie. He had terrible dreams and ended up with a drinking problem.

Elayne's father Ed Elder was a lot like his son. He had his own real estate brokerage company. Mr. Elder was a big sports fan, and we spent many hours together watching sports on television. We got along famously. The situation with Elayne's mother, however, was 180 degrees the other way. She and I didn't see eye to eye about anything. I thought she was overly protective of Elayne and that Elayne was spoiled as a result. Mrs. Elder was a meddler, and that caused problems in our marriage. Further, Elayne didn't like all the travel and separation a baseball career demanded. We later separated and were divorced in 1951 while I was playing for the White Sox. I had my faults, as Mrs. Elder was quick to point out, but in the final analysis Elayne wasn't cut out to be a baseball wife.

Elayne went on to have a successful second marriage, just as I have. I appreciate the fact that she did a good job of raising our son Robby and never tried to poison him against me. As a result, he and I have a great relationship.

After the war, during the 1946 season, our young daughter, Robby Ann, was stricken with a brain tumor that proved to be terminal. Robby Ann was not quite three years old when she became ill and was hospitalized at Johns Hopkins. She was in a coma in the intensive care unit for quite some time. I missed several games during that period. It was a very difficult time for Elayne and me. Little Robby Ann passed away during the season. Only those who have lost a young child can comprehend what it is like and how the loss affects you emotionally.

At the end of the 1944 baseball season in Norfolk, we had a Naval World Series that went seven games. The stands were almost always packed with sailors when we played the Air Station, and we provided a lot of entertainment for them.

Unless you were trained for some kind of specialized job, the base couldn't retain you for an indefinite period. I was trained to teach the Doppler radar system in the anti-submarine warfare class. I taught the naval officers to identify enemy submarines on the Doppler so they could drop depth charges. We also pulled guard duty, and I was paired with Paul Runyon, the professional golfer, who was a fine guy. We had night duty and would walk around guarding the barracks and that dreaded swimming pool where I'd tried to learn to swim.

We knew, however, our time would come and we'd be shipped out. The word came in October 1944 that thirteen of the players on our base team were being sent to Hawaii. I was shipped out on the *USS Afoundria*, a troop ship, along with about thirty other ballplayers including Johnny Rigney, Mickey Vernon, Virgil Trucks, Bob Klinger, Vinny Smith, and Hank Fernster. Mickey Vernon was seasick from the day we boarded the ship until we docked in Hawaii seven days later.

Once we got to Hawaii, the Navy split us up and assigned us to different naval stations on Oahu. I was stationed at Aiea Heights Hospital, which was the largest naval hospital outside the continental United States, along with Billy Herman, Pee Wee Reese, Buddy Blattner, and Eddie Shokes. Bill Dickey, the great Yankee catcher, was the officer-in-charge of all the athletes. With so many major league players stationed in Hawaii, the teams there were loaded. We arrived in the fall, so we had time to build a ballpark and get it in shape by spring. We'd go up into the hills and pull Bermuda grass, and then bring it down and plant it strand by strand. It wasn't long before we had a beautiful ball diamond.

We stayed in Marine barracks with many professional athletes. Max Patkin, who later became the second Clown Prince of Baseball, was among us. Al Schacht was the first, and I saw them both perform. Al, a former Washington Senator pitcher, was funny, but I thought Patkin was funnier. Every Friday and Saturday at the Royal Hawaiian Hotel, Patkin put on a dance for sailors who were there on R&R from their tours in the Pacific. Max Patkin was a great dancer who would put on a very entertaining performance with some young girls. On Sundays he'd go into the recreation centers in Honolulu and dance as well, always to great applause. In the barracks, he'd spend a lot of time playing ping pong with Bobby Riggs, the noted tennis player, who was also stationed with us.

While I was stationed in Hawaii, my right leg started bothering me. I'd always had a problem with my right knee from a high school football injury, and a few years earlier, in 1942 when I was playing a game in Baltimore, my kneecap slipped out of place. The Orioles sent me to see Dr. George Bennett, who was the team physician and the chief orthopedic surgeon at Johns Hopkins Hospital. He examined my knee and said it was all right, but told me I had a big bone tumor on my leg and that one of these days I might have to have it removed. Dr. Bennett told me that until it started bothering me I should leave it alone.

When my leg started hurting in Hawaii, I went to see a Dr. Walerus at the Aiea Naval Hospital, and after examining and X-raying my leg, he told me the tumor should be removed. That got my attention since my baseball career could be at risk from an operation of that magnitude. I wanted to talk with the chief surgeon of the hospital, and I wanted to talk with Dr. Bennett in Baltimore. I wrote Dr. Bennett and told him what the naval orthopedic surgeon had recommended. Dr. Bennett answered that if my leg was bothering me, I certainly should have the bone tumor removed. Dr. Bennett, however, told me to show his letter to the doctor who would do the operation. In the letter, Dr. Bennett told Dr. Walerus to be very careful in removing the tumor because he had seen the peroneal nerve, which controls the lifting of your foot, growing through the tumor. If it wasn't handled carefully, the nerve could be damaged, which would be a disaster for my baseball career.

I showed the letter from Dr. Bennett to Dr. Walerus, who let me know he didn't need any assistance. He said, "I know what I'm doing, and I don't need anybody else to tell me how to do an operation." I was still apprehensive about the operation, so I went to see the chief surgeon of the hospital, Captain Gray. He assured me Dr. Walerus was a competent surgeon, but if it would make me feel better, he himself would stand in during the operation. With that assurance, I went through with the operation. They gave me a spinal block, and I was able to talk to both surgeons during the procedure. They assured me it was going well.

Two or three days after the operation I noticed a numbness in my foot. I mentioned it to Dr. Walerus, who assured me that the numbness would go away and told me not to worry about it. Then the numbness increased, and I began to have severe pains from my knee to my foot. I knew my foot wasn't going to be all right, and the problem wasn't going to go away. I couldn't even raise my foot. Dr. Walerus didn't want to admit it, but he'd injured the nerve during the surgery, leaving me with what is called "foot drop," the very problem Dr. Bennett had warned him about.

After about three weeks, the Navy doctors decided to send me back to the continental United States. I finally went to see Captain Gray, who was most apologetic. He said the only man he knew anywhere, in or out of the service, who might be able to fix me up was Captain Wink Craig, who was the chief neurosurgeon at Bethesda Naval Hospital in Bethesda, Maryland. He said, "Eddie, don't let anybody touch you until you get back to Bethesda."

I'd contrived a way to walk using an Ace bandage, some rubber bands, and a safety pin. I'd wrap a bandage around my calf and attach the rubber bands to my shoelace. Then I'd pull up the rubber bands, and put the safety pin through the bandage and the rubber bands. The rubber bands held my foot up, and I was able to walk without dragging my foot. Even so, it looked like this was the end of my baseball career. But I guess I've always had a lot of blind faith. I believed that if I got to Bethesda, Dr. Craig was going to repair the damage and make me well.

I flew back to the United States on a huge Pan American Clipper. Soon after I shipped out, most of the other ballplayers were sent to different islands in the South Pacific to conduct recreational events for our troops. They organized baseball teams and did a great job of providing physical outlets for our boys. They didn't carry guns but contributed to the war effort in a positive way nonetheless.

The Clipper carrying me back to the mainland took off and landed on the water and had sleeping berths just like a railroad Pullman car. My first stop after landing in San Francisco Bay was the Oak Knoll Naval Hospital in Oakland. There two neurosurgeons with good reputations, Dr. Livingston and his son, wanted to operate on me. I remembered what Captain Gray told me, however, so I refused the operation. I told them I wanted to go to Bethesda, but they came back in a few days and told me there were no beds at Bethesda. The closest place they could find to send me was to Quantico, Virginia, to a small Marine hospital. When I checked into the hospital in Quantico, I was told that the closest they had to a nerve doctor was a psychiatrist. My response was that I didn't want to see a psychiatrist and I didn't want anybody there to work on me. All I wanted was to get to Bethesda Naval Hospital.

The psychiatrist came around anyway and told me there wasn't any chance of my getting into Bethesda so they were just going to discharge me. That really shook me up; I didn't want a discharge because I wanted to see Captain Craig in Bethesda. Then I called Dr. Bennett in Baltimore because he was familiar with the whole history of the operation. Not surprisingly, Dr. Bennett was a good friend of Dr. Craig's. In no time, Dr. Bennett had it set up for me to be transferred to Bethesda. The very next day a new station wagon arrived at Quantico to transfer me to Bethesda.

Captain Craig and I had a long visit, and he told me he no longer performed operations. He told me, however, they had two of the finest young neurosurgeons anywhere, Dr. Hunter Sheldon and Dr. Pudenz. Dr. Sheldon would perform the operation and Dr. Pudenz would assist. It took some time to schedule the procedure, but finally I was operated on in June of 1945. When the nurses came in to prep me for the operation, they told me Dr. Sheldon was out of town, but that Dr. Pudenz was going to do the operation. I said, "No way. Either Dr. Sheldon operates on me or I'm not going to have it." They tried to talk me into it, but I resisted with all my might. Then they gave me a couple of pills that had something in them, because after I took them it didn't matter to me who operated on me. I again had a spinal block and was able to talk to Dr. Pudenz during the entire operation. I was foggy from the anesthesia, but I was trying to impress on him the importance of doing a good job.

It turned out Dr. Walerus had stretched the nerve in my leg when he performed the operation in Hawaii. That caused what's called a neuroma, which is like gristle in the nerve that keeps the nerve fibers from growing. From the point of the neuroma, I didn't have any nerves growing down my leg and, as a result, had lost control of my foot. So Dr. Pudenz had to cut out an inch of the nerve in my leg and very delicately suture the nerve back together so that the nerve fibers could grow.

Afterwards, Dr. Pudenz told me the operation had gone well and that I'd be able to play ball again. I don't know if he really believed that, but that's what he said. I had to be in a cast for six weeks with my leg bent back towards my buttocks with a stick in the cast to keep me from extending my leg. It was terrible. About all I could do was lie on one side in bed for six weeks. It was the longest six weeks imaginable.

I was in a hospital ward with thirty patients, most of whom had been wounded in combat. Their wounds were much worse than my paralyzed leg. When I was feeling sorry for myself all I had to do was look around at the other patients and I felt lucky by contrast. The guys in the ward were good guys, and we got to know each other and developed a lot of camaraderie. And we had terrific nurses who took good care of us.

My wife Elayne was living in our home in Baltimore about thirty miles from the hospital. She visited me often, and my ward mates got to know her. Elayne was a very pretty girl, and the other guys looked forward to her visits. Most of them didn't have many visitors because they weren't close to their homes, and they liked seeing Elayne.

Finally six weeks passed and the doctors took off the cast. The sight of my leg shocked me. It was dwarfed. All of the muscles were shrunk. I had to walk on crutches and suffer through physical therapy for an extended period of time. Finally, Dr. Pudenz and Dr. Sheldon said they'd done all they could for me. The Navy discharged me so I could go back to Baltimore and let Dr. Bennett take over my therapy.

Dr. Bennett fixed me up with a brace to sleep in at night that would stretch the muscles in my leg by holding my foot at a right angle so as not to let the bedcovers push it down. He also provided me with a spring brace for my shoe to hold my foot up when I walked. Dr. Bennett told me that if the operation had been successful, and if the nerve really was repaired, the nerve fibers would grow back at the rate of one inch per month. The therapy in Baltimore started in September, so I had six months before spring training started with the Cleveland Indians. We determined that if the nerve grew six inches, it would have grown far enough before spring training to give me some use of my leg. If not, I was prepared to go to spring training with a brace on my leg.

*Chapter 5*
## INTERNATIONAL LEAGUE MVP

performed my exercises faithfully and did everything Dr. Bennett told me to do. Around the first of the year I began to get some feeling back in my foot, and I could even lift it a little bit, which was very encouraging. My foot continued to improve right up to the first day of spring training in February 1946. Just like Dr. Bennett told me— right on the money—my leg came back. I was able to throw my brace away on the first day of spring training. I was again able to run and hit and do the things I had to do to play baseball.

Of course, I was thankful to the good Lord. I was both pleased and elated that I had the possibility of resuming my career. The Indians' spring training was in Clearwater, Florida, at Jack Russell Stadium, named for my fellow Parisian who had told me not to save money on my stomach. Jack had pitched for fifteen years in the big leagues and had become one of the city fathers in Clearwater. I did a lot of running in spring train- ing to try to strengthen my leg and foot as much as I could. But I was so happy to have the brace off my leg that running was a pleasure. My whole world was beautiful even though my future was still in doubt. There were those who thought that I'd never play again. But I had a chance, which is all I'd hoped and prayed for.

My fielding had improved tremendously since I first started playing. But I was rusty after not playing at all for a year. My timing was off, and it took me most of the spring to get any feel at the plate. Les Fleming was my chief competition for the first-base job. Les had come back from the war during the 1945 season and had hit .329 in about a third of the season. He wasn't a very good fielder, but in the end, the club decided to keep him because of his hitting.

At the time major league teams traveled by train, and each player carried his uniform in a trunk tray. The players put all of their equipment and their uniform in a tray, and then the equipment men would pack the trays in trunks and put the trunks on the train to the city where we were to play next. So near the end of spring training every year, we would look for trays to be put on top of our lockers. If you had a tray above your locker that was good news because it meant you were going to go with the team. One day that spring I went into the clubhouse to find trays above a lot of lockers, but no tray above mine. I knew right away that I probably was going back to Baltimore, Cleveland's top farm club.

Sure enough, General Manager Roger Peckinpaugh told me in a few days that the club was sending me to Baltimore. Peckinpaugh said the club wanted me to be able to play regularly, and I wouldn't be able to do that in Cleveland with Fleming playing first base most of the time. So I bid the Cleveland Indians adieu in April 1946, and headed back for Baltimore, hoping that I'd have a good year, get called back up to the Indians at the end of the season, and stay in the big leagues from then on. Bob Lemon made the team as a pitcher, but Gene Woodling was sold to the Pacific Coast League.

I believed that 1946 was going to be a pivotal year in my professional baseball career. I'd been in the Navy for almost four years, and I'd had those operations on my leg. I wondered if I was going to be able to play a full season after my leg surgery and physical therapy. Now it was up to me to go back to Baltimore and prove I could play well enough to be a big leaguer.

Tommy Thomas was still the manager in Baltimore, which was a break for me. Tommy and I got along great, and I respected him as a baseball man. He was a wonderful man to play for. He didn't use signals like most third-base coaches. If he wanted you to bunt, he'd just yell at you to bunt. If he wanted you to hit, he'd just yell at you to hit the ball. He'd say, "Hell, the opposition won't believe me anyway if they hear me say those things."

Nineteen forty-six was the year Jackie Robinson began his professional career in the International League with the Montreal Royals, the top farm team of the Brooklyn Dodgers. His coming into the league at that time was a big event. A lot of folks were skeptical, wondering how integration was going to work, wondering what it meant to baseball in the future, not realizing what a big impact it was going to have. Jackie put his pants on one leg at a time just like everybody else, and he was a great player and competitor. He played extremely well for Montreal, hitting .349 to lead the league. It was evident he was headed for stardom with the Brooklyn Dodgers.

Even though Jackie was the first black player in the International League, he wasn't treated as badly as one might think. My teammates and the Baltimore fans didn't give him a bad time. We understood that the integration of baseball was significant. Our games against Montreal had a different feeling because Jackie was playing. We expected something to happen with the Baltimore fans, but nothing ever did. I know he had a much tougher time the next year when he broke into the big leagues.

Looking back on it, I admire and respect Jackie Robinson tremendously because it took a great amount of courage to be the first black player in Triple-A and in the big leagues. Jackie handled it well. In my opinion, Jackie Robinson and Larry Doby, my future teammate in Cleveland and the first black player in the American League, are right there with Dr. Martin Luther King in advancing the cause of African Americans.

I did prove I could play again in 1946 and showed I was ready for the big leagues. For the year I hit thirty-four home runs and drove in 123 runs to lead the league. The original Baltimore ballpark where I'd played in 1942 before I went into the service had burned down, and so we now played in Baltimore Stadium, which was a football stadium. The ball field was placed so that left field was very short, like the LA Coliseum when the Dodgers moved to Los Angeles in 1958. Although left field was short, right field had no end, almost literally. There was no fence, so the only way you could hit a home run in the right field stands was to hook the ball around the foul pole into the stadium seats. As a result, nearly every home run I hit in Baltimore went between or beyond the outfielders, meaning I had to leg them out.

We finished tied for third with Newark, nineteen games behind Montreal and a half-game behind the Syracuse Chiefs. Newark had an excellent team led by Bobby Brown and Tommy Byrne, but we defeated them in a one-game playoff for third. Then we lost in the playoffs to Syracuse, four games to two to conclude the season.

Bobby Brown had a great year, batting .341 and leading the league in hits. When it came time for naming the league's Most Valuable Player, it came down to Jackie Robinson, Bobby Brown, or me. Frank Shaughnessy, the league president, called me when the season was over and said it was a close race, but I'd won the Most Valuable Player Award over Bobby and Jackie. They were both great ballplayers, and it thrilled me to win the MVP award over them. I received a watch for winning the award. It still is one of my most prized possessions and is now on loan to the Babe Ruth/Baltimore Orioles museum in Baltimore.

I first met Bobby Brown at first base early in the 1946 season when we were playing the Newark Bears. It was the start of a friendship that has lasted sixty-four years and counting. In addition to being a fine player, well-known cardiologist, and former president of the American League, Bobby is a terrific storyteller. One story Bobby tells is about when he and his wife Sara were stationed in Japan during the Korean Conflict. While they were there Joe DiMaggio and Marilyn Monroe came over on their honeymoon. Marilyn was going to Korea to entertain the troops and needed some additional inoculations. Bobby was the only doctor Joe would allow to give Marilyn a shot in her rear end.

I became popular in Baltimore that 1946 season even though we spent most of the year battling the Syracuse Chiefs, Buffalo Bisons, and Newark Bears for second place, since Montreal ran away with the pennant. Late in the season we played Newark on Shriners' Night, and over thirty thousand fans came to the ball game. During the game I hit a ball far over the right fielder's head to no man's land and sprinted around the bases. I was back sitting in the dugout before the right fielder could retrieve the ball and throw it back in. It's amazing but even today whenever I meet someone from Baltimore of that generation, they remind me about that home run. Bobby Brown was on that Newark team, and he still frequently tells me he can't believe anyone could hit the ball that far.

At the end of 1946 I was called up to Cleveland and hit three home runs in only seven ball games. I hit my first major league home run in Cleveland off Freddie Hutchinson of the Tigers, my old Navy buddy. Then we went over to Detroit and I hit two home runs in one game against Hal White.

Cleveland's manager was the twenty-eight-year-old Lou Boudreau, who didn't seem to like me from the start and never talked to me or gave me any encouragement. He didn't seem to be happy to have me join the team. He may not have known how to encourage young players because of his own youth, but from the beginning we just didn't hit it off. Unfortunately, we had a strained relationship until I left the Indians. Lou was a fine player and a good leader. He had a top-notch coaching staff with Bill McKechnie, Muddy Ruel, Oscar Melillo, George Susce, and Mel Harder, who'd been a standout pitcher for the Indians, as our pitching coach. Boudreau, however, didn't know how to handle ballplayers, a major problem for a manager.

I had ended the 1946 season with a flurry of good play in Baltimore and had batted .407 with the Indians in twenty-seven late season at bats. I felt like I was ready to play in the big leagues. My leg continued to get stronger during the year, and I played in almost every game, except during my daughter's illness. Doctors examined me at the end of the season and told me they thought I had at least 90 to 95 percent use of my right leg, which is more than anyone had hoped for. So I proved that I was able to play, and that my leg could stand up under the stress of playing every day. I'd impressed the people in Cleveland enough so that they were expecting me to be their regular first baseman going into the 1947 season.

## Extra Inning

I needed a job the winter after the 1946 season. I heard that the Beth Thloh Community Center and School was looking for an athletic director. The job included coaching the boys' high school basketball team at their Hebrew School and conducting an exercise program for women in the synagogue. I applied for the job and was hired. I got to know many of the parents, and Meme Shavitz, the father of one of my basketball players, became a good friend. Meme and his wife had an infant son and I was invited to the bris, which is the Jewish celebration and circumcision ceremony at a Jewish hospital. Before the circumcision ceremony there was a huge party in a special room at the hospital. I was having a great time until the circumcision took place. When the baby was circumcised and I saw blood, I knew I was going to faint. I looked around for a place to land and spotted a block of ice over in the corner. I sat right down on that ice, and, fortunately, the cold saved me from fainting. My pants got wet, but at least I didn't keel over.

*Chapter 6*
## BIG LEAGUE ROOKIE

**B**ill Veeck bought the Cleveland ballclub during the 1946 season. I'd heard a lot about him, all of it good. He loved baseball. As a young man he hung around the Chicago Cubs while his father was president of the club. Later he got the urge to own a minor league club and bought into the Milwaukee Brewers of the American Association. He ran that team for a couple of years. Then, after the war, he was able to get some partners together, including my boyhood idol Hank Greenberg, and Bob Hope, to buy the Cleveland Indians.

Baseball was everything to Veeck. He didn't have any other businesses or means of livelihood. He either made his money or lost it in baseball. Baseball was his game and he was a master promoter. We'd heard he was a ballplayers' owner, and we were all excited that he bought the team. And he turned out to be exactly that. He was for the players first and would go out of his way to help one of them—financially or otherwise. He had a big, generous heart.

Bill had lost a leg as a result of World War II and had a wooden peg leg. He was a heavy smoker, and he often had great fun stubbing out a lit cigarette on his wooden leg to shock someone who wasn't aware of his condition. That trick was hard on his trousers, however.

Bill made just coming to the ballpark every day interesting with all of his Barnum and Bailey promotions. He had great ideas about how to attract people to the ballpark. One night, for example, he put on an Armed Forces Night with military marching bands from all branches of the service on the field before the game. He turned out all the lights after sixty thousand fans had entered the ballpark. It was absolutely dark in the stadium, and over the PA system he asked everyone to strike a match to show how sixty thousand matches would illuminate a huge place like a ballpark. Everybody in the park struck a match and the stadium lit up as bright as day; it was brighter than the stadium lights.

Bill brought in Max Patkin, the baseball clown. He also brought in a character named Jackie Price, who would ride around in a Jeep in the outfield and catch fly balls. Price would hang by his heels from a pole with a cross bar set at home plate and hit balls pitched to him. Jackie also carried a bunch of snakes with him. One time during spring training we were on the train heading from San Diego to Texas when Jackie brought a couple of his snakes into the dining car. The snakes scared the ladies and the waiters so badly that they ran up to the front of the train and wouldn't come back. Boudreau was so upset he had the engineer stop the train and put Jackie and his snakes off in some little town in the middle of Texas. That ended Jackie's tenure with the Indians.

Bill promised me at the beginning of 1947, my rookie season, that if I had a pretty good year, he'd give me a bonus. With about six weeks of the season remaining, I fouled an Allie Reynolds fastball off my right ankle and broke it, ending my year. At the end of the season, I decided I'd ask Veeck for the bonus anyway. I had what was considered a bad year in those days, but by today's standards, I would be entitled to a raise. I hit only .245 with 14 home runs and 52 runs batted in 318 at bats. Bill knew I wasn't making much money to start with, about $3,500 for the year. He gave me a $5,000 bonus — more than my salary. That's just the kind of big-hearted guy he was.

Veeck would sometimes come down to pitch batting practice wearing that wooden leg of his. If he wasn't throwing batting practice, he'd take his shirt off and sit around with the guys and tell stories. He was always available to the players. Any time a player had a problem or something he wanted to talk about, he could talk to Bill. If it was a money issue, Bill took care of his ballplayer.

Several years later when Bill owned the St. Louis Browns, he and I were together at the bar of the Chase Hotel in St. Louis during baseball's winter meetings. I put a $20 bill on the bar to pay for our drinks. Bill took my twenty and tore it into little pieces, saying he'd buy all the drinks.

Veeck's accountant was Rudie Schaeffer, who always said his biggest job was keeping Bill from giving all of his money away. Bill was an intelligent guy, but he didn't pay much attention to detail. He needed Rudie for that. Bill did make sure we went first-class everywhere. He was always doing something extra for the players, which set him apart from the other tightfisted owners. Every ballplayer on our team thought the world of Bill Veeck.

Bill sold the Cleveland franchise in 1949 and used the proceeds to buy the St. Louis Browns, taking over in July 1951. The Browns were a last-place club and, competing with the Cardinals, couldn't draw many people. Veeck did his promotional best to turn the franchise around. A couple of months after he took over, he put a 3'7" midget named Eddie Gaedel in to pinch hit in the first inning of the second game of a doubleheader against the Detroit Tigers. Gaedel hit for Frank Saucier, who was injured and couldn't play anyway. The Tigers' pitcher, Bob Cain, walked Gaedel on four pitches. Browns manager Zack Taylor immediately sent in a pinch runner for Gaedel, who left the field to enthusiastic applause. League president Will Harridge put an immediate stop to that kind of shenanigan and accused Veeck of trying to make a circus out of baseball.

That didn't even slow Veeck down. He was one of the first to shoot off fireworks at the ballpark and dreamed up all kinds of special promotions like hiring Vic Damone to sing, giving nylon hose to female fans, hosting ice cream and cake night, staging a Harlem Globetrotters' basketball exhibition before one game and a dance after another. He even came up with a "Grandstand Managers" night, in which he let the fans dictate strategy by flashing "yes" or "no" signs for bunts, hit and runs, or steal attempts. He signed the ageless Satchel Paige, who was forty-two years old, to pitch and provided him with a rocking chair, complete with canopy, in the bullpen.

Veeck was a maverick, and many in the baseball establishment were jealous of him because they didn't have his imagination.

The Indians finished sixth after Veeck took them over in June 1946. In 1947 we improved to fourth place with an 80–74 record with the addition of Joe Gordon, Dale Mitchell, Don Black, and, I like to think, me. On our first road trip east in 1947 I learned a valuable lesson. I hit my first home run in Yankee Stadium off Allie Reynolds. I was excited to hit a home run there where all the Yankee greats had played, and I couldn't help smiling as I rounded the bases. Next time up, Allie hit me on the elbow with a fastball, and I thought my arm was broken. There was no doubt that Allie was delivering a message, and from that time on, I never smiled after hitting a home run.

After being hit, I was unable to continue and left the ball game. Afterwards, Lefty Weisman, our trainer, took me into the Yankee clubhouse to get checked out by the Yankees' team physician. Even though I was in pain, I was awed by the experience of walking into the Yankee clubhouse and seeing DiMaggio, Dickey, Berra, and some of the other greats sitting in front of their lockers drinking their beers after the game.

In 1954 I was traded to the Yankees, and Reynolds was still there. I used to kid Allie about hitting me with that pitch. I'd say, "I know you did it on purpose." Allie would just chuckle. We became and stayed good friends, and when Allie was stricken with cancer in the early 1990s, Bobby Brown, who had also been Allie's teammate with the Yankees, and I drove from Fort Worth to Oklahoma City to see him. I told Allie he had to get out of his hospital bed so he could throw another fastball at me. Bobby and I went back up to Oklahoma City for Allie's funeral when he passed away in late 1994. Allie was of American Indian descent and Bobby gave a wonderful eulogy, which he ended with "Hail to the Chief."

As I mentioned, Bob Hope was one of the minority Cleveland owners, although he hardly ever came around. We got a Christmas card from him, which was a big deal since he was such a big star. I showed mine to all my friends. It featured a caricature of Bob on the front with his family sitting on his trademark long, sloped nose.

I'd heard and read about Bob Feller all my life, and when I came up to the Indians in '46 he was suddenly my teammate. I was in awe of him. Feller had broken into the American League with a bang in 1936 when he was only seventeen, striking out 15 in his first start. He struck out 18 against the Tigers in 1938 to set the major league record, pitched an Opening Day no-hitter against the White Sox in 1940, and had consecutive win seasons of 24, 27, and 25 before losing most of four seasons to World War II. He came back in 1946 without missing a beat, putting together a 26–15 record while striking out 348 to set another major league record.

Bob was the biggest name on the Indians' roster and was a little standoffish. It wasn't that he wasn't a nice guy, but he didn't joke around and hang out like the rest of the guys. He was just by nature a private person. He was cordial to me, but we never were close.

Bob had tremendous stuff with his overpowering fastball and knee-buckling curve. In fact, he was similar to Nolan Ryan after Nolan developed his breaking pitch. Occasionally, as with all pitchers, Bob would struggle. Once in 1948 he started a game, and on four pitches the first four hitters singled, doubled, singled, and doubled. Two runs were in, runners were on second and third, and nobody was out. Lou Boudreau walked out to the mound and was joined by Jim Hegan, the catcher. I trotted over from first base to hear the conversation. Lou didn't say anything to Feller, but asked Hegan, "Hey, Jim, what's the matter? Does he have it today? Does he have his good stuff?"

Without missing a beat, Hegan said, "I don't know, Lou. I haven't caught anything yet."

Another time, Boudreau visited the mound and stayed longer than usual. The umpire, Red Jones, an old country boy, came out to break up the meeting. Lou turned to him and said, "Red, what would you do in this situation?" Red answered, "If I had a field this big, I'd plant it all in watermelons."

Bob Feller owned his own plane, a Beechcraft Bonanza. An airport was located about a half-mile from Municipal Stadium near downtown Cleveland, and once in a while Bob would commute from his home in the suburbs to the game by plane. He had a small collapsible motor scooter he'd then ride over to the ballpark, right up to his locker in the clubhouse. One day, however, he flew in and forgot to put his landing gear down, landing on that Beechcraft's belly. After that, he didn't fly to the ballpark anymore.

I always felt sorry that World War II took so much out of the heart of Bob's career, as it did Ted Williams and some of others. I also think it unfortunate Feller never won a World Series game. He pitched a two-hitter in the first game of our 1948 Series against the Boston Braves but lost 1–0. He also started Game 5 of that Series, but, without his good stuff, ended with a no-decision in a game we eventually lost.

The Indians' next time in the World Series was in 1954, when I was with the Yankees. Cleveland won 111 games and finished eight games ahead of the Yankees, behind the big three of Bob Lemon, Mike Garcia, and Early Wynn. Bob, then thirty-five years old and battling a tired arm, still finished 13–3 as a spot starter. But Cleveland ran into a hot New York Giants team and was unexpectedly swept.

Feller was the winning pitcher in the 1946 All-Star Game in Boston, and his record in his five All-Star Games shows how dominant he was. Against the best the National League had to offer, Bob gave up only one run and five hits in 12 1/3 innings, striking out thirteen. His All-Star earned run average is a minuscule 0.73. Little wonder Lou Boudreau considered Feller one of the best clutch pitchers of all time.

In 1947 I roomed with Hal Peck, one of our outfielders and pinch hitters, who hailed from Wisconsin. In 1948 the club paired me with Joe Gordon, our second baseman, who'd won the American League Most Valuable Player Award in 1942 and was a many time All-Star. We became very good friends, and he never stopped trying to help me become a better player. Joe was the leader of the ballclub, the one we always looked to when things were going badly. He had a great sense of humor and could be very funny. Sometimes when he'd be in a bit of a slump, he'd say, "Give me a Thurman Tucker bat."

Thurman Tucker was a reserve outfielder, a slight guy who used a very lightweight bat. So Joe would go up to bat with a Thurman Tucker bat, and it seemed like he would hit a home run almost every time. It was amazing.

All the teams stayed at the Chase Hotel when they were in St. Louis. The Chase wasn't air conditioned, and St. Louis was often miserably hot in the summer. One evening in 1948 he and I came back to the sweltering room after a hot and humid afternoon game. Joe went into the bathroom, filled up two glasses with water, poured them on his bed, took off his clothes, and jumped in. "Roomie," he said, "this is how you cool off in St. Louis." I took his lead and followed suit.

Joe formed a singing quartet with our trainer Lefty Weisman, Jim Hegan, and me. Jim sang tenor, Joe baritone, Lefty bass, and I sang lead. We weren't bad; we sang all the good old harmony songs like "Those Wedding Bells are Breaking Up That Old Gang of Mine." We sang when we were waiting in a train station, in a bar, or in the ballpark. Several times when it was raining in Cleveland and the tarp was on the field, we got the microphone for the loud-speaker system and entertained the fans with our harmony while we were waiting to see if the game would be rained out. We enjoyed our quartet and became very close because of it.

I was thrilled when Joe was finally elected to the Hall of Fame in 2008. It was a long overdue tribute to a great ballplayer and a wonderful man.

Bob Lemon was my best friend on the team. We'd played together in Baltimore and both entered the service after the 1942 season. Bob showed promise as a pitcher in 1946 after the war years, winning four and losing five with a great 2.49 ERA as a spot starter and reliever. Early in 1947, however, he struggled so much that the Indians put him on waivers, and the Washington Senators claimed him. But Bill Veeck got angry when word leaked out that Lemon was going to Washington and revoked the waivers. It turned out to be one of the best baseball decisions Veeck ever made.

Bob and I were both struggling when he was put on waivers. We were in Boston to play the Red Sox, and I said to Bob, "Let's go out and have an early workout. You practice your curveball on me and I'll practice hitting it." So Lemon threw everything he had to me, and I tried to hit it. From then on Bob started pitching well and winning, ending up with an 11–5 record for 1947. It helped me as well, but not with the dramatic impact it had for him.

Years later when I was with the Yankees, the Indians came to town. I was dating my future wife Bette, and one evening I took her to meet my old teammates—Lemon, Hegan, Early Wynn, and a couple of others. We all went to dinner and ended up imbibing quite a bit. Then we retired to one of their suites and drank some more while we swapped stories. I finally got home about five o'clock in the morning. We'd been up most of the night, and we had to play that afternoon. Most of my drinking buddies were pitchers and weren't going to play. I was rarely hungover when I went to the ballpark, but I was that day. Luckily, I wasn't in the starting lineup. In the eighth inning, however, we were behind by one run with Ray Narleski, the Indians' ace relief pitcher, on the mound. We loaded the bases, and Casey Stengel sent me up to pinch-hit.

My former teammates and recent drinking buddies were all hollering at me out of their dugout. Most of the time I was a dead pull hitter, pulling the ball to right field. Well, Narleski wheeled a fastball toward the plate, and I didn't get around on it like I usually did. I did, however, manage to drive the ball down the left-field line. By the time the left fielder retrieved the ball, I'd struggled into third ready to collapse with a bases-clearing triple. Fortunately, Stengel sent in a pinch-runner. As I trotted by the Indians' dugout to get to our dugout, I gave my old buddies the raspberry. They were all tongue tied, while wondering how I could manage to hit the ball.

In 1947 a pitcher named Paul Calvert was with us for a little while, trying to earn a spot on the club. Paul was from Montreal, had a degree in accounting, and could speak several languages. He was also a very witty guy. We were playing a night game in Cleveland, and Paul had gone shopping that afternoon and bought himself a pair of red silk pajamas. He came to the ballpark right from his shopping trip, and during batting practice Paul decided he'd try on his new pajamas. Just as he got his pajama pants and pajama shirt on, manager Lou Boudreau walked into the clubhouse. He saw Calvert standing there in his red pajamas and asked, "What are you doing?"

Without pausing, Paul said, "Well, Lou, it's a night game, and I'm just getting ready for it."

Unfortunately, Paul was sent back to the minors a few days later. I think it had to do more with his pitching than his pajamas.

I figured since Boudreau was a young manager, he wanted to be associated more with older players, like Joe Gordon and Ken Keltner. He was extremely friendly with those guys. But with the younger guys, like Dale Mitchell and me, who were trying to make it in the big leagues, he didn't offer the support other managers might have. For example, Mitchell had led the Texas League in hitting in 1946 with Oklahoma City and had hit well in spring training in '47. At the end of camp, Boudreau told Dale he was going to be his center fielder. We weren't a month into the season, however, before Boudreau optioned Mitchell back to Oklahoma City. We were in Philadelphia when I saw Mitch on the elevator at our hotel. He was white as a sheet. I asked him what was wrong, and he told me Boudreau had sent him back to Double-A.

As it happened, Mitch was quickly back with us, in part because the Indians violated a rule in sending him to Oklahoma City. Since Baltimore was the highest affiliate of the Indians, they had first choice of any player who was sent out. When the Indians sent Mitchell to Oklahoma City, Baltimore complained. So the club brought Mitchell back to pack him off to Baltimore. However, Hank Edwards, one of our outfielders in Cleveland, got hurt the night Dale came back, so Boudreau put Mitchell into the lineup. Dale lashed three hits and was in the lineup for good, hitting .316 for the season. Then in our pennant-winning 1948 season, Mitch hit .336, third in the league, and clubbed 204 hits, second in the league behind Bob Dillinger of the Browns. So it was a mistake to send Dale out, but fortunately he made the most of his opportunity.

Even though I was struggling during my rookie year in 1947, I always hustled and never lost my desire or determination. I had confidence that eventually it would work out for me. Around midseason, Bill McKechnie, our veteran coach, came to me and said, "I know you're struggling. Why don't you go talk to Lou and tell him that you know you're struggling, but you want to stay in the lineup because you believe you're going to start hitting better." I took McKechnie's advice and went in and talked to Lou. He said, "Don't worry about it. You're my first baseman, and you're going to be our first baseman for the future." That was encouraging. The next day I hit a home run and got three hits in a doubleheader against the Detroit Tigers.

We traveled to Chicago for our next series, and word was that Larry Doby was coming in. Larry would be the first black player in the American League. I heard nothing more until the second day we were in Chicago, when Doby joined the team. We played the first game of a doubleheader, and Lou came into the dressing room between games and said, "Robbie, I want to borrow your glove. I want Doby to play first base." I told him he could borrow my glove, all right—but I was quitting. I couldn't believe what I was hearing. Two days before the manager had told me, "Don't worry about it. You're my first baseman," and I'd gone out and performed well. Doby had never even played first. He was a second baseman, and Joe Gordon, who was a seasoned veteran, wouldn't have minded at all if Doby played some second base. .

I was so mad I told Les Fleming, our other first baseman, "If Boudreau puts Doby at first, let's quit." I didn't want to be kicked around like that. Fleming said, "You can quit, but I ain't." But when the second game began, I stayed in the clubhouse. Fortunately, Bill McKechnie came into the clubhouse during the game and talked to me straight: "I understand why you quit, and your teammates understand as well. But the public isn't going to understand it that way. They're going to say you didn't want Doby to play because he's black. I think you're making a big mistake, and I don't want to see you play the rest of your career with that stigma on you." I then got it. I put my uniform back on and went back on the bench in the sixth inning. On my return to the dugout no one made any comment, but I got a couple of pats on the back.

Larry and I became friends, and I believe he understood that I threatened to quit because of my anger at Boudreau, not because he was a black guy coming in. He was a quiet, no-nonsense guy with loads of talent. He could have been an excellent first baseman (I'm happy it didn't turn out that way), but with his speed, arm strength, and ability he was an ideal center fielder. Larry was a good teammate and contributed greatly to the Indians' success.

I don't think Larry has ever gotten the recognition he deserves for being the first black ballplayer in the American League. He came into the major leagues the same year Jackie Robinson did, only a couple of months later, took the same abuse, and was under the same pressure. Jackie deserves all the credit in the world for what he did, but I don't understand why everyone overlooks Larry.

My season came to a premature end in early August when we were playing the Yankees at home. Allie Reynolds was pitching and threw me a low inside fastball that I hit squarely down into my right ankle. The blow numbed my foot and ankle immediately. I tried to continue my time at bat but couldn't. I limped into the clubhouse and waited on the trainer's table for the doctor to examine me. When he arrived, he manipulated my ankle and told me that he didn't think it was broken, but that I should go have it X-rayed anyway. I showered, got dressed, and drove myself to the doctor's office for X-rays. They told me to wait in the waiting room after the X-ray. I was sitting reading a magazine when they came out with a wheelchair and said, "This wheelchair is for you. You have a broken ankle."

They drove me to a hospital, admitted me, and put my leg in a cast to below my knee. I stayed in the hospital overnight. They told me I'd have the cast for six weeks, so I knew my season was over.

It was a disappointing way to end my rookie year in the big leagues. I hadn't been hitting the way I thought I could, and had hoped to improve over the last third of the season. Instead, I was sitting at home.

### Extra Inning

Nineteen forty-seven was my first full year in the big leagues, and I was still in awe of a lot of the stars. Early in the year Joe DiMaggio reached first base and surprised me by saying. "Hey, Eddie, you and I are having the same problem with our hitting."

I was surprised Joe knew my name but I said, "Yeah, Joe, what is that?"

He said, "We aren't getting the bat out in front soon enough. We're both late with our swings."

I agreed and was thrilled he would notice the way I hit and take the time to say something about it to me.

*Chapter 7*

## A MAGICAL YEAR IN CLEVELAND

We finished in fourth place in 1947 with an 80–74 won-loss record, seventeen games behind the pennant-winning Yankees. My wife Elayne was pregnant and we decided to spend the winter in Cleveland so that she could remain with the same obstetrician. I worked for the Indians that off-season selling season ticket packages. Nineteen forty-eight started off wonderfully with the birth on February 1 of our son William E. Robinson III, whom we called Robby.

I was unhappy with the year I'd had in 1947 and so I went into spring training in 1948 with a good deal of apprehension. I was in for a shock when I arrived in Tucson. I discovered that my dad was there and had taken a job as an assistant clubhouse attendant. I still don't know how he got the job, but he was very pleased to have it. I hadn't seen or heard from him in over a year. I was dismayed and embarrassed at his having such a menial job, but my teammates were great about the situation.

My dad was a raging alcoholic, and I was afraid sometime during spring training he would show up drunk. It only happened one time, and I was spared embarrassment by Joe Gordon, my roommate. One afternoon while I was away Dad came down to the team hotel, obviously inebriated, and ran into Joe, who hustled him upstairs to our room and put him to bed. When I arrived back at the hotel I saw Joe in the lobby, and he told me that my dad was upstairs asleep in my bed. I thanked Joe for taking care of my dad, and we let my father sleep it off. He woke up and left and never had another problem all spring. When spring training was over, Dad headed back to Texas while we barnstormed north to Cleveland.

I didn't see my dad again until June of 1951 when I was playing for the White Sox. We were playing a Sunday day game in Chicago, and one of the ticket takers came up to the clubhouse before the game and told me that there was a man at the gate who said he was my father and wanted to see me. I went down and there was my dad, looking down and out. I got him a seat for the game and afterwards took him to my hotel, the Conrad Hilton, and got him a room for the night. The next day he got cleaned up, and I took him out and bought him a whole new wardrobe. I rented him a room in the YMCA, right behind the Hilton, so we were neighbors.

We were at the beginning of a two-week home stand, so I saw a lot of Dad during that stretch. He'd come to the games, and then we'd go out to eat together afterwards. He was on the wagon then, and I enjoyed spending that time with him. Before we left for the next road trip, I was able to get him a night watchman's job through a friend of mine who owned a trucking company. When I left for the road trip he was doing great with his job and wasn't drinking. When I came back ten days later from the road trip he'd lost his job, pawned his clothes, didn't have a dime, and was about to be evicted from the YMCA. I said, "Dad, we can't do this. You've got to go back to Texas." I bought him a train ticket and put him on a train to Dallas. It was the last time I saw my dad alive.

I was with the Yankees in July 1954 when I received a call that my dad had died of a heart attack near downtown Dallas. I flew to Dallas to identify the body and then arranged for and attended his funeral in our hometown, Paris, Texas. Dad was sixty-five years old.

Over the winter of 1947–48 Bill Veeck brought in my boyhood hero Hank Greenberg as a vice president. There was some talk Hank might spell me some at first base. Hank had played for the Pittsburgh Pirates in 1947 and at thirty-six years of age had hit twenty-five home runs for the Bucs. But Hank announced he was through as a player and wanted to learn about the front office side of baseball. Tris Speaker, the legendary center fielder from Hubbard, Texas, was with us that spring as a coach and worked with Doby and our other outfielders. We had a strong spring, and coming into the season we knew we had a good team. But I don't think any of us thought we'd become World Champions, which, of course, is precisely what did happen. It helped that Lou Boudreau at shortstop, Joe Gordon at second base, Ken Keltner at third, and Dale Mitchell in left field all had career years.

It would have been hard to foresee how great our pitching, which had been pretty good but not spectacular in 1947, would become. We had close to the same staff with Bob Feller, Bob Lemon, Don Black, Steve Gromek, Al Gettel, and Eddie Klieman. Gene Bearden, a lanky southpaw up from the Oakland Oaks of the Pacific Coast League, had a good spring but wasn't even in the starting rotation when the season began. Although he'd won sixteen games with the Oaks after not making our club in 1947, no one could have predicted the role he would play for us in '48. He'd not only win twenty games, but he'd get better as the season wore on and would become our late season go-to-guy on the mound.

Late in the spring, Veeck took a flyer on Russ Christopher and purchased him from the Athletics for $25,000. Russ was a veteran pitcher who'd compiled a 10–7 record and 2.90 ERA out of the bullpen for the A's in 1947. His health was precarious, however, because of a weak heart that made him susceptible to respiratory problems. He was battling pneumonia when Veeck bought him, but by the start of the season he was ready to go. He ended up having a great season for us out of the pen and was our main late-inning reliever.

The Cleveland fans must have sensed something because 73,163 came out for our April 20 opener against the St. Louis Browns, the largest opening day crowd in history. We gave them reason to return as Bob Feller shut out the Brownies on two hits to win 2–0. That performance propelled us to a blazing start; we won our first six games, prompting Joe Gordon to tell me we were going to win the pennant. Ken Keltner, coming off two mediocre years, hit home runs in our first four games, and after the first week of the season Lou Boudreau was batting a lusty .519. After Joe's prediction, however, we proceeded to lose four straight before resuming our winning ways.

Connie Mack's Athletics also bolted out of the gate. Going into a May 24 double-header against the Yankees, we were 17–7, one game ahead of the A's and two ahead of the Yankees. Our infield started fast at the plate, and Boudreau was still over .400. Keltner was leading the league with twelve homers and was hitting .326. Joe Gordon already had twenty-six RBIs, and I was off to a good start, hitting .304 and driving in some runs. We split the doubleheader with the Yankees in front of over 78,000 fans, and we knew we were in a pennant race.

The Athletics were still hot on our tail when they came to Municipal Stadium for a four-game weekend series starting on June 19. We lost the first game Friday night 5–4, but won 4–0 on Saturday before only 15,000 fans. Folks must have been anticipating the doubleheader Sunday when we had Feller and Lemon pitching. Almost 83,000 fans crammed into the stadium Sunday, breaking the all-time single day attendance record, to watch us win both games, the second on a four-hit shutout by Bob Lemon. We emerged from the weekend series with a lead of three and a half games on the Yankees and four games on the Athletics. It would be the largest lead we'd enjoy all season.

We were in New York to play the Yankees on the day in June 1948 when the Yankees retired Babe Ruth's famous number three. Our visiting clubhouse was behind the third base dugout, which had been the Yankees' clubhouse when Babe played. When the Yankees moved over to the first base clubhouse, the team didn't move the individual lockers. The Babe's locker was still in the third base clubhouse with his name on top and the doors closed. Babe wanted to dress one last time in his own locker, so he used our clubhouse on that day. He dressed and then sat in our dugout and talked to us before the ceremony. He had his personal physician with him. Babe spoke in a raspy voice, the result of the throat cancer that would soon take his life. He appeared to be a little shaky, and as he started up the dugout steps to go onto the field, I grabbed a bat out of the bat rack and handed it to him for support. He used the bat as a cane while he walked out to home plate and leaned on it during the ceremony. There is a famous picture of the Babe gazing toward center field, resting on that bat with his famous number three on his back.

When he came back to our dugout, he handed me the bat and sat down. I don't know why, but I asked the Babe to autograph it for me. He was happy to sign it and then shortly after walked back to the clubhouse.

Beginning in 1952, I owned a restaurant in Baltimore called Eddie Robinson's Gorusch House. I displayed the bat there for several years with a photo of the Babe walking back to our dugout. As the years went on, that type of baseball memorabilia became quite valuable. Barry Halper, who was a friend of mine and a minority partner in the Yankees, had a huge Babe Ruth collection. Barry had always said that if I wanted to sell the bat, to let him know. I had no idea what the bat was worth, but after about thirty years of holding onto it, I decided to test the market by quoting a price to Barry I knew he wouldn't pay. I called and told him I was thinking about selling the bat and wanted $10,000 for it. He surprised me by saying, "I'll have the money to you tomorrow." I was dumbfounded, but there wasn't much I could do but send him the bat. The last time the bat was auctioned it brought over $125,000. So selling that bat was one of the many dumb moves I've made. It now resides in Bob Feller's museum in Van Meter, Iowa.

On June 30 in Detroit, Bob Lemon continued his dominant pitching, no-hitting the Tigers in an hour and thirty-three minutes. We scored two runs off Art Houtteman in the first for the only scoring in the game. We couldn't shake the A's or the Yankees, however. On Saturday July 3, Boudreau and I homered to help Bob Feller to an 8–2 win over the Browns, and on the Fourth of July we were a game and a half in front of both the Athletics and Yankees, with a 41–24 won-loss record.

Bill Veeck was never one to stand pat, and he signed the legendary Satchel Paige on July 7, 1948, as the first black pitcher in the American League. By this time Satchel was well over forty years old, but he could still pitch. He was a great guy, and everybody loved him from the minute he joined us. We were in Chicago when we signed Paige, and the fans knocked the gates down in the hopes they'd see him in his first major league game.

Satch was a funny-looking guy on the mound, tall and lanky and limber. He didn't have great stuff anymore, but he had finesse and could change speeds and had perfect control of his pitches. He threw a hesitation pitch in which he would step toward home plate and release the ball late to fool the hitter. He could still get hitters out.

Paige's first big league appearance was in relief of Bob Lemon on July 9 against the St. Louis Browns in Cleveland. He pitched two scoreless innings after allowing lead-off hits in both innings, entertaining the crowd with a variety of pitching motions on the mound. After several more relief appearances, Boudreau started Satch at home against Washington and their ace Early Wynn on August 3 before a full house of 72,434. It was an important game: we were now embroiled in a four-team race (the Red Sox had come on like a house afire) and were one-half game out of the lead.

Even the imperturbable Paige must have been nervous because after Eddie Yost popped up for the first out, he walked Al Kozar and Gil Coan, which was highly unusual for Satch. Eddie Stewart then slammed a drive off the fence in right-center field for a triple to drive in both runners. But Satch quickly settled down and retired the side to get out of the inning. We took the lead on a home run by Jim Hegan, our catcher, in the sixth inning. Paige had allowed only one more run when Boudreau sent Hal Peck up to pinch hit for him in the seventh. Peck promptly smacked another home run to put us up 5–3. Eddie Klieman pitched a scoreless eighth and ninth to give Satch his first big league win.

The victory pushed us back into first place for the first time in ten days. At least we were statistically in first place, by .002 percentage points. Only .006 percentage points separated the top four teams. It was the closest race in baseball history to that point.

After an off-day we again defeated the Senators 3–0 behind the pitching and hitting of Gene Bearden. We got exactly three hits against Ray Scarborough, and all three were home runs. Jim Hegan hit two and Bearden hit the other. We played great defense and turned a record six double plays. I participated in all six and tied the record for first basemen, while Joe Gordon was in on five of them, tying the second base record.

The downside was that Lou Boudreau was banged up and knocked out of action on a collision at second base as we headed into a four-game weekend home series with the Yankees. We hung on to win the first game 9–7 on Friday night before a crowd of over 71,000, snapping Eddie Lopat's nine-game winning streak. On Saturday, however, Vic Raschi threw a four-hit shutout to beat us 4–0 behind Joe DiMaggio's two doubles, three runs batted in, and steal of home. That brought us to the Sunday doubleheader where we squared off before a crowd of 73,484. We trailed 6–1 heading into the bottom of the seventh of the first game. Ken Keltner walked, but Yankee starter Frank "Spec" Shea retired the next two batters. Then John Berardino and I both slugged home runs to close the gap to 6–4.

We kept the inning going after my home run, loading the bases on two hits and a walk. With Yankee ace relief pitcher Joe Page in the game, Boudreau, who couldn't run much and whose right thumb was so sore he could scarcely hold the bat, put himself in as a pinch hitter for Thurman Tucker. He promptly smacked a ground ball single up the middle to tie the score 6–6. Lou then brought in Satchel Paige to hold off the Yankees, and Satch got them out in the eighth. In the bottom half, I came up again with two outs and one on against the Yankees' Page. Earlier, in late May, he'd struck me out with the bases loaded in the ninth to save a game for the Yankees, but this time

I connected for my second home run in as many innings to send us into the lead 8–6. Satch and Russ Christopher retired the Yankees in the ninth, and we had a dramatic come-from-behind win.

The second game pitted Steve Gromek against the Yankees' Bob Porterfield, a young phenom making his major league debut after going 15–6 at Newark in the International League. The game was scoreless in the bottom of the fifth when I knocked my third home run of the day over the right field fence to give us a 1–0 lead. The Yankees tied it in the sixth, but we squeezed ahead in the seventh when Hal Peck hit a line drive off Porterfield's pitching hand to drive in our second run. Eddie Klieman held the Yankees at bay for the last two innings to give us a doubleheader sweep and a two-game lead over New York. That ended one of my most memorable days in baseball.

The Yankee series completed a home stand in which we won nine of twelve, including six of eight against the Yankees and Red Sox. I batted .395 for the twelve games, and the team's and my confidence in our ability to win the pennant were riding high. We were headed next to a western road swing, and I continued my hot hitting in Detroit on Monday, blasting a three-run homer to help Gene Bearden defeat the Tigers 5–3. We struggled some for the rest of the trip, however, playing about .500 baseball and dropping out of first place.

On August 13 in his second start, Satchel Paige pitched us back into the league lead, shutting out the White Sox 5–0 before 51,000-plus fans in Chicago. Boudreau trotted Satch out against the White Sox again one week later, this time at home before a record night crowd of 78,382. The Sox came close against Satch but still couldn't score. We scratched a run off Bill Wight in the fourth inning and hung on for an important 1–0 victory. It was our eighth win and fourth shutout in a row and extended our scoreless innings streak to thirty-nine, only two short of the major league record for a team. For the season, Paige would finish with a 6–1 won-loss record and a stingy 2.48 earned run average in spot duty to help spark our run to the pennant.

Satch sometimes had problems with his stomach and took pills to control his indigestion. That year he was pitching a great game against the Senators in Griffith Stadium when he suffered from indigestion in the sixth inning. He couldn't find his pills. We all scurried around looking for them, and Bob Lemon finally found them in the clubhouse. Bob hurried out with two pills and a glass of water and handed them to Paige just before he went out to pitch the seventh inning. Satch told Bob he was only supposed to take one pill, but Bob said for him to take two because they'd do him twice as much good. So Satch swallowed both pills and went out and finished the game.

Bob Lemon extended our scoreless streak to forty-seven innings and broke the American League record the day after Satch's shutout, blanking the White Sox for eight innings. We led 2–0 heading into the ninth, but Bob gave up a walk and home runs to Aaron Robinson and Dave Philley to push the Sox ahead 3–2. We couldn't score in the bottom half, and in a matter of minutes had lost our shutout streak along with our winning streak.

Our momentum broken, we lost a doubleheader to the last place White Sox the following day and then dropped four of six in Boston and New York. We continued to scuffle, and after the Labor Day doubleheaders on September 6, were in third place, four and a half games behind the Red Sox and three behind the Yankees.

One of our hitters thought it was time for desperate measures and suggested we try to get the visiting catcher's signs. We picked a spot in the Municipal Stadium scoreboard in center field, and placed one of our pitchers out there with a telescope sitting on a tripod. Our pitcher would let us know when he had the opposing catcher's signals. We had one of the grounds crew dressed in a white uniform sit in the bleachers alongside the scoreboard. For the hitters who wanted the signals, he'd hold his legs together for a fastball, spread them for a curveball, and get up and walk around if he didn't have the sign.

Some of our hitters, including me, didn't want the signs. Our pitcher who was sitting in the scoreboard once asked me why I didn't want to know what pitch was coming. I told him I didn't look for specific pitches because Rogers Hornsby, who was with us in spring training as a coach and was one of the greatest hitters of all time, had advised me to just hit what I saw. Of course, Hornsby was so good he could just react to the pitch. I probably shouldn't have followed his advice because I wasn't as good a hitter and needed all the help I could get. I should've been looking for pitches.

Joe Gordon, Ken Keltner, and some of the others may have benefitted from getting the signs, but it sure didn't help me. Of course, we didn't have the signs on the road, and it had no impact on the playoff game against the Red Sox in Boston or in the World Series. Over the years a number of teams have been accused of stealing signs from the scoreboard, such as the New York Giants in the old Polo Grounds, the Brooklyn Dodgers in Ebbets Field, and the Cubs in Wrigley Field. But I've always thought sign stealing from way out there was overrated, and that it rarely if ever has had any impact on the outcome of a game.

Our local sportswriters counted us out after our early September swoon, but we didn't give up. We came home for a long home stand and ripped off six wins in a row heading into a September 13 home makeup game against the Browns. Don Black, one of our spot starters and relievers who'd shared a house with Elayne and me the previous year, started on the mound for us. Early in the game he came to bat and swung at and missed the first pitch. He immediately grabbed his neck, staggered around in a small circle, and said, "What hit me?" He then collapsed at the plate. Lefty Weisman, our trainer, ran out of the dugout and I followed, thinking my former roomie was in real trouble. Don was semi-conscious, but Lefty wanted us to help him walk off the field so that his wife, who was in the stands, wouldn't worry. I said, "No. We're going to carry him off," because I thought Don was in bad shape. We called for a stretcher and carried him into the clubhouse, where we put him on the training table. Don was making a loud guttural noise when he breathed. The team physician, Dr. Edward Castle, arrived and said Don was making the death rattle. He didn't think Don would live long enough for us to get him to the hospital. An ambulance arrived quickly and sped away with Don. We were left in shock, wondering and worrying about Don, but with a game to play.

Before the end of the game we received word that Don had had an aneurysm rupture in his head. It had apparently stopped bleeding, and he had a chance if they could keep it from bleeding again. Don didn't regain consciousness until after the World Series, but then he began to improve. He was finally released from the hospital a few months later and seemed to be normal. He tried to pitch the following year but was not successful and had to retire. Sadly, Don would die before his time in 1959 at the age of forty-two.

Don's illness shook us up, and we were worried about him, but the nature of baseball is that there's always a game to be played the next day. Further, we were in the midst of a ferocious pennant race with a crucial game to be won almost every day. We had to face the Yankees, who were in town for a single game, the next afternoon. We lost 6–5, leaving the tying and winning runs on second and third in the ninth inning. But the Indians were nothing if not resilient that year. We turned around and won six straight games again, sweeping the Senators and Athletics, who were finally starting to fade. We went 12–2 on our home stand and were right back in the pennant race, a game behind the Red Sox and a half game ahead of the Yankees with nine games remaining.

The Red Sox followed the A's to town for a single game scheduled for the afternoon of September 22. Bill Veeck talked the Red Sox into playing a night game instead so that he could hold a special donation night for Don Black, with all the proceeds going to Don and his family. Although the game would be a huge draw, Bill wanted to insure the largest crowd possible. With Bob Feller pitching in the biggest game of the year, we drew 76,772, and Don received over $40,000 from the Indians. No one could doubt that Bill Veeck was the best players' owner ever.

Feller, who'd struggled earlier in the summer with injuries, was on his game that night, holding the Red Sox without a hit until the sixth inning. We cruised to a 5–2 win and into a first place deadlock with the Red Sox with identical 91–55 records. It was the first time since August 25 that we'd been in the top spot.

We had eight remaining games, three in Detroit and then two at home versus the White Sox, before the Tigers came to town for a season-ending three-game week-end series. For reasons I've never understood, Boudreau benched me after Labor Day, replacing me with Walt Judnich, a thirty-one-year-old veteran. But in Detroit, I was back in the lineup, with Judnich moving to right field, Larry Doby over to center, and Thur-man Tucker the odd man out. We lost, however, to Detroit 4–3 in the first game of the series. Incredibly, when the dust settled that day, we were in a dead heat with the Red Sox and Yankees, all of us with a 91–56 won-loss record.

We bounced back again, beating the Tigers 9–3 and 4–1 behind Bearden's knuck-leball and Feller's return to form. At the end of the weekend we were one game ahead of both the Yankees and Red Sox. We were off on Monday before hosting the White Sox on Tuesday and Wednesday. Now Boudreau really went for it, starting Bearden and Feller each on only two days' rest. It worked, as we won both critical games, 11–0 and 5–2. Feller struggled in the second game, and we fell behind 2–0 until the sixth, when a walk and consecutive homers by Joe Gordon and Ken Keltner catapulted us into the lead.

Heading into the last weekend of the season, we were a game and a half in front of both the Yankees and Red Sox. Two victories out of the remaining three games with the Tigers would clinch the pennant; one win would insure a tie and a playoff game. Bob Lemon, who'd pitched over 290 innings that summer, took a 3–2 lead into the top of the ninth of the opener on Friday afternoon. We were three outs from clinching a tie for the pennant, but Bob and two relievers couldn't hold the Tigers in the ninth, and we lost 5–3.

Our lead was now one game over the Red Sox and Yankees, who, while off on Friday were playing each other on Saturday and Sunday. Our loss to Detroit meant that the pennant wouldn't be decided until the 154th game on Sunday, since either New York or Boston had to win on Saturday. Gene Bearden, pitching for the third time in eight days, again came to our rescue on Saturday, shutting the Tigers out 8–0 on a dark, cold, and windy day. It was his nineteenth win and sixth shutout of the season. I hit a home run in the sixth against Dizzy Trout, who was pitching in relief of rookie Lou Kretlow. I'd been struggling at the plate since being reinserted into the starting lineup, so it felt good to contribute again.

At Fenway Park in Boston the Red Sox had defeated the Yankees 5–1 behind the pitching of Jack Kramer and a home run and double from Ted Williams. The pennant race was down to two teams; if we won on Sunday we would go to the World Series, but if we lost and the BoSox won, we would end in a dead heat and would have to head to Boston for a one game playoff on Monday.

Unfortunately for the Indians, that's exactly what happened. The Red Sox again conquered the Yankees, 10–6, fueled by two doubles from Williams and a home run from Vern Stephens. On a cold and windy but sunny day, Boudreau selected Feller to start for us on three days' rest. Bob had won nine consecutive starts and would be after his sixth straight twenty-win season. Facing us would be the Tigers' southpaw ace Hal Newhouser, who was also throwing on three days' rest after beating the Browns for his twentieth win the previous Wednesday.

To put it simply, Feller didn't have it while Newhouser was almost unhittable. My fourth inning single was the only hit we managed for the first six innings. By that time we were down 6–0, and Bob was long gone from the game, having given up four runs in the first inning. We ended up losing 7–1 and sending a crowd of 74,181 shivering fans home disappointed. For the year we'd drawn an amazing 2,620,627, an attendance record that stood for more than thirty years.

Since we'd lost a coin flip several days earlier, we had to head to Boston right after the game for the playoff game the next day. It was not a happy thought. We'd gone 18–5 on the stretch run and still hadn't quite won the pennant.

In our meeting after the game, Boudreau asked us our opinion of who should start the playoff game. He told us his choice would be Bearden, even though he would be throwing on one day's rest and even though a left-handed starter had not pitched a complete game in Fenway Park all season. After some silence Joe Gordon spoke up and said, "Lou, we went along with you for 154 games and finished in a tie. There's not a man in this room who two weeks ago wouldn't have settled for a tie. I'm sure we can go along with you for another game. You've done a good job handling our pitching all year, and I think you should go with your choice." We all agreed with Joe's sentiments, and that was the end of the discussion.

We then headed to the train station for the overnight trip to Boston. Our wives stayed behind. If we won the playoff they would follow the next day, which would be an off day before the World Series started against the Boston Braves, who had swept to the National League pennant by six and a half games behind "Spahn and Sain and Pray for Rain." Several of my teammates got a little tipsy on that train ride to Boston. In fact, we had to undress one of them and put him in his berth. I won't mention any names, but the next day he hit two home runs.

Amid much speculation, Red Sox manager Joe McCarthy selected thirty-seven-year-old veteran right-hander Denny Galehouse to start against us. Although McCarthy's choice was then and has continued to be much second-guessed, Galehouse had pitched well against us and knew his way around the block in big games. He'd been instrumental in the St. Louis Browns' run to the 1944 pennant and had pitched two complete games in the World Series that year against the Cardinals, winning 2–1 and losing 2–0.

Boudreau surprised me and everyone else when he posted the starting lineup. He did seek me out to tell me he was going to stack our lineup with right-handed hitters. Of course, Fenway Park's Green Monster in left field was an inviting target for all hitters from the right side. It was unorthodox, but he inserted Bob Kennedy, who had been mostly a pinch-hitter, in right field and Allie Clark at first base. It was the first time Clark had ever played first base; he didn't even own a first baseman's glove. That meant I was on the bench for the biggest game of the year, but I tried to stay positive, knowing that if we got ahead I'd probably be put in for defense.

The wind was blowing out to Fenway's Green Monster in left. In the top of the first Boudreau lifted a ball to left, and the jet stream carried it just over the wall for a home run. The Red Sox tied it in the bottom half of the inning on a double by Johnny Pesky and a single through the hole at shortstop by Vern Stephens. Bearden was shaky again in the second, but with Feller and Lemon warming up, got out of a two-on, two-out jam by getting Dom DiMaggio to ground sharply to Keltner at third. A base hit by DiMaggio and Bearden would probably have been out of the game.

The game remained tied 1–1 until the top of the fourth when Boudreau and Joe Gordon led off with base hits. Ken Keltner was next. He came up looking for the bunt sign. There wasn't one, so he laced a 2–2 inside fastball off of the light tower behind the Green Monster for a three-run homer. With that, McCarthy yanked Galehouse and put in Ellis Kinder, who'd gone 10–7 for the Red Sox. Larry Doby greeted Kinder with a drive off the top of the Monster for a double. After Kennedy sacrificed Larry to third, Doby scored our fifth run on a ground out to short by Jim Hegan.

Boudreau had me take over first base in the bottom of the fourth, ostensibly for defense since we had a solid lead. I think Allie Clark must have been relieved to have been taken out. He'd been so nervous about making an error while playing an unfamiliar position that he literally could not sit down in the dugout between innings.

In the top of the fifth Lou hit another home run against the screen over the Monster to stretch our lead to 6–1. In the bottom of the sixth Bobby Doerr clubbed his 27th homer of the year with Ted Williams aboard to narrow our lead to 6–3. We loaded the bases in the top of the seventh with only one out but couldn't score. In the eighth inning, however, we cobbled together another run, helped immeasurably by a two-base error by Ted Williams, who dropped a long fly ball from Bearden after a long run.

Bearden continued to make great pitches with runners on base to hold the Red Sox at bay. In the top of the ninth, I led off with a single into the hole at shortstop. Vern Stephens got his glove on the ball but couldn't make a throw to first. Boudreau then singled to left, his fourth hit of the ballgame. Kinder wild pitched us to second and third and then intentionally walked Joe Gordon. I then scored on a double play grounder by Keltner to make the score 8–3.

In the bottom of the ninth, Bearden allowed only a walk to pinch hitter Billy Hitchcock. With two outs, Birdie Tebbetts hit a chopper that Keltner at third cut off. Kenny threw to me at first in plenty of time, and we had the pennant at last. We mobbed Bearden near the pitching mound, who looked sort of surprised that we were celebrating. I later learned that Gene had lost track of the innings and thought he had another inning to go. For some reason, I thought to keep the ball Keltner had fielded and thrown to me for the pennant-winning last out. I still have it, over sixty years later.

Bearden's complete game win topped a remarkable pitching streak—four complete game wins, including two shutouts, in our last eight games. He'd twice pitched and won with only one day's rest. If there had been a Cy Young Award in those days, Bearden would have won it hands down. And, as the World Series would prove, he wasn't done yet.

In the tumult in our clubhouse afterwards Bill Veeck was so emotional he could only say "thank you" to us. Most of us headed to our hotel, the Kenmore, for a victory party. Kenny Keltner was feeling his oats after his great season and was the life of the party. He and Joe Tipton even got in a brief altercation with each other, but five minutes later all was forgotten and they were buddies again.

Winning the pennant was a huge relief. We'd endured a long, trying, and hard-fought pennant race with Boston, New York, and Philadelphia. The pressure all summer was intense, and the intensity grew, ending with that one-game all-or-nothing playoff. As Joe Gordon said, we were "playing for a shit house or a castle," and it was like the world had been lifted from our shoulders.

Tuesday was an off-day, thankfully, and although we worked out at Braves Field to prepare for the World Series, we were all so hungover it wasn't much of a workout. We were the favorites, but the Boston Braves were something of a Cinderella team as well. They had overcome the favored Brooklyn Dodgers and St. Louis Cardinals behind the strongest hitting and the best pitching in the league. Besides Johnny Sain, who had led the majors with twenty-four wins, and Warren Spahn, Bill Voiselle and Vern Bickford were dependable starters. Al Dark was Rookie of the Year at shortstop, hitting .322, while right fielder Tommy Holmes had batted .325. Bob Elliott had driven in one hundred runs while playing third base. Unfortunately for the Braves, about a week before the end of the season, their slugging left fielder Jeff Heath, who was hitting .319, broke his ankle in a horrific accident sliding into home plate against the Dodgers in Ebbets Field. His baseball career was for all intents and purposes through. Marv Rickert replaced Heath in the lineup for the Series. Marv had a sore right hand and wore a golf glove while batting, to my knowledge the first player to ever wear a glove to hit.

The Series opened on October 6 with Bob Feller facing Johnny Sain. Bob had won nineteen games, breaking his streak of five twenty-game winning seasons in a row (not counting 1945, when he pitched only nine games after his discharge from the Navy). He'd overcome a subpar first half of the season, holding a 9–12 record in late July, to win ten of his final thirteen decisions in our push to the pennant.

Both pitchers were on their game in the opener. Feller didn't allow a hit through five innings, and through seven the Braves had only one hit, while we had just four scattered singles against Sain. In the bottom of the eighth Bob faltered slightly and walked Bill Salkeld, the Braves' catcher, to start the inning. Braves' manager Billy Southworth sent Phil Masi in as a pinch runner, and Mike McCormick sacrificed him to second, setting the stage for one of the most controversial plays in World Series history.

Boudreau had Feller walk Eddie Stanky intentionally to set up a force play. With Sain batting, Feller whirled and threw to Lou, sneaking into second on a timing play to pick off Masi. At least that's what everyone in the ballpark thought except second base umpire Bill Stewart, who called Masi safe. We argued and argued, to no avail, of course. Photos later showed Masi was out by about a foot, but Stewart's vote was the only one that counted. Feller retired Sain, but with two out Tommy Holmes smacked a hard ground single to left. Masi beat the throw to the plate, and we were down 1–0.

In the ninth Boudreau flew out to center, and Gordon fouled out to Al Dark at shortstop behind the third base line. We then got a break when Bob Elliott threw Keltner's bouncer about ten feet over Earl Torgeson's head at first. That put Keltner on second with two outs, the same situation the Braves had had the previous inning. Sain, however, struck Walt Judnich out on three pitches to end the game.

We'd wasted Feller's two-hit masterpiece on a very controversial call. The '48 Indians, however, could overcome adversity. The next day Bob Lemon defeated Warren Spahn 4–1 to even the Series at one game apiece. Ironically, another pick-off play proved pivotal, but this one went in our favor. In the bottom of the first the Braves scored on an error and two singles. With only one out, Bob Elliott occupied first base and Earl Torgeson was on second with Marv Rickert at the plate. With Torgeson leading off second, Lemon and Boudreau worked the same timing pick-off play that should have nailed Masi the day before. Torgy was a dead duck, and this time the umpire called him out, squelching the Braves' rally. Bob settled down after his shaky first inning, scattering six hits. We got to Spahn for two runs in the fourth and a run in the fifth to take the lead for good. Another run in the ninth on a single by Bob Kennedy provided the final margin.

Bill Veeck had apparently convinced Braves' owner Lou Perini to play the World Series in seven consecutive days, without any off days for travel, ostensibly to save money. It meant we took the train after Game 2 overnight to Cleveland to play Game 3 the next afternoon. We had Gene Bearden ready to go on three days' rest since his shutout in the playoff game. Boston started Vern Bickford, an eleven-game winner that year. Gene's knuckleball was still dancing, making it virtually unhittable, and he had great control. Bickford had good stuff but was wild, putting men on base with walks. We scored in the third inning on a Bearden double and an error to go ahead 1–0. In the fourth, I and then Jim Hegan followed a walk with one-out singles to chase Bickford and make it 2–0. Bearden made it hold up, throwing another complete game shutout by scattering five hits and walking no one.

We felt pretty confident going into Game 4 at home with a two-games-to-one lead. Billy Southworth came back with his ace Sain on two days' rest. Boudreau pulled another surprise by calling on Steve Gromek, a side-arming right-hander who had pitched well late in the season while putting together a 9–3 record.

Boudreau's first inning double scored Dale Mitchell to get us a quick 1–0 lead. Larry Doby homered off a Sain change-up in the third to stretch our margin to 2–0. It was the first World Series home run by an African American, although none of us were thinking about that at the time. Gromek was superb, allowing only a seventh inning solo homer by Marv Rickert. It was all over in an hour and thirty-one minutes, and we were ahead in the Series three games to one. I had a good day, going two for three but did not figure in the scoring.

For Game 5 we had Bob Feller pitching against the Braves' veteran Nelson Potter, who'd been an effective late-season pickup for Boston. With all his career accomplishments, Bob had yet to win a World Series game. It would've been most fitting for him to close out the Series in front of the home crowd. Most of us believed he should've won Game 1 but for Bill Stewart's bad call.

A record crowd of 86,288 jammed into Municipal Stadium, ready to celebrate with us. Unfortunately Feller struggled from the start, giving up two singles and a home run by Bob Elliott to open the game. Mitchell retaliated with a lead-off dinger in the bottom of the first, but Elliott homered again in the third to stretch the Braves' lead to 4–1. We rallied to take the lead 5–4 in the fourth, chasing Potter with a four-run surge propelled by Jim Hegan's three-run homer. That blow prompted Southworth to bring in Warren Spahn, who shut the door on us, giving us only a hit and a walk in 5 2/3 innings of relief.

Meanwhile, Feller battled on but just didn't have it. Bill Salkeld tied the score 5–5 with a solo home run in the sixth. Then in the seventh the roof caved in. The Braves tagged us for six runs off Feller and three relievers to put the game away 11 to 5. Satchel Paige came in to get the last two outs of the inning in what would be the only World Series appearance of his storied career.

Since we lost Game 5, we were back on the train to Boston to play Game 6 the next afternoon. We had Bob Lemon ready to go on his normal three days' rest, and Southworth countered with Bill Voiselle, who had held us to one hit in 3 2/3 innings in relief in Game 3. Voiselle had the highest uniform number in baseball. He lived in a little town called Ninety-Six, South Carolina, and wore number 96 on his jersey in its honor. On that afternoon both pitchers had good stuff, but we broke through in the top of the third with a run on doubles by Mitchell and Boudreau. The Braves got even in the bottom of the fourth on a two-out run-scoring single by Mike McCormick.

The game remained tied until our sixth, when Joe Gordon led off the inning with a home run. Before the inning was over, Thurman Tucker had drawn a walk, I had singled him to third, and Hegan had driven him in with a one-out ground out to put us ahead 3–1. We now had a little breathing room. In the eighth with Spahn in for Voiselle, Keltner and Tucker singled to put two men on. I always hit lefties well even though I batted left-handed, and here I proved it, knocking a single off Spahn to drive in Keltner and push our lead to 4–1.

It turned out we'd need that extra run. The Braves mounted a comeback in the bottom of the inning, starting with Tommy Holmes's single and a one-out double by Earl Torgeson to put runners on second and third. When Lemon walked Elliot to load the bases, Boudreau brought Bearden in from the bullpen. Pinch-hitter Clint Conatser slugged a long drive, which Tucker tracked down more than four hundred feet from the plate in deep center field. It was almost a home run, and Holmes scored easily from third after the catch. Phil Masi, hitting for Bill Salkeld, then blasted a double high off the wall in left, driving in Torgeson and putting runners on second and third with two outs. The score was now 4–3.

The first two batters against Bearden had ripped the ball to the farthest reaches of Braves Field, and the tying and go-ahead runs were in scoring position. Mike McCormick, a good right-handed hitter, was up next, but Boudreau stayed with the southpaw Bearden, who, after all, had been our best pitcher down the stretch. McCormick slapped the ball sharply up the middle, but Gene managed to glove it and toss to me at first for the third out.

We could do nothing against Spahn in the top of the ninth, but went to the bottom of the inning needing only three more outs to win the World Series. Gene walked Eddie Stanky to start the inning, and it looked as if those outs might be hard to come by. We caught a break, however, when pinch-hitter Sibby Sisti popped up a sacrifice bunt attempt that our catcher Jim Hegan grabbed about four feet in front of the plate. Connie Ryan, running for Stanky, had broken for second, so Hegan threw to me at first before Connie could get back. All of a sudden we had two outs and no one on base. Tommy Holmes flied out to Bob Kennedy in left field, and we were World Champions.

After the game, we boarded the train to return to Cleveland, and the celebration began almost immediately in the dining car. Bill Veeck had loaded the car with champagne, beer, and other alcoholic beverages, and we were all soon in a very good mood. Johnny Berardino, who had already had some bit movie parts, got up on one of the dining car tables and recited his Captain Bligh speech from *Mutiny on the Bounty*. Everyone was having a great time. Veeck, who was feeling no pain, didn't like my wife Elayne's hairdo, so he rubbed ice cream on her hair and then doused it with champagne. That made her angry, but she got over it quickly and was a good sport.

The champagne flowed until the wee hours. Elayne and I left the party around midnight, and when we went to the dining car for breakfast the next morning, champagne was still dripping from the ceiling. Veeck had a sizeable bill to pay for the damage we wreaked on the dining car.

When we arrived in Cleveland the next afternoon, we were ushered through an overflow crowd at Union Station to convertibles waiting to take us downtown to Euclid Avenue for a victory parade before an estimated 500,000 people. There was a wall of people with just enough room for us to creep down the street. Throngs of people were looking out every window, throwing confetti. It was a momentous occasion for the city of Cleveland and for us.

The next day the players went by the Municipal Stadium to pick up their gear and head home for the winter. It was sad to say goodbye because we all knew that the '48 Indians would never be together again. We'd shared so much adversity and yet had accomplished so much we were like a family. As it turned out, I was one of the first to leave the Indians' organization.

Elayne and I returned to Baltimore for what turned out to be an eventful winter. My World Series share turned out to be almost $6,800, which helped us purchase property in Towson, Maryland, and begin building a beautiful home there.

Looking back, Lou Boudreau had a phenomenal year in 1948 in leading us to the pennant. He managed, batted .355 as our shortstop, and won the American League Most Valuable Player Award. It was an exceptional feat. His great year in '48 had a lot to do with his later being voted into the Hall of Fame, an honor I believe he deserved. In my mind, however, he was still a mediocre manager, even with all our success in 1948. Perhaps it's just sour grapes, since we never got along well and my time in Cleveland was to be short.

The '48 Indians had some outstanding performances, so Lou didn't do it all by himself. People forget that Dale Mitchell, who's mostly remembered for making the last out in Don Larsen's perfect game in the 1956 World Series, batted .336 in 1948 as our starting left fielder. Kenny Keltner and my roomie Joe Gordon also had huge years. Ken slugged 31 home runs and drove in 119 runs, while Joe topped him with 32 dingers and 124 RBIs. Our infield of Keltner, Boudreau, Gordon, and me had driven in 432 runs, one of the few infields ever to top 400. (I was a distant fourth on that list.) We also had terrific starting pitching with Bearden's career year and twenty wins, another twenty wins from Bob Lemon, who also won two World Series games, and nineteen wins from Bob Feller. Steve Gromek, Sam Zoldak, and Russ Christopher were all outstanding as spot starters and in relief.

I'd hit .300 for the Series, the second highest average on the Indians after Larry Doby's .318, and had driven in what proved to be the winning run in the decisive sixth game off Warren Spahn, so I was very pleased I had contributed to our winning the World Series.

### Extra Inning

Near the end of the 1948 season we were playing the A's in Philadelphia, and Gene Bearden was pitching for us. Eddie Joost, an intelligent hitter who drew a lot of walks, reached first base. During a brief delay, Eddie said to me, "You know, we're stupid to be swinging at that knuckle curve Bearden throws because it's always a ball." Joost was right; the pitch came to the plate about knee high and quickly broke down and out of the strike zone. Word got around, and the hitters stopped swinging at that pitch after the '48 season. Bearden was never again as effective.

*Chapter 8*
## AN ALL-STAR YEAR IN WASHINGTON

**E**ven though we won the pennant and World Series in 1948, I didn't have a great year, hitting .254 with sixteen home runs and eighty-three runs driven in. I guess the Indians thought I was expendable. After the season Cleveland had a chance to get Early Wynn and Mickey Vernon, who were both coming off mediocre years with the Senators. In November, the Indians had traded Joe Tipton to the White Sox for Joe Haynes, a pitcher. Haynes was the son-in-law of Clark Griffith, who owned the Senators. Mr. Griffith wanted Haynes in Washington, so the Senators and Indians negotiated a deal where they traded reliever Ed Klieman, Joe Haynes, and me for Mickey Vernon and Early Wynn. It turned out to be a hell of a deal for Cleveland: Wynn became a perennial twenty-game winner, and Mickey Vernon continued to be one of the best first basemen in the league.

Of course, I had mixed emotions about leaving Cleveland. I hated to leave a championship team and my teammates for the Senators, who had finished in seventh place, forty games out of first in 1948. I was happy, however, to get away from Municipal Stadium in Cleveland, where I had never hit well, and to get a fresh start with a new manager. I would also be playing only forty miles from my home in Baltimore.

The manager of the Senators was Joe Kuhel, who had been one of the best fielding first basemen in the majors during his playing career. Clyde "Deerfoot" Milan, who had tried to sign me before I graduated from high school, was one of the coaches, along with future Hall of Famer Rick Ferrell. I thought Milan had gotten his nickname because he'd been a great base stealer in his playing days. He had been, stealing eighty-eight bases in 1912 and seventy-five the next year. But one day I asked Clyde where "Deerfoot" came from.

He said, "Well, Eddie, I used to do a lot of hunting in the winter back in Clarksville, Texas. There was a big buck with a huge set of antlers that I frequently saw but never could get a shot at. Each winter my goal was to bag that big buck. One day, after several years of trying to get him, I was out hunting and heard a noise behind me. I turned around and there's that big buck standing right behind me looking me in the eye.

"I was surprised, but I raised my gun, took aim, and fired. But the damn gun misfired. The click of the misfiring startled the buck, and he started running right at me. I was so angry my gun had misfired that I grabbed it by the barrel and as the buck went by I swung at him. I hit him right across the nose and broke my rifle in two. The blow only stunned the buck a little, and he kept right on going, so I took off running after him.

"I was gaining on him and finally got close enough to get my finger in his rear-end but I never could get close enough to crook it. I just wasn't quite fast enough. And that's how I got the name Deerfoot."

Although I'd hoped to get off to a good start with my new team, I began the 1949 season slowly and had my average barely above .200 when we were in Boston in late April. I was trying not to guess what pitch was coming, but just to react to the ball. It wasn't working. I didn't hit particularly well in '48, and now I was off to a bad start in 1949.

My system of just reacting to the pitch went back to spring training in 1948, when I was still with the Indians. My roomie, Joe Gordon, had asked me one night after we were in bed if I ever guessed what pitch the pitcher was going to throw. I told him, "No, I've always been told not to guess. I tried it once in the Eastern League and it didn't work. So I just get ready for the fastball and try to get a good pitch to it." Joe said, "Well, one of these days you're going to discover that the hardest balls you hit are off pitches you're looking for."

That conversation made an impression on me. The next day I made sure I got a seat next to Rogers Hornsby, who was in spring training with us as a hitting instructor, on the bus as we headed from Tucson to Phoenix to play an exhibition game against the Cubs. I figured Rogers's opinion on guess hitting was worth listening to. I related what Joe had told me and asked Hornsby if he thought I should guess hit. He said, "Hell no. Hit what you see." Since Hornsby was probably the greatest right-handed hitter of all time, batting over .400 three times with a .358 lifetime average, I decided not to be a guess hitter.

We had a rain delay that April day in Boston in '49, and after a while the game was called. All the players dressed and drifted out of the clubhouse and pretty soon only Joe Kuhel, Clyde Milan, and I were left. We started talking about hitting, and Joe asked me if I ever looked for certain pitches. I told them Joe Gordon had asked me the same question and what Rogers Hornsby had said about guessing. Then Kuhel said something that made good sense to me and probably saved my major league career. He said, "Eddie, it's not guessing; it's figuring, looking for a certain pitch until you have two strikes. If the pitch he throws you isn't the pitch you're looking for, you don't swing at it." Joe knew I was a fastball hitter so he continued, "In your case, with two strikes, look for the fastball and try to adjust to the other pitches."

He used Joe Dobson, a pitcher with the Red Sox, as an example. Kuhel said, "Dobson knows you're a fastball hitter, and he has an excellent curve. If you come to bat with men on base, what do you think he'll try to get you to hit?"

I said, "A curve, of course."

Joe said, "Don't you think you have a better chance to hit his curve if you're looking for it? Almost every time at bat you'll get at least one pitch you're looking for, and if you're ready for it, you'll hit it solidly." Clyde Milan agreed with Joe, and it turns out they were exactly right.

I put their theory to work the very next day. In batting practice I asked the pitcher to throw me curves and off-speed pitches. I practiced hitting them and discovered that if I was ready for a curve I could hit it. My hitting improved immediately and my batting average began to climb. I started hitting better and with more authority.

Not too long after that conversation we went to Cleveland to play a series against the Indians. Bob Feller pitched against us. He knew I had trouble hitting the curve ball, and he had a great one. I came to bat with the bases loaded and figured he'd throw me a curve. He did, and because I was looking for it I smashed a triple into the right field corner to drive in three runs. I can still remember standing on third base looking over at Bob. He was standing on the mound with his hands on his hips, staring at me, and he said, "Eddie, how the hell did you hit that pitch?"

That conversation I had with Joe Kuhel early in the 1949 season was a revelation to me and was the key to my future success as a hitter. Up to two strikes, if I didn't get my pitch, I'd take it. Then with two strikes I'd guard the plate, in my case, looking for the fastball and fighting off other pitches.

During that conversation about hitting, Kuhel had told me to watch Ted Williams hit because he thought that was Ted's philosophy as well. A couple of years later I had the chance to talk to Ted during a World Series and sure enough, he looked for a pitch he could handle up to two strikes. He carried it a step further, however, and looked for his pitch in a certain part of the strike zone.

Ted, of course, loved to talk hitting and was the best hitter I've ever seen. Many other players felt the same way, because when Ted took batting practice before a game, all the visiting players would stop what they were doing when he stepped into the batting cage. They'd watch him hit and then continue to warm up after Ted had taken his swings. Williams hit a lot of sinking line drives. Joe Kuhel had our second baseman play fifteen feet out onto the right-field grass when Ted came to bat. Williams impressed me one day in Griffith Stadium when he hit a sinking line drive right at Sherry Robertson, our second baseman. Although Sherry was way back on the outfield grass, he didn't come close to catching the liner.

In '49 I continued to hit well after that rainout in Boston, and as a result I was voted to the All-Star game as the starting first baseman for the American League. It was a thrill to play with guys like Joe DiMaggio, Ted Williams, and George Kell. Since I played first base, I'd seen all these guys up close and had exchanged a few words with them. But it was still very exciting to walk into my first All-Star clubhouse that year.

I had chatted with Joe DiMaggio a few times when he got on first base in my three years in the league and had visited him at the Johns Hopkins Hospital in Baltimore the winter before when he'd had his heel operated on. We hit it off and warmed up together before my first All-Star game in 1949 and then again before the 1951 All-Star game. I thought Joe was a good guy and enjoyed his company.

The 1949 All-Star game was played in Ebbets Field in Brooklyn with Lou Boudreau as the manager, since Cleveland had won the pennant the year before. I have to admit that I derived great satisfaction in making the All-Star team that Boudreau was to manage. After the troubles we'd had in Cleveland, it felt good to be his starting All-Star first baseman.

We scored four unearned runs in the top of the first inning off Warren Spahn, and I contributed, lining a single to right field to drive in Joe DiMaggio with our second run. I played into the eighth inning but didn't get any more hits. We led 11–7 so I finally asked Boudreau if he wanted Billy Goodman of the Red Sox to play some. Lou let him finish the game. The excitement of being chosen an All-Star starter and playing with all those great players, many of whom I had worshiped as a kid, was something I've never forgotten.

I was selected for the All-Star game in 1951 and was again voted a starter in 1952, both when I was with the Chicago White Sox. In the '51 game in Detroit I pinch hit for Ferris Fain late in the game and grounded out. The 1952 game was played in Philadelphia but was rained out after five innings. I struck out against the National League starter Curt Simmons but did get a hit off the Cubs' Bob Rush to drive in a run, but we lost 3–2. That was my first encounter with Mickey Mantle, who was selected to the team as a reserve. He was just a twenty-year-old kid who was in his first full year with the Yankees. He was a well-built, tow-headed, innocent-looking youngster and one of the strongest, best-looking players I'd seen—he was a young Adonis. Mickey could do amazing things on a ball field—run like lightning and hit a ball over the moon. He was an incredible talent.

In 1953 I was selected to the All-Star squad by Casey Stengel as a member of the Philadelphia Athletics. The game was held in Crosley Field in Cincinnati. We were losing 3–0 when Casey asked me to pinch-hit for Mike Garcia in the top of the eighth inning against Murry Dickson. I hit a line drive right at Enos Slaughter in right field, just as a ball got away in the bullpen. Umpire Bill McKinley in right field called time right as I was hitting the ball. He ruled that the play was dead even though Slaughter caught the ball. That meant I could hit again and actually got two at bats. Unfortunately, I made another out, flying out to Slaughter again. So the time-out didn't make any difference—except that I got to hit twice and make two outs, though only one counted.

I met Eddie Mathews for the first time at that All-Star game in Cincinnati. He was only twenty-one and was in the Navy reserves. He showed up for the game wearing a white bell-bottom sailor uniform. Mathews was not quite as compact as Mickey Mantle, but as an opposing player he seemed to have all the tools. Many years later I hired Eddie to manage the Atlanta Braves when I served as general manager there.

I enjoyed playing in All-Star games. We traveled to the city hosting the game the day before, which gave me the chance to get acquainted and hang out with the All-Star players from the other teams. Then walking through the hotel lobbies, fans would recognize me and ask for my autograph. It made me feel special. It was a thrill to be there and to be associated with all of those famous guys from other teams. It made me feel like I was one of the best players of the game and gave me a lot of confidence. The players had a good rapport and went all out to win for the prestige of our league. We wanted to be the best.

Beginning about 1950 the National League started winning most of the All-Star games. I don't know of any reason for it except that the National League was quicker to bring in black players. Many good black players were out there, and the National League teams signed blacks earlier and in greater numbers. I believe the integration of major league baseball had a big impact on the caliber of play, adding players with major league ability who took the place of white players with lesser talent. After Jackie Robinson broke the color barrier with Brooklyn in 1947, the Dodgers soon signed players like Don Newcombe, Roy Campanella, and Joe Black. The New York Giants quickly followed suit with Monte Irvin and a kid named Willie Mays, both of whom are in the Hall of Fame. Pretty soon guys like Ernie Banks, Hank Aaron, and, a couple of years later, Frank Robinson, were making a significant impact in the National League.

In contrast, the New York Yankees, the best team in the American League in the late 1940s and 1950s, didn't integrate until they brought up Elston Howard in 1955. Of course, Larry Doby and Satchel Paige both joined the Indians in 1948, but the American League teams were generally slower to integrate. The American League, however, did do a good job of scouting and finding players in Latin American countries. In 1952 with the White Sox, I played with Minnie Minoso in the outfield and Hector Rodriguez at third base, both of whom were from Cuba. Minoso became something of a legend and was in the major leagues well into his forties. We had Luis Aloma, also a Cuban, who was a terrific relief pitcher. In his four-year major league career, from 1950 to 1953, Luis put together an 18–3 lifetime won-loss record. Our shortstop was Chico Carrasquel, a fine ballplayer from Venezuela, who was a regular shortstop for ten years in the big leagues.

The major leagues had a few Latin players before the war, but it wasn't until the 1950s that scouts began to scour Latin America for ballplayers. After Jackie Robinson broke the color barrier, clubs began to look for talent from the Negro Leagues. Jackie Robinson also paved the way for the major leagues to scout and sign black Latin players like Minnie Minoso. That fed on itself, because as more and better baseball was being played in the Latin countries, teams could now scout and sign any talented player from Latin America, and that too improved the quality of major league baseball. It all started in 1947 when Branch Rickey, with Commissioner Happy Chandler's tacit approval, signed Jackie Robinson.

I enjoyed batting against National League pitchers in All-Star games to try to get the feel of the pitching differences in the two leagues. Robin Roberts and Curt Simmons impressed me as opposing pitchers, Robin for his great command of his pitches and Curt for his terrific stuff. I read about the players in the National League, but never had a chance to face them except occasionally in a spring training game.

In those days American League pitchers were more hard-throwing, fastball type pitchers, while the National League pitchers seemed more cunning, throwing more curveballs and change of speeds. Then by the middle 1950s it switched, and the National League became the dominant league with the better pitchers into the 1960s. Fireball hurlers like Sandy Koufax, Don Drysdale, Larry Jackson, Bob Friend, Jack Sanford, and then Bob Gibson came into the National League.

Of course, one big difference in the way the game was played in those days and today is the enhanced role of relief pitchers. In the 1940s and 1950s, pitchers were expected to go nine innings and often would throw more than three hundred innings a season. Relief pitchers were pitchers who weren't good enough to break into the starting rotation. Today a starting pitcher throws five or six innings, then a couple of set-up men pitch an inning or two before the star closer finishes the game, rarely pitching more than an inning. So instead of seeing the same guy for eight or nine innings like we did, a hitter now has to face at least three pitchers most of the time—starter, set-up man, and a closer— making it considerably tougher on the hitters.

We had guys who threw hard and who would have been good relievers, but it just wasn't the style of play. The emphasis was on the guy who could pitch nine innings. There were some exceptions like Joe Page of the Yankees and then Jim Konstanty of the Phillies, both of whom enjoyed great success as relief pitchers. Elroy Face was an outstanding relief pitcher for the Pirates in the 1950s and early 1960s. Shortly after I stopped playing, the Yankees had great relief pitchers like Ryne Duren and Luis Arroyo, and the Red Sox developed Dick Radatz, who was 6'6" and could throw a ball through a brick wall.

About the same time platooning became more common, where a right-handed hitter would play against a left-handed pitcher and a left-handed batter would play against a right-handed pitcher. Casey Stengel of the Yankees was a big advocate of shuffling the lineup and giving guys rest. We major leaguers used to pride ourselves on playing every game even when we were tired, and most managers seemed to want the regulars to play every game if we were able to play. But Stengel would play guys in different positions and platooned players, using left-handed hitters against right-handed pitchers and righty hitters against southpaw pitchers. The Yankees were so successful with this strategy that other managers began platooning, too, significantly changing the way the game was played.

**Extra Inning**

I always loved to run into Ted Williams after our playing careers because when he saw me he'd invariably say, "Hey Eddie, you know you are still the most underrated hitter I ever played against." Ted had a big booming voice so it always delighted me that all my friends could hear him.

Shortly before Ted passed away in 2002, I ran into Ted's son John Henry while attending a Major League Baseball Alumni meeting in Tampa. I asked John Henry how his dad was doing, and he said, "Come on. We'll call him up." Ted was glad to hear from me and invited Rich Hand, who had played for Ted when he managed the Texas Rangers, and me to his home in Hernando, Florida, for a visit. We gladly accepted and spent about three hours reminiscing with Ted. During the conversation, Ted suddenly asked me, "Eddie, when you used to just tick a real good fastball, did you ever smell wood burning?"

That surprised me and I told him, "No, I never did."

Ted almost jumped out of his seat. He said, "You never did? I used to smell it all the time."

I said, "Well, I guess you had a little more bat speed than I did."

Ted autographed a ball for me, probably one of the last balls he ever signed. He died within a year, and I was grateful for the opportunity to have had one last visit with him.

Here I am at about two years of age.

The Paris Coca-Cola Bottlers in our fancy red satin uniforms in about 1937.
I'm third from the left in the front row.

My mother, Hazel Hammer Robinson.
She was a great lady.

Warming up for the Paris High Wildcats. That is my buddy George Stephens, behind me punting. A year later I was in the stands when George suffered a ruptured spleen while playing for the Paris Junior College Dragons. He died two days later.

My high school graduation picture from 1938.

The 1941 Elmira Pioneers of the Class A Eastern League. I'm in the front row, fourth from the right with a bat in front of me. Sal Maglie, who became a star pitcher with the New York Giants, is in the second row, third from the left.

Taking a hack with the Baltimore Orioles in 1942.

My only baseball fight and I didn't start it. In 1942 Montreal Royals pitcher Max Macon punched me because I had stepped on him when he covered first base and put his foot in the middle of the bag. I'm trying to retaliate.

The day I made the big leagues, September, 1942. I'm on the left with Ted Sepkowksi, who came with me to the Cleveland Indians from the Baltimore Orioles. After the 1942 season it would take me a World War and five years to get back to the major leagues.

Before I was injured, I was fortunate to get to play a lot of baseball in the service. Here I am suited up for the Norfolk Training Station team with Benny McCoy and Don Padgett, both major leaguers.

I'm happy about the home run I hit in the Naval World Series on September 15, 1943, against the Norfolk Naval Air Station.

I'm not sure what we're looking at, but that is Tommy Thomas, my manager with the old Baltimore Orioles. He was a man I greatly admired.

Our Cleveland coaching staff in spring training 1948 included four current or future
Hall of Famers: Bill McKechnie (far left, back row); Lou Boudreau (middle, back row);
Tris Speaker (front row, left); and Hank Greenberg (far right, front row). A Hall of Fame case
could also be made for Mel Harder (back row, second from left).

Here I am relaxing with Joe Gordon, my first big league roommate, and Ken Keltner in the clubhouse between games of a doubleheader after a win in 1948. Note we are drinking soft drinks and eating sandwiches. I was thrilled when Joe was finally elected to the Baseball Hall of Fame in 2009.

June 13, 1948. The Yankees officially retire Babe Ruth's uniform number 3.
I'm to the right of the Babe, applauding on the top step. I've just handed Babe the bat he will use
as a cane to get to home plate and back. Two months later, the Babe was dead.

I'm stretching at first for Bob Lemon's throw, but Alvin Dark is safe at first for a bunt hit in the first inning of Game Six of the 1948 World Series. We edged the Boston Braves 4 to 3 behind the pitching of Lemon and Gene Bearden to wrap up the World Series.

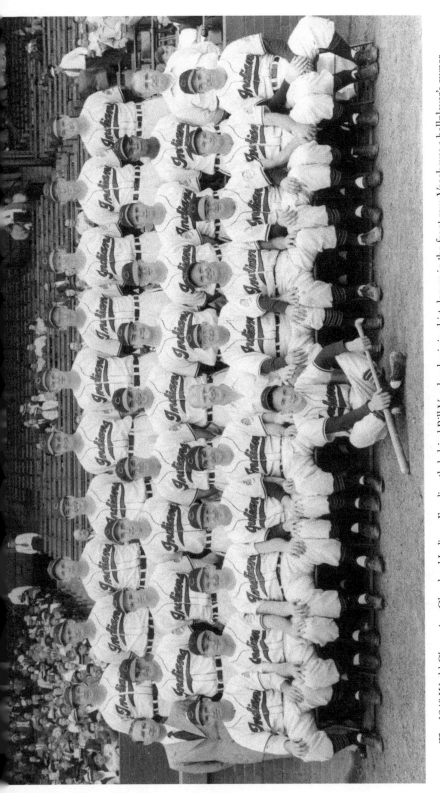

The 1948 World Champion Cleveland Indians. I'm directly behind Bill Veeck, who is in shirt-sleeves in the front row. Veeck was a ballplayer's owner if there ever was one. Larry Doby, the first African-American to play in the American League, is in the second row, second from the right.

President Truman threw out the first pitch to open the 1949 baseball season, and I was lucky enough to catch it. President Truman's wife Bess is to his immediate right. Clark Griffith, the long-time owner of the Washington Senators, is between us.

With Joe Kuhel, my manager with the Senators. His approach to hitting helped turn
my career around and made me an All-Star.

Signing autographs in 1949. I'm still signing sixty years later.

*Chapter 9*
## WITH THE PALE HOSE

lthough I had a good year with Washington in '49, hitting .294 with eighteen home runs and twenty-seven doubles, we had a bad team. We won only fifty games, lost 104, and finished last, forty-seven games out of first place. We hoped for better in 1950 with a touted thirty-three-year-old rookie pitcher from Cuba named Connie Marrero joining quality starters Sid Hudson and Ray Scarborough.

The Senators opened the season at home a day ahead of everyone else, with President Truman throwing out the first pitch. The president stood up in his special box on the first base side, and all the Senators lined up along the first base line hoping to catch his throw. It glanced off a couple of guys, and I was able to grab it on the deflection. I then had the privilege of taking the ball over to the president and asking him to autograph it. I still have the ball and the photo of President Truman autographing it as he stood next to Clark Griffith and me.

Unfortunately, I got off to a slow start in 1950. I had a great spring but caught the flu near the end of spring training. When the season opened I was weak and didn't have any pop in my bat. Then, on May 31, thirty-six games into the season, I was traded to Chicago with my good friend and buddy Ray Scarborough and second baseman Al Kozar for Bob Kuzava, Cass Michaels, and John Ostrowski. I wasn't happy with the trade because Comiskey Park was a tough place to hit in. The right field fence was 352 feet from home plate, and the wind often blew in, making it even farther.

Red Corriden was the White Sox manager, having replaced Jack Onslow about a month into the season. Red was fun to play for, but we were not a very good club.

Nellie Fox was the second baseman, who, at the time was a skinny little guy who didn't look like much of a player. He wasn't someone I'd thought would one day end up in the Hall of Fame.

Ray Scarborough, with whom I was traded, became my roommate, and we developed a lasting friendship. Ray and I ended up living in the Conrad Hilton, right across from Grant Park. At the time, it was the largest hotel in the country. Ray was battling a sore arm and struggled on the mound, but that didn't keep him from being one of the best bench jockeys of all time. For example, one day we were playing in Cleveland, and the Indians brought in Marino Pieretti to pitch in relief. Pieretti was a short, stocky little right-hander, and when he came in, Scarborough jumped up from the bench and yelled, "Pieretti, you are the only man in baseball who wears a sixteen-inch collar and a size 2 hat." That cracked up the Cleveland players as well as our entire bench.

When we played the Yankees, Ray would yell at Yogi Berra when he came to bat, and when Yogi looked over, Ray would hang by one hand from the dugout roof and scratch his chest like an ape. Yogi would laugh out loud and step into the batter's box. More often than not, he'd make us sorry we kidded him by knocking a base hit.

Scarborough had a very large nose, and the other bench jockeys in the league called him pickle nose. They'd yell, "Hey, pickle nose, you're the only guy in baseball who can hang by his nose and pick cherries with both hands."

We finished behind Washington in sixth place in 1950 with a 60–94 record, although I batted .311 after joining Chicago and hit twenty-one home runs for the year. During that season, Elayne and I began to have serious marital problems, which culminated in our separation and ultimate divorce that winter. Elayne continued to live in the home we'd built near Baltimore, and I was able to remain in close contact with my son Robby, who was now two years old.

In 1951 Paul Richards became the manager of the White Sox, replacing Red Corriden, and he quickly turned our downtrodden outfit to respectability. All we knew about Richards when he joined us was that he'd been a very successful minor league manager. As a player, he'd been a good defensive catcher but a weak hitter with only a .227 batting average in eight big league seasons. He started managing in the minor leagues as a player-manager when he was twenty-nine, before returning to the major leagues as a catcher during World War II. He played eighty-three games for the champion Detroit Tigers in 1945 and caught all seven games of the World Series. We had heard he was a no-nonsense type of guy, which, it turns out, was putting it mildly.

Richards invited many of us to come meet him in Palm Springs, California, in a pre–spring training camp a few days before our regular spring training camp began in Pasadena, California. We quickly learned that Richards was a very thorough baseball man. He worked quite a bit with the catchers because he had been a catcher. But he made sure that the rest of us worked on every aspect of the game, such as cutoff plays, pick-offs, and base running. Nellie Fox was our second baseman, and Richards brought in Joe Gordon, who had just retired after a stellar career, to work with Nellie on turning the double play. We ran drills constantly so that the fundamentals became second nature. Those sound fundamentals helped us win a lot of games that year. Paul Richards turned out to be the best teacher I encountered in all my years of baseball.

Paul was a very quiet, rather stern individual. He was a scholarly kind of guy who read a lot. He didn't drink much and was never seen in a bar. He didn't pat players on the back or make a big fuss over anyone. If you did well you wouldn't get much praise, but he also wouldn't embarrass you in front of the other players. If you fouled up he would call you into his office and talk to you. He might also make you work on one of your weaknesses after a game. Sometimes if we were in a batting slump, he'd have the whole team take batting practice after a night game or even after a Sunday doubleheader. If we'd messed up a run-down play, we'd work on that after the game.

He also had a knack for developing pitchers. He was given a lot of credit for turning Hal Newhouser into a two-time MVP when both were with Detroit during the war years. Paul could also take pitchers of mediocre ability and make winners out of them. If a pitcher had a decent arm, Richards could generally help him with a new pitch or perhaps a different philosophy that would help him improve significantly. In 1951 Richards handled the pitching staff magnificently and got the most out of what we had. As a result, we finished eight games above .500, in fourth place after finishing thirty-four games below .500 the year before.

Marv Grissom, one of our starters in 1952, was a good example of how Paul could figure how to get the most out of pitchers. Marv would start out the game strong but falter in the later innings. In those days good starting pitchers typically completed about one-half of their starts. Some of the guys thought Grissom couldn't pitch in tight situations with the game on the line in the late innings.

One day Paul said, "I'll find out whether he's got it or not." He took Grissom out of the rotation and began bringing him out of the bullpen in the late innings. Marv pitched wonderfully and became one of the top relief pitchers in baseball for about the next six years. He just didn't have the stamina to pitch complete games, but when he came out of the bullpen fresh, he was tough to hit. As a result, Grissom, who was a great guy, had a successful big league career.

I had a strong rapport with Richards and thought he liked me. I think he intuitively knew I liked playing for him. In fact, I enjoyed playing for Paul more than any manager I ever played for. He was my kind of manager. I thought he was an extremely knowledgeable baseball man, and I wanted his approval. I wanted him to think I was a good player and was playing well for him—and it turned out I did play well in both 1951 and 1952. I did just about anything a manager would want a player to do—hit for a good average, drove in runs, and played every day. I knew Paul appreciated it. We became friends, not off the field, but at the ballpark. I loved that White Sox team. By 1952 we knew what Paul was like and what he expected of his players. Everything was easier, and so the team played well that year, finishing in third place with an 81–73 record.

Paul had an air of confidence in his managing ability and carried himself in a way that made us feel like he was the best manager around and knew what he was doing. If he believed we could win, so did we. We were proud he'd selected us to be his regulars. He had an answer for every question. In arguments with umpires, he always knew the rules as well or better than the umpires did. Furthermore, he had that knack for getting the most out of his players and pitchers, even the mediocre ones. If you ask any of his players who was the best manager they ever played for, a majority would say Paul Richards.

Tony La Russa, one of today's most highly regarded managers, was heavily influenced by Paul Richards when La Russa was managing the White Sox and Richards was working for the White Sox front office. La Russa often says Paul Richards had a big impact on the way he manages. Other top managers like Dick Williams played under Richards. Luman Harris managed in Houston and coached and managed in Atlanta under Paul. Earl Weaver, whom I thought was a brilliant manager, managed in the

Baltimore organization when Richards was the general manager and manager. Earl was able to observe Paul in spring training every year and certainly learned from him. Earl was a studious guy, one of the first major league managers to keep statistics on how his players and players on other teams did against each other. He was well informed and forward thinking. He was the first manager in the major leagues to use the radar gun to measure his pitchers' velocity. He'd gotten the idea from Danny Litwhiler, the long-time coach at Michigan State. Litwhiler was using the radar gun to time the velocity of infielders' and outfielders' arms, and Weaver decided to use it for pitchers.

Bill Veeck also respected Paul Richards. They had a pact that if Veeck ever acquired another major league club he'd make Paul the manager, and he did. Many years later Veeck bought the White Sox and made Paul the manager. I thought Paul and Bill were very sharp guys who had respect for one another and worked well together.

Later, when I was a farm director in charge of player development for Houston and then Atlanta, I emphasized fundamentals the way Richards did. For instance, we signed Joe Morgan when I was in charge of player development with the Astros. Joe had quick hands. In fact, they were too quick. He wanted to catch and get rid of the ball too fast. He had a little flip in his glove that caused him to fumble balls when taking them out of his glove. Paul Richards had him not just take a few extra ground balls during batting practice or after infield practice with the shortstop, Sonny Jackson. Instead he made Morgan field and throw one hundred ground balls to the shortstop covering second every day. Exactly one hundred, no less, every day and sometimes twice a day during spring training. I copied that idea with my minor league players in their training drills to great success.

If a player had a weakness Richards would make him work on that weakness, not just fifteen or twenty times but a hundred times and then a hundred times more. He didn't do this with every player, however. He worked with the players he thought had the ability to overcome their weaknesses, those he could develop. It was effective. Joe Morgan, for example, is in the Hall of Fame.

I'm not sure if that type of repetition is done today, but I kept following Paul's system as closely as I could when I became a general manager. When I worked for Paul I kept a notebook on the way he ran the team. I wrote down when he had meetings, what he told the players, and what he had them do to improve their skills.

Of course, managers today learn under different systems in the minor leagues before they become big league managers and have their own ways to instruct. They don't know how Paul Richards did it, so unfortunately his method of teaching may be lost. Under his direction, we wouldn't dare start a game without taking infield practice. We didn't clown around but took infield practice as if we were playing the game. In my playing days we came out early to watch the opposition's pregame practice in order to see how well the outfielders threw and how well they moved.

Today if a club takes infield practice it's an event. You might watch a whole series where neither team takes infield practice. If they do, they often just go through the motions. I can't believe that approach makes for better play. Of course, if I were making $5 million a year I might not care about infield practice either. If a manager told a player today he was going to have to catch a hundred ground balls, he'd think he was being made an example of. But if Paul Richards required a player to take extra ground balls, the player would have been grateful because he wanted to improve. Ballplayers in those days wanted to play well because playing well meant more money next year. Improving one's performance was the only way to earn more money—so players were willing to make every effort to get better. I'm not sure the incentives are the same now in the time of multi-year guaranteed contracts. In the old days, players didn't resent the extra work. A ballplayer might have moaned about having to take extra batting practice after a game, but he knew it was best for him so he went out and took the extra swings.

Paul has often been characterized as aloof and as a know-it-all. He *was* aloof, and I thought he knew and taught more baseball than any other manager in the American League. He was close to those who worked for him and had a host of other close friends. He didn't go out of his way to make friends, but he was loyal to the friends he chose. Although he could seem humorless, he was a great storyteller and was fun to be with. He hardly drank at all but occasionally would have a martini with friends. I liked and admired him and miss him a lot.

The White Sox trained in Pasadena, California, at Brookside Park, which was across the street from the Rose Bowl. One day in spring training in 1951 a pretty, curvaceous girl showed up at camp, accompanied by her agent. They'd arranged to have publicity photos taken with Gus Zernial, one of our star players. Gus was a big, good-looking guy and was a home run hitter to boot. Gus spent a lot of time that day with the starlet and the photographers. Afterwards we kidded him and asked him if he'd gotten her phone number.

No one knew who the gal was until the next week, when all of us received auto-graphed pictures signed by Marilyn Monroe. My picture was signed "With love to Edi, Marilyn Monroe." I didn't know who she was and immediately tore the picture up, thinking that I didn't want a picture from someone who can't spell "Eddie." Not a good move on my part.

Nineteen fifty-one marked the beginning of the Go-Go White Sox. We had players like Chico Carrasquel, Jim Busby, Nellie Fox, and Bob Dillinger, who were fast and could steal bases. All except the first baseman. I stole exactly two bases in 151 games. I had improved over my 1950 performance when I set a record for a 154-game season by stealing exactly zero bases in 155 games. We had a tie game and later made it up to account for the extra game, enabling me to set that ignominious record.

Nellie Fox became my best friend on the White Sox. It never occurred to me that he'd make the Hall of Fame because at first he had trouble making the double play. We'd bet a Coke doing pickups before games. We'd throw each other balls in the dirt to work on catching short hops. Whoever missed the most short hops owed the other a Coke.

I could catch a pop fly, but I don't think Nellie thought I could because he wanted to catch all the pop-ups. We also developed a trick play. A couple of times ground balls went through my legs and Nellie fielded them behind me and threw to the pitcher who was covering first for the put-out. Nellie called that our trick play. Doc Cramer taught Nellie how to bunt, and one year Nellie beat out twenty-seven bunts for base hits.

One day during batting practice in Yankee Stadium, Nellie swung at a high inside pitch and ticked the ball squarely into his left eye. His eye swelled up and closed imme-diately, and we were afraid he was seriously injured. He was taken to the hospital, where they found no severe damage, just a very black eye. He returned to the ballpark and sat on the bench for the rest of the game. Nellie raised such a commotion on the bench, yelling at the Yankees, yelling at our players, that he made a pest of himself and got on Paul Richards's nerves. The next day Nellie's eye was still very swollen, but Paul put him back into the lineup, saying, "I've got to play him; I can't stand him making all that noise on the bench."

Early in the 1951 season, Frank Lane, our general manager, engineered a three-team trade that got us Minnie Minoso, a rookie outfielder from Cuba, from the Indians. Minnie was a terrific addition to the Go-Go Sox and was on his way to the Rookie of the Year Award. He batted .326 and led the league in triples with fourteen. He was strongly built, could run like the wind, had a strong arm, and played all-out every day. He could also hit the ball a mile. In his first at bat on the day he joined us, Minnie crushed a line drive that carried over the center-field fence in Comiskey Park. Not many players ever accomplished that hitting feat.

Minnie was not only a great talent but he was also a wonderful teammate with a great sense of humor. He stood very close to the plate in an open stance, which resulted in his getting hit by pitches frequently. Once after he had been hit a couple of times in a game, he came into the clubhouse afterwards, stripped off his uniform, grabbed a pint of milk, and standing naked in the middle of the clubhouse, poured it over his head, saying in a loud voice, "I'm going to make myself white so they won't throw at me so much."

Minnie and Doc Cramer, our first base coach, kidded each other a lot and became good friends. One day Minnie asked Doc if he would go with him to a Lincoln dealership to help him pick out a car. Minnie ended up buying a big Lincoln and was going to drive it back to Comiskey Park. Doc hopped into the backseat and told Minnie, "I'm not riding in the front seat of a big new car with a black guy. You have to chauffeur me back to the ball park." Minnie got a big kick out of that, and the next day came to the ballpark with a fancy chauffeur's cap, saying that if he was going to drive Doc around he needed to look the part.

Although we became known for our speed, we had some sluggers when I joined the White Sox. Occasionally we'd have a before-game home run–hitting contest with the opposition. I would be in the contest with Gus Zernial, before he was traded, or Minnie Minoso, or one of our other players. One day Luman Harris, one of our coaches who became a great friend of mine and who was always pulling tricks, said, "Why don't we freeze the balls the other team is going to hit. We'll hit the warm, lively balls and win."

So we did. We put the balls for the other team in the freezer and would take them out long enough to thaw the cover so that they couldn't tell the balls were frozen. After that, we never lost a home run–hitting contest at Comiskey Park.

Frank Lane was responsible for making the franchise into a winner. He had taken over in 1949 and orchestrated the trade for me during the 1950 season. He hired Paul Richards as manager, in my view a stroke of genius. Then he made a series of very good trades, earning his reputation as "Trader Lane." In doing so he molded the Go-Go Sox. In addition to the Minoso trade (which cost the White Sox outfielders Gus Zernial and Dave Philley), Lane put together the best double-play combination in the league by plucking twenty-one-year-old Chico Carrasquel out of the Dodger chain and, in one of the most one-sided trades in history, swapping reserve catcher Joe Tipton to the Philadelphia Athletics for Nellie Fox, who was then an unknown rookie second baseman. Baseball people often point to the 1964 Ernie Broglio for Lou Brock Cards–Cubs trade as the most one-sided in history, but I'm not sure that Tipton for Fox doesn't at least match it.

Frank Lane put together a fine team in Chicago in the early '50s. He was so successful early on, however, that he got carried away with trading and made a number of bad deals that ended up hurting the club. But for the '50, '51, '52, and '53 White Sox he did a fine job.

Although I loved playing in Chicago for Paul Richards, I was traded again after the 1952 season. Frank Lane and I had our differences. He never wanted to pay me what I thought I should be paid, even though I felt like I'd given him a couple of great years. In 1951 I hit 29 home runs, drove in 117 runs, hit .282, and made the All-Star team. In 1952 I played every game, was the starting first baseman for the American League in the All-Star game, and batted .296 with 22 home runs with 104 runs batted in, which was only one RBI behind Al Rosen's league-leading 105.

I was the first White Sox player and the seventh overall to hit a ball over the right-field roof at Comiskey Park in the forty-one-year history of the stadium, connecting off Al Widmar of the Browns. It put me in pretty good company; the first six who cleared the roof were Babe Ruth, Lou Gehrig, Jimmy Foxx, Hank Greenberg, Ted Williams, and Mickey Mantle.

The ball landed in the parking lot behind the right-field stands. A fan was parking his car and picked it up and brought it to the clubhouse after the game. I still have the ball. That dinger even earned me an appearance on the Dave Garroway television show that same evening. They wanted me in uniform, so I went to the studio and put on my full uniform, spikes and all.

Old Comiskey Park was a tough place to hit home runs because the wind often blew in from right field off the lake and would knock high fly balls down. Occasionally you could smell the stockyards at the ballpark, which was good news for hitters because it meant a south wind that would push the ball towards the outfield fences. We hitters called that stockyard stench the sweetest smell on earth because it meant the wind was blowing out.

The Stockyard Inn was one of the best steakhouses in Chicago. The management there gave two certificates for a steak dinner to any White Sox player who hit a home run. In 1951 I treated one or another of my teammates to steak dinners many times.

I tied the club record for homers that year and set the franchise record for left-handed hitters. Gus Zernial had hit twenty-nine homers for the Sox the year before as a right-handed hitter. I had the twenty-nine dingers going into the last weekend of the season and was eager to hit number thirty and break the tie. Paul Richards, however, called me into his office and said, "You don't really want to break that home run record, do you?"

I said, "Heck yes, I'd really like to." We were playing the Browns in St. Louis. I'd hit a lot of home runs there, and thought I was pretty certain to break the record. Also, I'd played in over two hundred consecutive games at that juncture. I would go on to play every game for the next two years, which would have given me a consecutive game streak of over six hundred games.

Paul said, "Well, I'm sorry, but I want Boyd to get some playing time and I'm going to start him."

Bob Boyd was a rookie first baseman the club had brought up in September. He went on to have a solid big league career. But I didn't get a chance to break the record. Even so, I was satisfied. My left-handed home run record stood for twenty-six years until Oscar Gamble broke it in 1977. In the interim the team had moved home plate out about five feet to make it a little easier to reach the fences. That makes a difference, and I was happy to have the record for as long as I did.

I became a fan favorite in Chicago. Some of the fans got together and decided to have an Eddie Robinson Day. It was orchestrated by Herb Castle, a dear friend of mine. He and his wife and daughter lived in Chicago and were huge White Sox fans. Before one of our home games, they presented me with a shiny new Cadillac convertible and many other gifts. My teammates gave me a beautiful Browning Winchester

Model-12 Magnum shotgun. It was a great duck and geese gun that I treasure to this day.

Beforehand Herb had gone to Frank Lane and asked him if he wanted to give me something from the club on my day. His response was, "Hell no, he's making enough money already." The club ended up giving me a bouquet of flowers, but Lane stayed on the cheap side. In those days, if a player was given a day in his honor, the club usually chipped in with a nice gift.

After the 1951 season I asked for $35,000 for 1952. Lane offered $30,000, and we had a hard time getting together. There weren't many guys in the league making that much or more, and $30,000 was a raise from the $25,000 I'd made the year before. But I think Frank resented the fact that I was threatening to hold out and hold his feet to the fire to get more money. What I did wasn't uncommon. Every year players had arguments with their clubs, but clubs had a tight hold on players because of the reserve clause. We didn't have any real leverage. We only had one choice. If a ballplayer didn't want to sign for what the team offered, he held out. And if he held out, he didn't go to spring training but kept negotiating with the club. Most players needed the money and wanted to play, so they finally came around and signed close to the club's figure. There weren't many players who held out for very long. They'd hold out maybe until spring training opened, and within a day or two they'd capitulate and sign. In this instance, Frank Lane finally came around a little, and we settled for $32,000 right before the start of spring training.

It was tough for players to negotiate contracts in those days. The story was that Bob Dillinger, who had hit over .320, was trying to negotiate his contract in the late 1940s with Bill DeWitt, the general manager of the Browns. DeWitt told Dillinger, "We finished last with you and we can finish last without you."

In 1952, my second full year with the White Sox, I got a call at my apartment from a woman who called herself Pete (pronounced "Peetee") right after I got back from spring training. I asked her how she got my number, and she told me she had called Railway Express, knowing they'd be delivering our trunks to us. Pete told me she was going to marry me, and that she already had a room in her house set up with a rocking chair for me. She knew I liked to hunt and said she had a shotgun for me.

I'd never heard from her before, but I quickly became suspicious and a little nervous about her. She kept calling me and began writing me letters. It was scary, especially since Eddie Waitkus had been shot in Chicago in 1949 by some gal he didn't know. She plugged him at the Edgewater Beach Hotel and almost killed him. Although Eddie came back and played in the big leagues, he was never the same.

Pete would call me and tell me she'd been to the game and complain that I wasn't paying any attention to her. She even sent a long telegram to me at the ballpark saying that I had caused her to love me and that I wouldn't pay attention to her. I'd never spoken to her and didn't even know what she looked like.

Then I began to look for her in the stands and spotted her. She'd sit on the third base line, looking down the first base line at me the whole game. It was disconcerting, but there wasn't anything I could do about it. She was an attractive lady, but I never spoke to her.

She wrote me frequently for several years, and her letters became more and more bizarre, very religious and emotional. For some reason she came to hate Ted Williams and the Yawkeys, who owned the Boston Red Sox. She'd ramble on about a lot of ball-players. Then she'd write about the outer world and people from outer space who were on earth. She'd go into long dissertations about the stars and the moon. My teammates couldn't believe I got these kind of letters. Pete, however, was never violent or threatening. She wrote me that Ted Williams and I were two of the few athletes chosen to go up in a flying saucer. And once she mailed me a book about flying saucers that had landed on earth, which I actually read. Still it was worrisome to be getting these strange letters all the time. After I got married again in 1955 she stopped writing, and I thought I was rid of her.

Ironically, when I was with the Yankees in the mid-1950s, Phil Rizzuto began receiving letters from a "female fan" similar to the ones I got from Pete. Phil would read the letters to us in the locker room, and we all got a big kick out of them. His were less bizarre and more romantic than mine, and I don't think he had the worry that Pete caused me.

I hadn't heard from Pete for years until my wife Bette and I moved to Houston in 1962 to help start the Colt .45s franchise. On the day we moved into our new home there, I received a dozen red roses from her. Later when I was the general manager of the Texas Rangers, the New York Mets contacted me with the startling news that Pete had become Casey Stengel's housekeeper. The Mets were trying to get some information about her because they were afraid that she was trying to take advantage of Casey. After Stengel died in 1975, Pete claimed Casey's estate because Casey's wife Edna had died previously and the Stengels had no children. I told the Mets what I knew about Pete and gave them the letters I had from her. Thankfully, after twenty years, I've never heard from her again.

## Extra Inning

Frank Lane used to sit by himself in the upper deck of the right field stands to watch part of the games. We could see him up there all alone. One day during the 1952 season he was sitting out there, and we all saw him. He no sooner left than I hit a home run that landed in the very seat he had been sitting in. I knew it was the seat he'd been sitting in because that seat was down, and all the other seats were pushed up. Frank and I were having contract problems at that time, and I remember thinking I wished he'd still been sitting there so that the ball would have nailed him.

*Chapter 10*
## A YEAR IN PURGATORY, ER, PHILADELPHIA

After the 1952 season Frank Lane and I started talking about a contract around December. I wanted my $35,000 again, and he wasn't going to pay it. I was living in Baltimore and was divorced by then. It never occurred to me that I might be traded. After the three productive years I'd had there, I thought I was an integral part of that ballclub. We had finished third in 1952 and were improving every year with guys like Nellie Fox, Chico Carrasquel, Minnie Minoso, and Billy Pierce. I knew Paul Richards liked me. But on January 27 I was listening to the radio and talking on the phone when I heard, "Eddie Robinson has just been traded to Philadelphia for Ferris Fain." That trade shook me to the point that I don't think I was ever as good a player after that. It was very disappointing to be traded to a bad club from an up-and-coming team like the White Sox, especially since I had contributed to their improvement.

After I heard about the trade on the radio, I called Richards and asked him what happened. I said, "I thought I was more or less a fixture with the White Sox."

Paul said, "Eddie, I didn't want to trade you. But Lane was determined to move you. He thinks your leg won't stand up to playing every day for very long, and Fain is healthy; he's led the league in hitting the last two years, and was available. Frank insisted on the deal."

That's how it goes sometimes in baseball. I moved on and reported to the Athletics, who trained in West Palm Beach, Florida. I signed a two-year contract for $35,000 a year. I was told it was the most the A's had ever paid a ballplayer, and I went to training camp very pleased with my contract.

I enjoyed my new teammates, and we had some fun during the spring. One day after practice several of us were doing wind sprints from the left-field foul line to the center-field flag pole. Lloyd Fisher, one of the lawyers who had represented Bruno Richard Hauptmann in the famous Lindbergh kidnapping case, was a big ball fan and was very friendly with the players. On this day he was out in left field kidding us about having to run sprints while he stood comfortably in the shade. I suggested to Dave Philley, Loren Babe, Gus Zernial, and the other guys that we take Lloyd's trousers off and run them up the flag pole. And that is exactly what we did. We then ran into the clubhouse, leaving Lloyd out there by himself where he had to walk out to the flagpole in his skivvies and retrieve his pants. Fisher didn't buy us any more dinners the rest of the spring.

Once the season began, however, I found that I didn't care for the city of Philadelphia and, to make matters worse, we didn't have a good team. I liked all the guys, but we struggled on the field all season, finishing in seventh place, forty-one and a half games out. It was a big change from playing in Chicago; the Philly fans were the roughest I'd ever seen. I'd never known fans like that. They're still pretty tough, but they were the toughest in those days. The A's didn't draw a lot of people, and those who came were constantly berating us, yelling at us and calling us bums, along with a lot of unprintable names. Their favorite expression was, "Hey, ya bum ya."

Fain didn't like the trade either. He didn't like Chicago, and early in the year broke his toe kicking first base in anger and missed about a month of playing time. He ended up hitting only .256, about seventy points below his average the year before. I hit only .247, about fifty points below my '52 average, but I drove in 102 runs and hit twenty-two home runs. That tied the record for home runs by a left-handed hitter in Shibe Park, which had a high fence in right field. Other than not hitting for a high average, I had a solid year. But I could tell I was starting to wind down as a player.

When you play in a city with hostile fans and you're trying your very best and they're not giving you any credit and you don't like the city and you didn't like the trade that brought you there—nothing much is good about playing baseball. You become disgruntled and unhappy, which is what happened to me. The A's had some terrific guys on the ballclub, and Jimmy Dykes was a fine man and a great manager. We had Elmer Valo, who would run through a brick wall to catch a ball, Dave Philley, from my hometown area in east Texas, Gus Zernial, Bobby Shantz, Ray Murray, and a bunch of other good guys.

Gus was the left fielder for the Athletics that year. A group of gamblers sat out in the left-field stands during every game. They bet on everything. Sometimes they'd bet on whether the pitch would be a strike or ball or whether a batter would get a hit or not. All the while they rode the left fielder unmercifully. They were especially rough on Del Ennis, who played left field for the Phillies and was a fine player. Del was from Olney, a Philly suburb, but those gamblers were still on him all the time.

Zernial was a big guy, over 6'2", and a little clumsy, but he could hit a ball a mile. Those gamblers rode him constantly. The next year, after I had been traded to the Yankees, Gus dove for a ball in Philadelphia and landed on his shoulder, breaking his collarbone. He didn't get up, and everyone ran out to see if he was badly hurt. My former teammates told me that they found Gus lying on the grass with a smile on his face. He said, "Fellas, don't worry about me. I know I've broken my collarbone. But that's not all bad. I won't have to listen to those sons-of-bitches in the bleachers for six weeks while I get well." That's how rough it was in Philadelphia. Thank goodness I just had to stay there one year. I've always regarded it as a lost year in my career.

Eddie Joost was the longtime shortstop for the A's, and the players on the team could see that he was out to get Jimmy Dykes's job. But Jimmy was such a nice unassuming guy that he didn't pay any attention to Joost's shenanigans. It bothered us to watch Eddie undermine his manager so blatantly. As a result, I never had any respect for Eddie Joost. He got the manager's job the next year, but the A's finished in the American League basement, sixty games out of first place. He was fired after the season, and before long was out of baseball.

Bobo Newsom was winding down his long and illustrious big league pitching career and was quite a character. He had broken in with the Dodgers back in 1929 and was back in the big leagues with the A's in 1953 at age forty-five. Although Bobo had won over two hundred games in the majors and was a great competitor, he'd get so nervous on the mound he would almost shake. I recall one time when he got in trouble early in the game, so I walked over to encourage him from my position at first base. Bobo called everybody Bo and he said to me, "Bo, I'm so nervous, I don't know if I can throw that ball over the plate anymore or not." It turned out that 1953 was the last of twenty years Bobo spent pitching in the big leagues.

Bobo had some real peculiarities. He hated it if there was anything on the mound that might distract him. Sometimes opposing players would tear up a newspaper and sprinkle it on the mound as they ran in from their positions at the end of an inning. Bobo would come out to warm up and refuse to pitch until the grounds crew picked up every piece of paper.

Bobo was also a know-it-all. One day on the train in 1953, our third baseman Loren Babe, Bobo, and I were talking about how to wring a chicken's neck. Bobo said, "Babe, I'll tell you what I can do. I can take a chicken's head off and he'll never move a muscle. He'll never flop around on the ground like they normally do when you wring a chicken's head off."

Loren said, "No way. Any time you pull a chicken's head off, he's going to flop around on the ground."

Bobo said, "Okay, I'll just bet both of you five dollars that I can do it."

We took the bet and arranged to have dinner at Loren's house in Philadelphia so that Bobo could show us his trick. After the game on the appointed day, we went over to Loren's house. His wife had bought a live chicken for the occasion, so we took the chicken out to the backyard and gave it to Bobo. Instead of wringing the chicken's neck, Bobo proceeded to pull the chicken's head straight off. As he did, he held the chicken's wings close to his body. He then laid the headless chicken flat on the ground with its feet up. It never moved.

Bobo was from rural South Carolina, so I guess that's how they killed chickens down there. In any event, Loren and I paid off. But it wasn't a total loss. I got a chicken dinner out of the deal.

We all loved ole Bobo. He was a fun guy to hang around. When he retired from baseball he went down to Orlando, Florida, and bought and ran a bar until he died in 1962.

Ray Murray was one of the catchers on that 1953 A's team who was also a character. Ray and I had been friends since 1948 when he was briefly with the Indians. One day we were playing the Yankees, and Yogi Berra was at bat with the bases loaded and a 3–2 count. There were two outs, so I was playing back at first base to try to stop any hard ground ball Yogi might send my way. Well, Yogi hit a towering pop-up right in front of the plate. I drifted in towards the infield grass, certain that Murray was going to catch it. When the ball hit its zenith, I heard Ray yell, "Come on, Eddie!" That meant he wanted me to catch the ball, so I ran as fast as I could toward home plate. I dove for the ball, but it hit the ground just out of my reach. Fortunately I didn't get my glove on it, and it bounced foul. If it hadn't, all three runners would have scored, since with two outs and a 3–2 count, they were off with the pitch.

Boy, was I grateful that pop fly bounced foul. The Philadelphia fans gave me the raspberry every chance they got, and they would've had a great time riding me if three runs had scored because I missed a pop fly.

Once that year we were playing the White Sox in Chicago, and Ray Murray was again catching for us. Ray was letting umpire Larry Napp know he didn't think much of Napp's ball and strike decisions. They were jawing back and forth. Then, all of a sudden, Murray called time, turned, and faced Napp. Ray then proceeded to pull his mask off and lay it on home plate, followed by his chest protector and shin guards. Then he got down on his knees on home plate facing Napp and started praying, "Dear God, please give this umpire one good eye so that he can call a strike."

Napp, of course, became irate. Manager Jimmy Dykes ran out and Napp said, "Do something with this guy. We can't have this going on."

Dykes took his hat off, put it over his heart, and said, "You can't ever interrupt a man while he's praying."

It was a great show and one of the funniest episodes I ever saw on a ball field. Napp threw both Dykes and Murray out of the game, but it was worth it.

My Philadelphia A's teammates elected me the club's player representative in 1953, maybe because they knew I could be outspoken. In any event, by then television was still new, but was becoming a major source of conflict for the owners and the players. The 1947 World Series was the first to be televised, and the players rightly believed radio and TV were going to provide considerable future revenues. The players had gotten together in 1946 and formed an association to put together a pension plan and force the owners to contribute to it. At that juncture a few players might have had radio and television money in mind, but not many. A pension plan would give us some security for the future, because most players had not attended college and didn't have any employable skills after they finished playing.

Anyone who'd played in the big leagues after 1942 did have a pension plan. It was set up so that the armed service years from World War II were included, so, for example, I got credit for my three years in the Navy. By 1953 the Players' Association had a good group of player representatives, guys like Bob Feller, Allie Reynolds, Robin Roberts, and Carl Erskine, but the association itself didn't have any outside person to lead us. Judge Robert Cannon of Milwaukee served as our legal counsel but only on a part-time basis. After the 1953 season, the players' reps, including Bob, Allie, Robbie, Carl, and I, traveled to Atlanta to meet with the owners to negotiate getting a cut of the radio and television money. We wanted Judge Cannon to participate in the meeting, but the owners refused, telling us they'd meet with the players only, not with our lawyer. We in turn refused to meet without the presence of Judge Cannon and so flew home without meeting with the owners.

The confrontation in Atlanta was the players' first real breach with management. I was never a player's rep again. I was traded to the Yankees the next year, and Allie Reynolds was well entrenched as the Yankees' player rep. More than ten years later Marvin Miller, primarily through the efforts of Robin Roberts, was hired as the head of the Players' Association. Under Marvin the players progressed from an association to a bona fide union as the relationship between the players and owners became more contentious. Nobody would refer to it as a union in the beginning because "union" was considered a dirty word.

Through the reserve clause, players were under the control of management and didn't have any bargaining leverage. A player had to play for his team or not play at all. There was no free agency, so a player could hold out for more money but eventually had to sign with his club for what he was offered or not play.

The owners had a death grip on baseball players that changed only after Marvin Miller came in. The players had never dealt much with management before 1953. They'd given us a few crumbs, a little of the All-Star Game money and World Series money. But when it came to making a sizeable commitment, the owners didn't want to talk. After that non-meeting in Atlanta, the conflict between management and the players began to get serious, and the association began to work hard to gain acceptance.

When Marvin Miller took over, the players got tougher and tougher and more and more powerful until today, the worm has pretty much turned. Now the players' union runs the game, and it's the owners' hands that are tied. The owners must go through the players' union to make any kind of change. Perhaps the most notorious example is the recent blockage of drug testing by the Players' Association, which had a lot to do with the steroid scandal of the 1990s and early 2000s.

I sometimes wonder whether the owners or the union really wanted to stop the home run surge of the steroid era. It attracted record crowds, particularly after the devastating strike of 1994 when the World Series was cancelled and many fans were disaffected, and from the union's perspective, it helped jack up salaries even more.

Baseball has always been a business, and the means by which the owners made their money. For the most part, baseball teams had not been one of the assets of a corporate ownership. The owners had depended on baseball for whatever money they made, so it was understandable that they wanted to keep a tight rein on the game. In most cases the owners had been involved in baseball for many years and, before television and radio, didn't make that much money. The owners were dependent on gate receipts to produce revenue, and used the reserve clause to keep their costs down by assuring that no free market existed that would give players significant bargaining power.

Until Dave McNally and Andy Messersmith played out their option and had an arbitrator strike down the reserve clause in 1975, the owners did not fully realize the potential power of the Players' Association. They didn't feel like they had to give the players anything out of the goodness of their hearts. But after Marvin Miller came on and McNally and Messersmith were granted free agency, it all changed quickly. The owners were forced to cede some of their bargaining power with the players. Television and radio money began to impact baseball revenues, and a new breed of owner came into baseball when some older owners sold out to large corporations.

Corporate CEOs were successful in their businesses and believed they could bring their type of management to baseball. The strategy didn't always work. These new owners didn't want to listen to their general managers, who were baseball lifers and understood what could be done to save baseball from union control. For example, the owners agreed to arbitration, which has negatively impacted the game and helped escalate salaries. Of course, greed played a large role. Teams like the Dodgers, the Giants, and the

Braves had moved into lucrative new markets and were drawing mostly packed houses. The owners recoiled at the thought of player strikes or stoppages because it would cost them significant revenue.

After the old line of owners got out of the game, their successors were unable to stand up to the Players' Association. The owners' group became more and more fragmented, with the big-market teams pitted against the small-market teams. The union took advantage of the fact that management couldn't agree on any important issue. The owners lacked cohesiveness then, and, it appears to me, they still do.

The Players' Association pension plan is one of the best plans in existence for those former major leaguers who qualify. Today, any player who spends one day in the big leagues is vested in the plan. Formerly, however, a player needed four years of big league service to be vested. I have been on a crusade through the Major League Baseball Players' Alumni Association (MLBPAA) for the last several years to include players who helped start the pension in the late forties and early fifties but who lack the required four years of big league service. Those players contributed part of their salaries to help get the union started. Although they can opt to get their contribution back, I believe that the union, which has well over $2 billion in its pension fund, should vest those players who were so important to the success of the union. Dan Foster, who is the chief operating officer of the MLBPAA, and the Players' Services Committee are helping me in my quest.

Near the end of the 1953 season, Eddie Lopat, the Yankee pitcher, and Frank Scott, a promoter, asked me to join the Eddie Lopat All-Stars for a postseason barnstorming trip to Hawaii and Japan. They put together a great team, and I was honored to be included. On that team were six future Hall of Famers: Robin Roberts, Yogi Berra, Eddie Mathews, Nellie Fox, Enos Slaughter, and my old pal Bob Lemon. The rest of the club were no slouches either. We had Harvey Kuenn, Billy Martin, Curt Simmons, Mike Garcia, Hank Sauer, Jackie Jensen (who was then with the Senators), Lopat, and Gus Niarhos.

We flew to Hawaii right after the World Series and spent a week there, staying in the Royal Hawaiian Hotel. I hadn't been to Hawaii since I was in the Navy. We palled around and hung out on the beach and had a great time. We also played a few games against a team Roy Campanella had put together called the Roy Campanella All-Stars, before heading on to Japan. We were billed as the greatest team ever to visit that country, and we received a hero's welcome when we landed in Tokyo. We lost the first game 5–4 but won all the rest against Japanese professional and all-star teams before heading to Okinawa and the Philippines, where we played a few games against our service personnel. It was a wonderful trip and allowed me to start enjoying playing baseball again after the rough season in Philadelphia.

## Extra Inning

Jackie Jensen and Billy Martin were two of my teammates with the Eddie Lopat All-Stars that toured Japan after the 1953 season. Jensen had a fear of flying that eventually caused him to end his playing career early. On our trip back from Japan, Jackie had a sleep mask on and had finally managed to fall asleep. Billy Martin noticed that Jackie was sleeping and put on one of the plane's oxygen masks. Then he shook Jackie and yelled, "Jackie, we're going down We're going down!"

Ballplayer humor can be very cruel.

*Chapter 11*
## FROM THE OUTHOUSE TO THE PENTHOUSE

After that miserable year in Philadelphia, December 16, 1953, was one of the happiest days of my baseball life. That was the day I was traded to the Yankees in a big multi-player deal. I went with Harry Byrd and several minor leaguers to New York for infielder Jim Finigan, first basemen Vic Power and Don Bollweg, outfielder Bill Renna, catcher Al Robertson, and pitcher John Gray. It was like a breath of fresh air to get out of Philadelphia, but going to the Yankees was beyond my wildest dreams. They won the pennant almost every year, and I thought with their World Series bonus every year I could make some pretty good money.

When I reported for spring training, however, I found that the Yankees already had Joe Collins and a twenty-three-year-old rookie named Bill "Moose" Skowron, who I could see had a great future, to play first base. The Yankees weren't sure Skowron was ready, but he turned out to be outstanding. In fact he hit .340 in eighty-seven games his rookie year. It was obvious that Moose was going to be the regular first baseman for the Yankees for years to come.

The Yankees trained in St. Petersburg, Florida, at Miller Huggins Field, which, surprisingly to me, looked like a high school playground. I had assumed the mighty Yankees would have a first-class training facility. We took all our hitting practice and drills at Huggins Field and then played the exhibition games at St. Petersburg Park, where the St. Louis Cardinals also trained.

We stayed at the old Serena Hotel, which featured dinner music and was frequented by retired people. The old folks would have dinner and then sit in the lobby and listen to the music. It was a new experience for me. The Yankees had been training there for years; they didn't let the music or the old people bother them. I don't know if we bothered the old people or not.

Bill Virdon was my roommate that first spring. He was just twenty-two and hadn't played any big league ball. We were both single, and one night during spring training we were out having a drink at a bar when we met two gals who volunteered to drive us back to our hotel in St. Petersburg. The girl who was driving must have been drinking because she kept driving faster and faster, making me very nervous. I kept telling her from the backseat to slow down. She kept going faster, and so finally I lost my cool and whacked her in the back of the head and said, "Stop this goddamned car!" She stopped immediately, and Bill and I got out and had a long walk back to the hotel. Whenever I see Bill, he still says, "Slow down, slow down" to me.

Bill was a good center fielder prospect, but the Yankees had a young guy named Mantle in that position. So they traded Bill and a couple of others in April 1954 to the Cardinals for Enos "Country" Slaughter. Virdon became Rookie of the Year with the Cardinals in 1955 and went on to have a fine career with the Cards and Pirates before becoming a successful big league manager with the Pirates, Yankees, Astros, and Expos. He is also remembered for hitting the ground ball in Game 7 of the 1960 World Series that struck Yankee shortstop Tony Kubek in the throat and opened the door for the Pirates' comeback victory.

The Yankees were a loose bunch. I'd rented a Volkswagen to drive during spring training, and one day I came out of the clubhouse to find that some of my teammates had picked my Volkswagen up and put it between two poles so I couldn't drive it out. I think Whitey Ford and Don Larsen were two of the guys who were responsible, but I never found out for certain who all was involved.

In contrast to Paul Richards's approach with the White Sox, we didn't go through any fundamentals with the Yankees. When the Yanks got you as a player, they figured you knew how to play, and that's what you were supposed to do. If you couldn't play, the club didn't keep you around very long.

I was proud to be a Yankee. They had history and tradition and had won five straight World Series before I joined them. The 1954 season turned out to be unusual, however. We won 103 games, more than any other Stengel-managed team, but still lost to Cleveland by eight games. The Indians set a record by winning 111 games, but then managed to get swept in the World Series by the New York Giants. It was a crazy year.

I went to the Yankees thinking I'd play a lot, but with the glut of talent at first base I became a pinch hitter and a part-time player. In 1954 I played in eighty-five games and led the league with fifteen pinch hits. Pinch hitting, by the way, is not an easy job. I recall one doubleheader where I took batting practice at 11:30 in the morning and then pinch hit at 8:00 that night. But I helped the team, and I played well when I did play. Even though I didn't play much, I loved being in New York. The Yankees expected to win every game. And, most of the time we did. It was a feeling I'd never experienced with a ballclub before.

One of my Yankee teammates was Gene Woodling, who had been a good friend since our Cleveland days. Gene loved to needle teammates and would really work on me. Since I'd been the regular first baseman everywhere I'd played until I got to the Yankees, Woodling would come over and sit by me in the dugout and say, "Eddie, you thought you were going to play when you came over here, didn't you? You thought you'd waltz in and be the first baseman, didn't you? And here you sit on the bench. I'll bet that really bothers you, doesn't it?" Gene would go on and on, agitating me and having a great time doing it.

Casey Stengel was a different kind of manager from anyone I had ever played for. He never gave any instruction. He never told a player anything to try to improve his play. He frequently would not be on the bench when we were going through pregame workouts. And he held very few team meetings. We saw more of Casey on the train when we were traveling from city to city and during the games than any other time.

He had his quirks. For example, he would get angry if an opposing pitcher was throwing sinker balls and we were swinging at low pitches and hitting ground balls. He'd yell, "Quit hitting at those damn grounders."

The Yankees were a team comprised of players who were interchangeable. Gil McDougald could play short, second, or third. Jerry Coleman could move to short or second. Yogi Berra could play left field as well as catch, and the outfielders could play different outfield positions. Joe Collins, a first baseman, could play the outfield. Casey also had a good bench. He'd call on a pinch hitter any time during a ballgame, and had any number of ways he could change the lineup. I'd hit for Rizzuto as early as the second inning. If we'd get men on base and Rizzuto would come up, I'd pinch hit. Stengel had a knack for making unorthodox moves to win games.

During the 1954 season, for instance, Bill Skowron was a rookie and hitting sixth in the batting order. We loaded the bases in the first inning with two outs, bringing Bill to the plate. The opposition changed pitchers, bringing in a right-hander to replace the southpaw who'd started. Casey said, "Eddie, get a bat and hit for Skowron." The look on Moose's face when he saw me walking up to hit for him was priceless. He couldn't believe it. I slammed a double to drive in three runs, which soothed Bill a little and made Casey look like a genius. Every time I see Moose, even today, he says, "Hey, Eddie, you remember that day in Yankee Stadium when you pinch hit for me in the first inning?"

I say, "Yeah, Moose. I remember."

Then Moose will say, "I'm glad you got a base hit. I would've been even madder if you hadn't."

Casey kept players stirred up by not playing them every day. Most wanted to play regularly, but he would platoon them or pinch hit for them. Sometimes even when a player was going good he'd take him out of the lineup. Using his bench gave him a stronger team and kept the players involved because everyone played frequently.

Casey was always entertaining the press. He'd sit on the bench and tell funny stories to the press, and we would sit close enough to listen to him carry on. He liked to speak in that Stengelese double-talk I never could understand. It was so crazy you'd have to write it down to remember it. The newspapers loved to write about him because he was such a colorful man.

Casey had some memorable sayings. He used to say that sex isn't bad for a ball-player; it was chasing it that took its toll. Another Stengelese standby was "Good pitching will stop good hitting and vice versa."

He could also display a sense of humor on the field. In spring training in 1955 Whitey Herzog, who later became a very successful manager, was a young outfielder trying to make the club. Casey put Whitey in to pinch hit in an exhibition game against the Tigers in Lakeland, Florida. Herzog promptly got a base hit and then stumbled over first base and sprained his ankle. It was bad enough that he had to be helped off the field. Casey came out of the dugout and said, "He's been playing baseball most of his life and he still doesn't know where first base is."

I'm sure some of the players didn't like Casey. Phil Rizzuto was his most outspoken critic. Stengel always said that a ballclub was comprised of twenty-five guys – twenty guys who liked you and five guys who didn't. He said one of the biggest tricks of managing was to keep the twenty guys who liked you away from the five guys who didn't.

Casey never was close to any of the players while I was there. I know he liked some of his players, and I'm sure he had his favorites such as Billy Martin. Because he had such a great ballclub, the players liked being in New York and liked playing for the Yankees. Stengel was a tough old bird, but he had a heart. He didn't embarrass you or tear you down. He'd be all happy and strut around when we were winning, which was most of the time. I recall one game in which we slugged a bunch of home runs. Every time we would hit a home run Casey would shake the player's hand when he came back into the dugout. When I hit a home run late in the ballgame and came around, he said, "Here, shake my elbow; my hand's tired."

One of the funniest stories I know about Stengel took place later, when I was working for the Braves in Atlanta and Paul Richards was general manager. The winter meetings that year were in San Diego. The major league draft of minor league players was on a Monday, the first day of the meetings. Paul called a meeting for 7:00 a.m. to discuss players we might draft prior to our going to the ten o'clock draft. Frank Gabler, who was a part-time coach and friend of Paul's and the coaches, got on the elevator with me to go to Paul's room. We got off the elevator and were walking down the hall, when there lying on the stairs was this guy passed out with his pants down. As we passed by Gabler said, "Look at that bum, passed out, drunk on the stairs. That's really awful." Gabler was no slouch as a drinker himself and may have found himself in the same situation a time or two.

Then Frank said, "Wait a minute. That ain't no bum; that guy's got alligator shoes on." So we stopped and walked over to check the guy out. It was none other than Casey Stengel, passed out, pants down around his knees. We pulled him up, but when we did his pants fell off. Then Gabler and I tried to help him back into his pants, planning to take him over to Richards's room and get some coffee in him. We were trying to help him with his pants but Casey was trying to put them on wrong side out. Gabler kept saying, "Casey, you're putting your pants on wrong side out." He said, "Young man, I've been putting my pants on for seventy years. I know how to put my pants on."

We finally got his pants on him right side out and, with one of us on each side of him, managed to guide him to Paul Richards's room. We poured some coffee down him and got him talking a little bit. Finally Casey looked over at me and said, "Eddie, call Edna up. If she answers, don't say anything." Edna was Casey's wife. Of course, he hadn't been to their room all night, so I wasn't sure what was on his mind. Apparently, he just wanted to know if she was in the room. So I called the room, Edna answered, and I didn't say anything. I just hung up. I said, "Yeah, Casey, Edna was in." So Casey drank some more coffee and left. At two o'clock that afternoon he was back in the hotel bar downstairs fresh as a daisy—fresh shirt, tie, and suit—joshing with the guys. He looked like he'd slept like a baby for eight hours.

Mickey McDermott was a hard-living left-handed pitcher who spent the 1956 season with the Yankees. Mickey told me that one night when the Yankees were on the road he came back to the hotel about 2:30 in the morning, thinking Stengel and the coaches would long be in bed by that time. He walked into the elevator and there stood Casey. As the elevator started up, Casey looked over at Mickey and asked, "Drunk again?"

Mickey said, "Yep, afraid so."

"Me, too," Casey responded. Then Casey got off on his floor. Mickey rode on up to his and never heard another word about his late hours.

Yogi Berra and I became good friends, as did our wives Bette and Carmen. When we were on opposing teams, we used to kid each other all the time. One time I offered to bet Yogi five bucks that we were going to beat them the next day and Yogi said, "Okay, you got a bet." We beat the Yankees, and the first time I walked up to bat the following day, Yogi handed me a five-dollar bill. I wonder what Commissioner Frick would have thought about that.

One day when we were teammates, we'd played a night game followed by a doubleheader the next day. I didn't want to take batting practice so I got to the park late. I was at my locker, putting my uniform on, when the players starting coming in after batting practice. Yogi came in and headed right for my locker. He said, "Eddie, where were you during batting practice? You really missed it."

I said, "What did I miss?"

Yogi said, "There were two streakers. They jumped onto the field at the right field foul pole and ran all the way into the stands at the left field foul pole. And they didn't have any clothes on."

I said, "No kidding. I guess I did miss it. Were they boys or girls?"

Yogi said, "I dunno. They had bags on their heads."

Of course, a lot of fun has been poked at Yogi over the years for his so-called Yogi-isms. One thing is for certain; Yogi is a lot sharper than people give him credit for. Many of his funny sayings do make sense, for example, "Nobody goes there anymore; it's too crowded" when talking about a popular restaurant.

People love to kid Yogi. But he is like a big old bear. The teasing just runs off his back and doesn't seem to bother him. He doesn't have to try to say those funny things he always says. They just seem to come naturally to him. Like when they gave him a day in his hometown, St. Louis, and he thanked the fans for "making this day necessary." Yogi loved to talk. When I was an opposing player and came to the plate, we would hold a regular conversation. He'd say, "Hi Eddie, how's Bette?"

I'd reply, "She's fine. How's Carmen?"

"Where you going to dinner tonight?"

"I don't know, how about you?"

"Bet you can't hit this pitch."

"Throw me a fastball, Yogi."

And on and on through the entire at bat.

Yogi remains a great friend and a national treasure.

I also became friends with Ralph Houk, who was a backup catcher. Ralph had been a Ranger during World War II and had seen a lot of action. He was called "Major" in deference to his war record. During rain delays, Ralph would keep us enthralled with stories about his war experiences. He was once captured by the Germans but managed to jump off the truck transporting him and escape back to the Allied lines to continue to fight.

Gil McDougald was probably my biggest surprise when I joined the Yankees. As an opposing player, you don't think you'd like certain guys and McDougald was one of those. He had a prissy manner, and when he'd get on first base he always complained to me about something. I thought, this guy is really stuck-up. As it turned out, when I became his teammate he was one of the nicest guys you'd ever want to meet and became one of my favorites on the team.

I was thirty-three when I joined the Yankees. Billy Martin and Mickey Mantle were younger and they palled around with some of the younger players. Houk, Woodling,

Phil Rizzuto, Jerry Coleman, Yogi, and Hank Bauer were of my vintage, so we naturally hung around together. We played a lot of poker. Yogi loved to gamble and played a lot of cards with us. Mickey liked to play poker and Billy Martin was usually in the game. We'd often play in our hotel rooms in the afternoon before a night game. If there was no poker game, Phil Rizzuto and I often spent the afternoon at the movies. Phil couldn't see enough movies. Phil loved double features, and many times we'd watch two movies before going to the ballpark.

Rizzuto was still the Yankee shortstop in 1954. He had a weak arm and it seemed like he could just barely get the ball over to first. But it would get there and beat the runner by about a half-step because he could get rid of it so fast.

I'd known Phil since our Navy days together. Phil was always the butt of jokes, just like the time we were in the Navy and played that nasty trick on him right before he got married. Phil was squeamish. If we were in the dining car someone could say something a little off-color or comment about the food not being properly prepared, and Rizzuto would have to get up and leave the table to keep from gagging.

Jerry Coleman was one of our veteran infielders and was coming off two years of flying combat missions in Korea. He flew sixty missions there and had flown over sixty missions as a dive bomber in World War II. He was the only big leaguer to see combat in both wars. In addition to being an American hero, Jerry was a fine ballplayer and teammate and I enjoyed his company. Growing up in San Francisco, Jerry had played with a southpaw pitcher named Bill Wight. Wight now pitched for Chicago, and the first time the White Sox came to Yankee Stadium, he was the starting pitcher. Before the game, Jerry went around and warned everyone about Wight's terrific pick-off move. He said, "You've got to be very, very careful. Bill Wight has the best pick-off move I've ever seen. If you just put your foot off first base, he'll pick you off. Stay very close to the bag or you'll be embarrassed by getting picked off."

Jerry played second base in the ball game, got on first base in his first time at bat, and was promptly picked off by Wight.

After his playing days, Jerry went on to have a Hall of Fame career as a broadcaster, and at age eighty-six is still doing the San Diego Padres games. He's a legend in San Diego, but I still enjoy reminding him about that pick-off whenever I see him.

Bill Dickey was the first base and hitting coach for the Yankees, and I liked him very much. He'd been an All-Star catcher on the great Yankee teams of the 1930s and is in the Hall of Fame in Cooperstown. In the late 1940s he had a lot to do with making Yogi Berra a top-drawer receiver. Bill and I became friendly before I came to the Yankees because we always visited during the games, since I played first base and Bill coached first for the Yankees. Bill would get me good theater tickets even when I was a visiting player.

Frankie Crosetti was our third base coach and a contemporary of Dickey's. He'd played shortstop for the Yankees for years until Phil Rizzuto took over. Then Cro, as we fondly called him, had stepped right into coaching third. There's no telling how many World Series rings Cro and Bill Dickey had between them, but you would need an extra hand to wear them all. Cro had a squeaky high voice and emitted endless chatter from the third base coaching box, complete with slogans and phrases that used to crack us up. Cro was always very much into the game, very intense. He also was a little on the tight side, and he wanted and expected World Series money every year. He didn't like it when we got way ahead in a game and started to relax and joke around. He'd tell us in his high pitched voice, "All right you guys, don't get gay when you're full of shit. You're messing with my money."

After the 1954 season I went barnstorming through the south with Ralph Houk, Whitey Lockman, Eddie Lopat, Gus Niarhos, Yogi Berra, Cal Abrams, and others. Tommy Byrne, who was a southpaw pitcher on the Yankees, rode with me in my new DeSoto convertible as we traveled through North and South Carolina playing exhibition games against semipro teams. Tommy, who was a good practical joker, and I got the reputation, probably earned, of driving fast. Our teammates would say, "You guys better slow down. You're going to have a wreck."

After one game the team stopped in a little town in North Carolina and had dinner. Tommy and I got through eating first and headed out to drive to the next town. We decided to pull a trick on the guys behind us. We found a place where there was a hill with a curve at the bottom. We pulled the car down into the ditch so that the car lights were shining up into the air. Then we threw both of the doors open. Tommy lay down on the side of the road and I hung my head out the door. We knew our teammates were in a car right behind us. Over the hill came a car that screeched to a stop and a man and woman got out. Then here came another car and three more people got out; we didn't know any of them. Somehow they were ahead of the players. I can hear Tommy now. He's lying there on the ground saying, "Go away. Go away. There's nothing wrong with us." And those good Samaritans were standing there looking at us, wondering why we were acting so strangely.

However, those bystanders made our little accident scene look even more realistic, because when our teammates did come over the hill they saw all these people and then saw our car. They screeched to a halt, piled out of the cars, and came running. They couldn't see any evidence of a wreck, but they knew there must have been one. I can still remember Cal Abrams looking down at me and saying, "You couldn't make that curve, could you?" With that, Byrne jumped up, ran around, and got in the passenger side. I sat up, cranked the car, and we yelled, "Bet you can't catch us," and took off in a cloud of dust, leaving all of them standing there in the road.

Yogi later said, "We'll never stop again for you guys. You can turn that vehicle upside-down and we're not stopping." They never forgot we'd duped them. We could've had a serious accident and they wouldn't have stopped. The following year we were in Hawaii, barnstorming again. We played a game and afterwards I was driving four other players to our hotel. As we were leaving the park, I discovered that our car had a flat tire, so I jumped out to wave down Yogi's car. I said, "Wait a minute. We've got a flat tire." Yogi said, "Don't believe that son of a bitch; they don't have any flat tire. It's a trick."

While I was playing for the Athletics in 1953, I got to meet Patti Paige. Patti was my favorite female vocalist, so I went to see her perform while she was appearing at a nightclub in Philadelphia. Afterwards the nightclub owner invited me to go backstage to meet her. He introduced me to her and to her manager, Stanley Kay, who also doubled as her drummer. Stanley was a baseball fan, and so the three of us agreed to have lunch the next day. Patti lived in New York, and after I was traded to the Yankees in December, we started dating.

It also happened that during that winter I traveled from my home in Baltimore to Cumberland, Maryland, to appear at a banquet. When I boarded the train to return to Baltimore the next morning, the coach was almost full. I noticed two girls sitting across from me. One of them was very pretty. I didn't say anything to them, however, and just read my book and later had lunch in the dining car. When the train arrived in Washington, everyone on the car got off except one of the two girls, the pretty one, who'd been sitting across from me. I introduced myself and said, "Looks like we're the only two left. I'm getting off in Baltimore, so why don't we go to the club car and have a drink?" The pretty girl said, "All right," and that is how I met Bette Farlow, the love of my life. It was my lucky day.

Bette was from Staten Island and was in her senior year at Hunter College in New York. I told her I was a ballplayer and had just been traded to the Yankees. We agreed to get together for lunch after the baseball season started in the spring. Bette was so attractive and so warm and friendly that I looked forward to seeing her again in New York.

I called her when I arrived in New York the next spring with the Yankees and made a date for dinner. That was the beginning of a wonderful lifetime relationship. Although I dated both Patti Paige and Bette during the 1954 season, in the fall of 1954 Bette won my heart and that was that. As I got to know Bette better and got to meet her friends, I learned that she had excelled academically at New Dorp High School on Staten Island and was one of the brightest students at Hunter College, which was then a very selective women's college. She was also an accomplished pianist. The more I learned about her the luckier I got.

The Yankees went barnstorming as a team to Hawaii, Japan, and Okinawa after the '55 season. We were to leave two days after the World Series was over, so Bette and I decided to get married on that off-day in-between and take our honeymoon on the trip. Johnny Kucks, one of our pitchers, and third baseman Andy Carey also got married on October 6, and we all flew to Honolulu on the seventh. How many newlyweds have thirty-five people with them on their honeymoon?

While we were at the Royal Hawaiian Hotel, Enos Slaughter, who had been married about five times, made his infamous remark about wives. He said, "Wives are like apples. Just shake a tree and another one will fall out." I wonder what his latest wife, who was with him on the trip, thought about that comment.

After a week in Honolulu we flew to Japan to play a series of games against Japanese professional teams. We were like the Japanese in that we did not want to lose face. We wanted to win every game, and we almost did. The closest we came to losing was a game that ended up tied. Whitey Ford was pitching and put the pick-off play on at second base. At least Whitey thought the pick-off play was on, but neither Jerry Coleman, the second baseman, nor Gil McDougald, the shortstop, was aware of it. Whitey whirled around and threw the ball as the Japanese player was taking his lead. The Japanese runner turned and slid into second base, but there was nobody there to catch the ball, which proceeded to clobber the second base Japanese umpire right in the head. He crumpled in a heap, and it took several minutes to revive him.

We were the first American team of any kind to go to Hiroshima after the atom bomb had been dropped there at the end of World War II. The city reminded me of a giant shopping center that had just been built. There were many new buildings and a lot of new cement streets. There were only a few recently planted trees. The whole town was flat because they were not erecting any tall buildings. We went to a monument and museum that depicted the horrible damage from the bomb. We saw, for example, silver coins that had been in a bank vault and had become fused from the intense heat of the blast into a giant paperweight. The museum was located right on ground zero.

We didn't leave the hotel that evening because the Japanese officials were nervous about the reaction of the locals if we wandered around at night. So we started a big poker game on the mezzanine of the hotel, and after a few drinks we were making quite a bit of noise. Stengel's room happened to be nearby. He finally decided to tell us to be quiet and startled us when he walked down the hall. He was in red silk pajamas and bare feet with his white hair all tousled. Charlie Silvera, who was just watching the game and not playing, looked up and with a big laugh said, "Here comes Santa Claus." That made Casey even angrier. He gave us a little speech about being quiet, and went back to his room and we went back to playing cards.

Many of the players had their wives on the trip. At one point, the wives went to a health spa while we went to Nagoya to play a game. We were supposed to meet our wives back at the health spa in two days. The game was at a huge American Air Force base, and afterwards we were invited to a dance at the Officers' Club. We went and had a big time with some of the officers and their wives. Some of them joined us back at our hotel, where we continued to drink at the hotel bar. I was sitting at the bar near this one gal who had been flirting with a lot of us, me included. Although I had no business doing it, I started tossing peanuts at her. She got mad and slapped me in front of the entire crowd. That was the end of that; folks started leaving and the party broke up.

Afterwards Billy Martin, Whitey Ford, and I were the only three left in the bar, along with the Japanese bartender. We were talking and one of us, I think it was Billy, had an idea. "Wouldn't it be fun to get everybody back down here?" So we started cooking up a plan and decided since the woman had slapped me in front of everyone, our teammates would assume that she was married. We figured if we called the rooms and told our teammates we were in a fight down at the bar and were outnumbered and needed help, the guys would come back down to help. We decided if we could get Yogi down first, we could get him to call others on the phone and they'd be more likely to believe him than Martin, Ford, or me. So we called Yogi first and put Whitey on the phone because he was more believable than Billy or I. Yogi wouldn't have believed me because of the faked car wreck the year before.

So Billy and I started yelling and banging chairs around and Whitey told Yogi that I was in a big fight and that he and Billy were helping, but we were outnumbered and needed help. Yogi said, "I'll be right there." It didn't take him two minutes to get down to the bar. He came down in just his pants and an undershirt without any shoes, ready to fight. He ran around the corner by the entrance and saw it was a hoax and started laughing. Then we put Yogi on the phone, and he called all the other players and coaches except Casey Stengel. We decided it wouldn't be prudent to call Casey.

When our teammates came to the bar they had to make a little turn at the entrance before they could see into the bar. To see the guys' faces when they made the turn and knew they'd been had was comical. The only two guys who wouldn't come down were Moose Skowron and Bob Cerv, two of the biggest guys on the team. They didn't believe us and wouldn't come down. Everyone had a big laugh, and the bar got busy again before we went to bed for good.

The postseason tour ended after a week in Hawaii and five weeks in Japan and Okinawa. Bette and I had decided that instead of coming home we'd continue around the world. While most of the fellas flew back through Hawaii, Bette and I had an itinerary taking us to Taiwan, Hong Kong, and Bangkok, Thailand. From Bangkok we traveled to India, Athens, Turkey, and Rome. While we were in India we visited a little town named Jaipur, about three weeks after we'd left Tokyo. We'd been to Bombay and were going to ride an elephant the next morning in this ancient little town. As we left our hotel to go to the elephant ride, we ran smack into Tommy Byrne, a left-handed pitcher for the Yankees, and his wife Sue. The Byrnes had made their itinerary without any idea of our travels, but there we all were at the elephant ride in Jaipur, India.

Bette and I left the next day with a car and driver for the long drive to Agra, India.

There we saw the Taj Mahal, constructed by Shah Johan to honor his wife. It is an unbelievable monument that took twenty thousand workers twenty years to build. We were lucky enough to see it in a full moon.

In Rome we stayed at the Roma Hotel. One afternoon Bette and I were out shopping and wandered into a tie shop. I heard a familiar voice from the back of the store and said, "Casey and Edna Stengel are in this store." Bette listened and said, "Yeah, that's Casey." Sure enough they soon came walking from the back of the store. We had dinner with Casey and Edna at our hotel that evening. So twice after we left Tokyo we randomly ran into other Yankees.

After we left Rome we took the train to Florence for a few days and then went on to Venice. From there we spent Christmas in Kitzbuhel, Austria. The Austrians were dressed in their long green Tyrolean coats and strange-looking green hats. From Kitzbuhel we traveled by train to the Volkswagen plant in Wolfsburg, Germany, to pick up the Volkswagen I had purchased before we left New York. We then drove the rest of the way through Europe, through the Netherlands and into Paris. We took the car ferry across the English Channel and spent three days taking in the sights of London before shipping our Volkswagen home and flying back to New York, almost three months to the day after we'd left. It was a terrific honeymoon and the beginning of a wonderful marriage.

## Chapter 12

## FUN AND GAMES WITH THE YANKEES

The Yankees went to spring training in 1955 after coming in second in 1954, although we won more games than any Stengel-managed team. We went back to St. Petersburg, and Elston Howard, the first black player on the Yankees, joined the team for his first spring training. We went through the normal routine, training at Miller Huggins Field and playing our games in St. Pete. Everyone was interested in whether Elston would make the team, and since he was a catcher, wondered how this would impact Yogi. Yogi was getting to the age where he needed a little rest behind the plate and could play the outfield some to keep his bat in the lineup. The day spring training was over and it was announced Elston had made the team, Ellie was so happy he broke out with hives. We went to the train station to head north—we were going to play exhibition games along the way—and Elston and his wife were at the train station to meet us. He was going on the train and she was going to drive to New York. Ellie was so excited that he got on the train with their car keys. We were about two miles out of town on the train when he discovered he had his wife's keys. I still don't know how she got to New York.

On our way north we stopped in Savannah, Georgia, to play an exhibition game against the Savannah Athletics, a Class A team in the Sally League. I played the first seven innings. In exhibition games a player would come out of the game and take a taxi back to the hotel to get dressed and wait for the rest of the team. The club had taxis waiting for us.

On this day the score was 9–0 in favor of Savannah when several of us including Jerry Coleman, Gil McDougald, and Yogi Berra, left in the eighth inning. Stengel was irate for letting these Humpty Dumptys get so far ahead of us. We got back to the hotel, showered, packed our uniform trays, and took them down to the lobby. Then we waited and waited for the rest of the team to return to the hotel and couldn't figure out what was taking so long. When the guys finally did get back, we learned that we'd scored nine runs in the ninth inning to tie the game and then scored a run in the tenth to win.

I had a strange but good year in 1955. We still had three first basemen, but the club knew that Skowron was its first baseman of the future, so I didn't get to play first much. I pinch-hit quite a bit and played first when Skowron was hurt. During one period I played several days in a row and hit great, including a bunch of home runs. For the year I had more RBIs than I did hits (42 to 36), and I hit 16 home runs in only 173 at bats, which is a major league record that still stands. Even though I didn't hit for much of an average, Skowron, Collins, and I tacked up some productive numbers from the first base position, with 41 home runs and 148 RBIs collectively.

Nineteen fifty-five was the year Mickey Mantle hit a ball thrown by Pedros Ramos off the facade in Yankee Stadium, which was the closest anyone ever came to hitting a fair ball out of Yankee Stadium. The home run ball bounded back onto the field, and after the game someone gave it to Mickey, who knew I had a restaurant in Baltimore. Mick yelled across the clubhouse, "Hey, Eddie, you want this ball for your restaurant?" I said sure, so he signed it and gave it to me, and I displayed it in my restaurant for many years with the Babe Ruth bat I'd gotten in 1948.

I had opened the restaurant in 1952. I was still popular in Baltimore because of my Most Valuable Player year in the International League in 1946. The restaurant was on Gorusch Avenue, a half mile from Memorial Stadium. It soon became a hangout for baseball and football players. Johnny Unitas, Alan Ameche, Gino Marchetti, Don Shula, Raymond Berry (from my hometown of Paris, Texas, and one of the best receivers I've even seen), Jim Mutscheller, and Art Donovan of the Baltimore Colts came in all the time. I even had a key club because private key clubs were popular in those days. I had a lot of sports artifacts in the restaurant, but I wanted sports paintings rather than just a bunch of glossy photos on the wall.

In 1956 Bette and I lived in one of her brother-in-law's apartments in Greenwich

Village. I may be the only Yankees player ever to live in Greenwich Village. Bette's brother-in-law, Joe Holzka, owned a four-story brownstone in the Village with an apartment on each floor, and we had one of the apartments. I could jump on the subway two blocks from the house and get off at Yankee Stadium thirty minutes later. It was a great setup.

One night we attended a party in the Village and met a group of artists, so I began to ask if anyone knew anyone who painted sports art. We were directed to Elaine de Kooning, who'd done a couple of basketball paintings. She lived in a studio in the Village and didn't have a phone, so I sent her a telegram and asked her to call me. She agreed to attend some Yankee games to sketch so that she could later paint from the sketches. She ended up producing some great abstract baseball paintings for my restaurant.

Elaine was the wife of Willem "Bill" de Kooning, one of the most famous abstract artists in the world. His paintings today sell for over a million dollars. Elaine was one of the first artists commissioned to paint President Kennedy's portrait, which today hangs in the Library of Congress. Hers is the only portrait of JFK actually sat for. Bette and I remained friends with Elaine until she passed away in 1989.

During the time I owned the restaurant, the only fight that took place there involved my Yankee buddies. Gene Woodling, Ralph Houk, and Hank Bauer were having lunch before they went to the ballpark when some patrons came over and asked for their autographs. The guys signed a couple, but then they wanted to eat their meal. One man, however, gave them some guff. So Woodling, Houk, and Bauer, who were all big strong ballplayers, jumped up and pinned the three autograph seekers right over the bar. That ended the scuffle and the autographs.

I owned the restaurant from 1952 until the fall of 1961, when Paul Richards asked me to go to Houston with him to start the new National League franchise there. I had a decision to make because if I stayed in Baltimore, I probably would've been in the restaurant business the rest of my life. I knew that if I went to Houston, I was choosing to stay in baseball, and that is what I did.

I decided to approach Brooks Robinson and Joe Hamper, who was the Orioles accountant and a frequent patron of the restaurant, about investing in the place. They decided to buy in and run the restaurant while I was in Houston. We formed a corporation, and they each purchased 24 percent, leaving me with 52 percent. We continued that arrangement for about five years. Brooksie was never really into the restaurant business, however, and didn't hang out there like I used to. So eventually we decided it would be best to sell the restaurant, although I hated to let it go. That old place had provided us with a nice livelihood while I was making the transition from player to coach to farm director to front office executive.

We had a tough pennant race against Cleveland and the Chicago White Sox in 1955 before finally clinching the pennant in Boston two days before the end of the season. We had a nice victory party at the Kenmore Hotel in Boston, where the visiting teams stayed. But victory parties with the Yankees weren't like they were with other teams. They were more subdued since the Yankees expected to win and usually did. In contrast, when the Indians won the championship in Boston in 1948, we'd had a celebration at the Kenmore that was a huge blowout compared to the Yankee party.

There would be no Yankee World Series victory party in 1955, however. That was the year the Dodgers finally defeated the Yankees in the World Series, the first time they'd ever won a Series. The Dodgers were ahead three games to two, but we went back to Yankee Stadium and won the sixth game 5–1 behind a four-hitter by Whitey Ford. In the seventh game the Dodgers were ahead 2–0 going into the sixth inning. We had the bases loaded against Johnny Podres when Yogi hit the ball down the left-field line, which he hardly ever did. Sandy Amoros somehow got over and caught it to keep three runs from scoring. On top of that, Amoros doubled Gil McDougald off second base to end the inning. We never mounted any other offense and lost 2–0.

In the sixth inning of that game, Casey sent me up to pinch-hit with two outs and Billy Martin on third base. For some reason, Billy decided to try to steal home. He took off with the pitch and was thrown out to end the inning. He jumped up and started arguing with the umpire that he beat the tag. Billy turned to me and said, "Eddie, wasn't I safe?"

I said, "Hell no, you were out. You shouldn't have been trying to steal home in the first place." Of course, I was unhappy because Martin had taken the bat right out of my hands.

So in my two full years with the Yankees we finished second and then won the pennant, but lost the World Series, losing to the Dodgers for the first time. I guess it was just time for Brooklyn to win.

## Extra Inning

Moose Skowron and Hank Bauer were roommates while they were with the Yankees. One day Skowron said to Bauer, "I had a terrific dream last night."

Bauer said, "Tell me about it."

Skowron said, "I dreamed I was at Yankee Stadium watching the old-time Yankees play. Babe Ruth, Lou Gehrig, and Bill Dickey were all there, and it was great watching them play."

Bauer said, "I had a good dream, too, last night. I dreamed that I was in a bar with Marilyn Monroe and another beautiful girl. We had a drink and were having a great time and wanted to continue partying but couldn't because we didn't have a date for the other girl."

Skowron said, "Why didn't you call me?"

Bauer said, "I did, but you were at the ballgame."

Chapter 13
## PLAYING OUT THE STRING

The 1956 Yankees were an exceptionally strong ballclub. We started the season near the top of the league standings and just got stronger as the season wore on. Moose Skowron had taken over as the regular first baseman. The team still had three first basemen with Moose, Joe Collins, and me, and I could see the handwriting on the wall in spring training. Joe had been with the Yankees since 1950 and was a little younger than I was. He also could play the outfield and I couldn't. I had been the main left-handed pinch-hitter, but I didn't think Stengel would go with three first basemen. But when the season started we were all still with the team.

We were all three still there on June 15, the trading deadline. That day I pinch-hit and hit a home run. I was very happy because I thought I was going to get by that trade deadline and stay with the Yankees. We were in first place by four and a half games, and it looked like we were a cinch to win the pennant again. I'll be darned if after the game I walked into the clubhouse, and Stengel said he wanted to see me. He told me I'd been traded to Kansas City. Casey said, "I appreciate what you've done for us. You've really done a good job, but we have three first basemen, and we feel like we need an outfielder." The trade involved minor league outfielder Lou Skizas and me for outfielder Bill Renna, pitcher Moe Burtschy, and cash. The Yankees sent Renna to their Richmond farm team and called up Norm Siebern, who would eventually become a starting outfielder for the team.

When I came out of the Yankee clubhouse that day, Bette was waiting for me. She immediately said, "What's wrong with you?" I told her, "I've just been traded to Kansas

City." We went out to dinner that night at the Penguin, our favorite little restaurant in Greenwich Village, where we knew the owner well. I was so distraught he invited us over to his house after dinner. Once we got there my tears started flowing. It was embarrassing, but I couldn't help crying about leaving the Yankees. Playing in New York had been such a great experience, and now I was headed from a first-place team to a team in the cellar.

The Athletics were in last place by six games. In addition, Lou Boudreau was the manager there, and I wasn't keen on playing for him again. It was hot and humid in Kansas City, and there was nothing to do in the daytime.

I did have some friends on the Kansas City club. Gus Zernial and Joe DeMaestri were there and several other guys I had played with before. But that didn't change the fact that it was depressing to go from first place by four games to six games in the basement. Then I got off to a terrible start with the A's. About the only bright spots were that I hit a home run off my former teammate Johnny Kucks in Yankee Stadium when we played the Yankees there, and later connected off Mickey McDermott when the Yankees came to Kansas City. Those were the only two home runs I managed for the A's. I finished the year batting only .204 in 226 at bats, and I knew I was about done. But I wanted to try to play one more year. I had the restaurant in Baltimore going for me, but I wasn't ready to get out of baseball.

It turned out I was traded again over the winter, this time to the Detroit Tigers. The deal made me happy because I always hit well in Briggs Stadium in Detroit. It was a major trade, with third baseman Jim Finigan, pitchers Jack Crimian and Bill Harrington, and me going to Detroit for pitchers Ned Garver, Virgil Trucks, and Gene Host, first baseman Wayne Belardi, and cash. The Tigers trained then, as now, in Lakeland, Florida, and Bette was pregnant with Marc, our first child. Jack Tighe was the manager of the club and John McHale was general manager. Jim Bunning, now a senator from Kentucky and a member of baseball's Hall of Fame, was in camp as a young pitcher on the team.

During that spring training I first started hitting the golf ball a little bit. I knew I was near the end of my baseball career, and I was eager to learn to play golf. Jim Finigan and I would go out to try to play, and we were terrible. But we enjoyed ourselves, and that was my initiation into golf. I had a decent spring on the ball field, better than on the golf course.

When we broke camp to head east we had two first basemen, Earl Torgeson and me. We were both veterans, had played against each other in the '48 World Series, and we were friends. But we were competitors, and both of us wanted to play regularly, even though we were probably both too old to be regular first basemen. Torgy was thirty-five and I was thirty-six, and at that time we were considered old, even ancient, ballplayers.

Nowadays, many ballplayers play until they're forty or more. But I have to admit that today's players keep themselves in much better shape, even without considering steroid use. When I played, we figured the winter was to rest, and we didn't do anything to stay in shape. We hunted and fished and worked at a winter job if we needed to. Spring training was to get in shape again. Today's players stay in shape pretty much year-round and keep their muscles well toned. It is to their credit and has added several years to their careers. But if you played until you were thirty-seven years old in my day, you'd lasted a pretty long time.

I didn't get off to a good start in 1957. The team was struggling, and Torgy was playing more than I was. I was mostly just pinch-hitting. About six weeks into the season, John McHale called me into his office and said, "Eddie, I may be doing the wrong thing, but we've decided to release you." That really shook me. I thought, "Is this the ignominious end to my playing career?" In those days when you were released, you received a month's pay and that was it.

I went home to Baltimore. I thought, "Should I try to hook on with another club or not?" I figured if somebody called, I would talk to them about playing some more. Bill Veeck was the first person who called. He was calling for his friend Morris Silverman, the owner of the Rochester Red Wings in the Triple-A International League. Silverman wanted to get into the International League playoffs every year for the additional revenue and thought I could help him get there if I would play the year out for the Red Wings. Bill said, "I know you'd like to be in the administrative end of baseball. If you finish the year with Rochester, Silverman has promised me he'll make you the general manager of the team next year."

That idea appealed to me, but I'd always thought that when I was through as a major league player I wouldn't go back and play in the minor leagues. I wanted to end my career as a major league player, rather than scuffle around in the minor leagues like I'd seen so many guys do. And I didn't have to because I had the restaurant, which was quite successful. So I told Bill I appreciated the offer, but I didn't want to go to Roches-ter. He understood, though he tried to talk me into going.

Then Kerby Farrell, the manager of the Cleveland Indians, called and wanted to sign me for the same money that I was making in Detroit—$20,000 a year. I talked it over with Bette, and we weren't sure what to do. We had Marc on the way, but we decided to accept their offer. I joined the team in Cleveland, and after one series at home the club traveled to Detroit. All of a sudden I was with the Indians playing the Tigers. Billy Hoeft, a southpaw, pitched the first game for Detroit and was one run ahead in the ninth inning. Farrell sent me up to pinch-hit with a man on base. I could hit left-handers. I always hit left-handers just about as well as I did right-handers, and not many left-handed hitters can. On that day, I promptly hit a line shot into the right-field bleachers to beat the Tigers. It would be the 172nd and last home run of my career.

The headlines in the papers said the Tigers had made a mistake in letting me go, which wasn't true at all. The Tigers did the right thing. I helped the Indians a little, but I wasn't any ball of fire. Gene Woodling, my old teammate and close friend, was on the team and that was enjoyable for me.

My most embarrassing moment on a ball field happened during the brief time I was with Cleveland at the end of my playing career. We were playing in Chicago, and the score was tied 1–1 late in the game. We had a left-handed pitcher named Bud Daley, who had a great move to first base. I was playing first, the White Sox had a man on first, and Nellie Fox, who was a hell of a bunter, was the hitter. I knew he'd be bun-ting, and I was intent on getting in to field the bunt to try to force the runner at second base. I held the runner as he took his lead, but I was poised to race in for the bunt. Daley came set and put that good move on and threw to first base. The next thing I remember is Bud yelling, "Look out!" He had the runner picked off, he had me picked off, and he had the umpire picked off. Nobody knew the ball was coming. When Bud yelled, the runner fell—not on the bag—he fell out on the base path where he had his lead. I fell and the ball hit Nestor Chylak, the umpire, in the neck and bounced over near our first base dugout. I jumped up and scrambled over to get the ball. The runner went to third while Chylak almost passed out, gagging and choking.

Minnie Minoso, the next batter, hit a fly ball to score the runner from third to beat us. I was embarrassed. I had played all those years and never been picked off by a pitcher while playing first base. I had earlier played with Bill Wight, who had the best pick-off move I'd ever seen. They used to say that if you patted your foot on first base, Wight would pick you off between pats. But Bud Daley's pick-off move was almost as good.

About two weeks later, Farrell sent me up to pinch-hit with runners on first and third in a game against the White Sox. I quickly grounded to second base. The White Sox forced the runner at second, but didn't relay the ball to first in time, so I was safe. I thought the ball beat me, however, so I turned around and just trotted back to the dugout like I was out at first base. I plopped down in the dugout, and Woodling quickly walked over, sat down beside me, and said, "What are you doing here? They didn't have you out at first base." So I jumped up and tried to reach first base before they tagged me, but they chased me around and finally did tag me. That little incident was almost as embarrassing as getting picked off by my own pitcher.

Our son Marc was born while I was with Cleveland. They called me in the dugout after he was born, and I got to talk to Bette. In those days players didn't even think about leaving the team for the birth of their children. After talking to Bette, I knew the baby was healthy and that everything was fine, but I really missed not being there when he was born. It wasn't long after Marc was born that Farrell told me the club was going to release me. So I was without a team again, but at least I was home full time.

We still lived in Baltimore. The St. Louis Browns had moved there in 1954, and the team had become the Orioles. When Cleveland released me, Paul Richards was the manager and general manager of the Orioles. As soon as I got home I went to see Paul and told him I'd like to work for the Orioles. I said, "I live here, I have my business here, I want to stay in baseball, and I want to work for you." Paul said he could probably arrange that, but they couldn't pay me much money. I told him that was okay. I just wanted to get my foot in the door and work my way into a front office job.

A couple of days later Paul came into the restaurant and told me he'd hire me for the rest of the year for $6,000 to play and coach and would give me $12,000 the next year to coach. I jumped at the opportunity. I finished out the year as a player-coach and appeared in four games for the Orioles. My last at bat as a major league ballplayer was against Cleveland's Hoyt Wilhelm and his knuckleball. It was an inauspicious way to end a career, hitting at Hoyt's knuckleball. In fact, Paul Richards knew it was going to be my last at bat and was laughing in the dugout as I went up to try to hit that knuckleball. Hoyt struck me out, and that was the end of my playing career.

## Extra Inning

In 1958 I was coaching for the Orioles when we acquired Hoyt Wilhelm from the Cleveland Indians. Hoyt started a game against the Red Sox in the middle of the season, and Larry Napp, who was slightly built, was the home plate umpire. In the middle of a hot day game a Red Sox batter fouled a knuckleball off the plate into Napp's private parts. He went down like a wet rag, and the trainers rushed out and bounced him up and down on the ground and got him ready to umpire again. Two pitches later, the same thing happened again. The trainers rushed out and revived him again. Napp stayed in the game behind the plate, although one of the base umpires offered to take over for him.

Two innings later, the same thing happened a third time. This time the trainers just grabbed a stretcher, ran out, loaded Napp on it, and took him to our training room.

## Chapter 14
### COACHING WITH PAUL RICHARDS AND THE ORIOLES

enjoyed being a coach, but I knew I wanted to be in the front office. I'd always harbored an ambition to be a baseball executive after I retired from playing. Paul Richards planned for me to be the hitting coach the next year, 1958, but he also wanted me to do some scouting so I could begin working my way into player development. It was a big adjustment, being a player one day and a coach the next. Players with whom I'd been very friendly were suddenly a little standoffish because now I was on the management side. It was a strange feeling. The players looked at me in a different light. It was as though they thought I might tell on them if I saw them drinking or out late. It seemed like they began to avoid me. As a result, I began to make new friends among the coaches. But I enjoyed doing some scouting for the first time and loved still being in baseball.

The Orioles trained in Scottsdale, Arizona. I had trained with Cleveland in Arizona for a couple of years, but didn't know anything about Scottsdale except from playing in exhibition games there. It did have the Pink Pony, a corner bar with swinging doors just like the old cowboy saloons. The town had persuaded the Orioles to come out to train and had built a ballpark right downtown. Today the San Francisco Giants train at that ballpark.

That first spring training I hung around some with Dizzy Dean, who was a friend of Paul Richards and lived in Scottsdale. Dizzy loved to play gin rummy, and one night he wanted me to be his partner. We were playing at Bill Wirek's house that evening. Bill was "the father of Scottsdale," a former mayor; he was the reason the Orioles trained there. Scottsdale was then nothing more than a small western town with gravel streets. Bill had gotten the ballpark built, attracted the Orioles, and become a friend of Paul Richards.

In any event, on that evening I partnered with Ole Diz and ended up winning $200, which was a good wad of money in those days. Dizzy was a lot of fun to be around, but he was a hustler. He'd hustle at cards and hustle on the golf course. Richards and he were quite a team on the golf course. They'd beat you just enough to make you think you had a chance the next time. They had the uncanny knack of giving you just enough strokes, but after the round of golf, you were always forking over money to them.

That was the first major league spring training for Brooks Robinson, and it was my job to help him with his hitting. His fielding was certainly never an issue. He could catch anything close to him. During one of our workouts, Richards was standing near the batting cage with a bunch of newspapermen while Al Vincent, one of our coaches, was hitting ground balls to Brooks at third base. Al was hitting ball after ball to Brooks and Paul said, "You know, that Al Vincent is an amazing guy. He's a great fungo hitter." The newspaper guys said, "Oh, is he?" Paul said, "Yeah, look. Everywhere Brooks Robinson puts his glove, Vincent knocks it right in there."

I spent many hours throwing batting practice to Brooks down in the batting cage. At first he tried to pull everything, but I tried to get him to stay back and not be out on his front foot so that he could hit the ball straightaway to right-center and left-center. After hitting only .238 for the Orioles, Brooksie started the 1959 season with Vancouver, our Triple-A club in the Pacific Coast League. He kept working on his hitting and after hitting .331 in forty-two games down there, came back up to the Orioles to stay. He became a dangerous hitter who could hit for average, slug home runs, and drive in runs.

The Orioles had Billy Loes, an eccentric pitcher who was trying to hang on after some good years with the old Brooklyn Dodgers. Loes was known as a screwball (he once claimed to have lost a ground ball in the sun while he was with the Dodgers) and marched to the beat of his own drummer. Richards always made the pitchers run from the foul line to the center-field fence, walk back to the foul line, and sprint again. One day Loes shouted to Paul, "Hey, Richards, we're not training for the Olympics. There's no reason we should have to run like this every day." Paul just ignored him.

One night in spring training Loes was pitching and was unhappy with the way umpire Ed Rommel was calling the game. They were jawing back and forth for a few innings, until in the fifth Rommel called a pitch a ball that Loes thought was a strike. Loes went storming toward home plate and Rommel jerked off his mask and stormed toward Loes with the intention of tossing him from the game. When they met, Loes walked right on past Rommel to the catcher, Gus Triandos, and said, "Gus, I don't think I better say anything to the umpire." Then Billy turned around and walked back to the pitcher's mound, leaving Rommel standing in front of home plate. Rommel, a former knuckleball pitcher with the Athletics, was a good umpire who knew how to get along with the players, and he got a kick out of Loes's antics.

Rommel had a great way to end player arguments. For example, if he was umpiring at first base and called a runner out on a close play, he'd say in response to arguments from the first base coach and runner, "Okay, I missed it. Now let's get on with the game." At that point there was nothing more for anyone to say.

One of our shortstops in 1958 and 1959 was Willie Miranda, who was a great fielder with an amazing arm. Willie could stand flat-footed at home plate in Memorial Stadium and throw the ball all the way out of the ballpark. Gene Woodling had a weak arm, so Paul Richards put Gene in left field and told Willie, "Every time a ball is hit to left field I want you to run as fast as you can and get as close to Woodling as you can." He told Woodling, "All I want you to do is catch the ball and throw it to Willie." That was how we protected Woodling's arm. Willie would run out towards left field. He could gun runners down from anywhere. It worked. The opposition never took the extra base.

Willie was as bad a hitter as he was good a fielder, in part because he had a fear of being hit by a pitched ball. To combat this, at the beginning of the '59 season Richards told Willie that he'd give him $100 every time he got hit by a pitched ball. Even with that incentive, Willie didn't get hit once all year. I don't think you could have hit him with a handful of rice. He was very tentative at the plate. But we needed somebody at shortstop who could catch the ball, and he could.

Our outfield those first two years wasn't strong. We had the veteran Gene Woodling in left field, Bob Nieman in right, and Jim Busby, followed by Willie Tasby, in center. Bob was a good hitter, but he was a selfish player. He was like a modern-day player. His batting average meant everything. We used to say that he knew what his batting average was each time he went to bat. In those days that ticked guys off. Ballplayers expected their teammates to be team players who were willing to sacrifice for the team.

I had the title of field director-coach, which involved working with minor league scouts and minor league teams. We were following a young ballplayer named Jerry Adair, an outstanding prospect from Oklahoma, who was playing semipro ball in Canada. Paul told me to go up there and bring him back to Baltimore when his season was over so that we could try to sign him. Richards said, "I understand the Red Sox are trying to sign him and I want first crack at him. So go get him."

I flew to Minnesota and tried to get a flight to Lloydminister, British Columbia, where Jerry was playing. There were no scheduled commercial flights, so the only thing I could do was rent a plane to get there. But I didn't hesitate. Paul had told me to get him, so I rented a plane. It was the last game of their season, and I'd never met Jerry before, but I cornered him. I said, "Look, I'm up here in a private plane and I know the Red Sox are trying to sign you. But Paul Richards in Baltimore wants to talk to you first. So I'm waiting here with this private plane, and when the game's over I want you to go back with me. You can talk to Boston tomorrow, but I want to get you back to Baltimore."

Jerry said he'd go with me. About the time we got through talking, however, up walked the Red Sox scout, Tommy Thomas, the same man who'd been my manager when I was with Baltimore's Double-A club in the 1940s. He asked me what was up, and I explained to him I was taking Jerry back to Baltimore because Paul Richards wanted to talk to him and that the Red Sox could talk to him later.

Tommy was flabbergasted. He couldn't drive a car, so I guess someone had driven him up there, and he knew I had knocked him out of the box. When the game was over, I got Jerry on the plane and we flew back to Minnesota. Then we caught a commercial flight back to Baltimore. I delivered Adair to Richards and Paul proceeded to sign him.

Jerry became our regular second baseman after playing some minor league ball. Even though the Orioles owners weren't thrilled about the cost of my renting a plane, I was off to a good start. Richards used to say I was the only scout in the big leagues who'd rent a plane to sign a player.

A little later, we learned the Giants were thinking of selling or trading Willie

McCovey, and Richards sent me to watch him play for the Phoenix Giants, their Triple-A farm club. Willie had a big looping swing, which he never got rid of. I thought, "That guy's going to have trouble in the big leagues hitting with that swing." The Giants decided to keep McCovey, and he is now in the Hall of Fame in Cooperstown. That error in judgment convinced me I needed to try to be more perceptive in my scouting. McCovey was so big and strong that he had great bat speed even with a loop in his swing.

The Orioles had a number of great pitching prospects in their minor league system, including Jerry Walker, Chuck Estrada, Bo Belinsky, Steve Barber, and Jack Fisher. Milt Pappas made the Orioles in 1958 at nineteen years of age and won ten games. I was amazed at all their talent. They all had great arms, and it wasn't hard to see that some of them would become quality major league pitchers. And they all did have good big league careers. Jack Fisher lost his first twelve minor league games but eventually had a fine career for the Orioles.

We had a few prospects in Pensacola, Florida, in the Alabama-Florida League, including Steve Barber. Steve was one of those wild left-handed pitchers who seemed like he was never going to be able to throw the ball over the plate. When I visited there, the manager, Lou Fitzgerald, told me he was going to pitch Barber because he thought I'd like his arm. Lou was right. Barber was impressive.

Fitzgerald was one of the best minor league managers who ever worked for me. The hallmark of a good minor league manager is whether or not the players he manages improve over the year. I knew when I sent a player with good ability to Fitz that the player would be ready to move up at least a notch the next year.

Afterwards I told Lou that since the Pensacola season was about over, I'd like to move Barber up to San Antonio, our Double-A club, so I could see him pitch against that level of competition. Barber pitched a couple of good games for San Antonio and did well. Steve lived in Washington, D.C., so I told Paul Richards we had a pitcher in San Antonio whom I liked and wanted to bring up. Paul said he didn't want to bring anybody in that late in the year.

I told Paul I'd promised the kid that we'd bring him up and take a look at him, since he lived in D.C. At that point, Paul told me to work it out with Luman Harris, one of our coaches, so I arranged for Steve to come over and work out. Richards didn't seem to want to look at him. After hitting practice, while the opposing team was taking batting practice, Luman and I took Steve and a catcher down to the bullpen to warm up. The more Steve threw the ball, the more excited Luman, who'd been a big league pitcher, got. Steve had great stuff, good movement, and could really pop the ball.

Luman said, "I'm going to go get Richards." He went into the clubhouse and told Paul, "Hey, you've got to come see this kid." Paul came out, watched him throw, and fell in love with him. Steve made the team the following year and won ten games as a rookie.

After the 1958 season, Paul decided he didn't want to continue to be both general manager and manager of the club. He didn't have the time to do both jobs. At his suggestion the team promoted Lee MacPhail, whom the Orioles had earlier hired away from the Yankees, where he headed their player development and minor league scouting operation. Although none of us knew him when he joined us, Lee turned out to be a great person to work for and an astute baseball man. He was well liked by everyone in the organization and did a great job for the Orioles.

During spring training Jim Wilson, our scouting supervisor in Southern California and Arizona, had identified a young pitching prospect. The Dodgers were after the same prospect, and Lee MacPhail and I decided we'd fly to Phoenix to talk to the youngster about signing with the Orioles. We flew from Baltimore and had a layover in Dallas, so we had a beer in the airport bar to kill some time. We got to talking about hitting and I began demonstrating to Lee things I thought were instrumental in making a good hitter. We got so engrossed in our conversation that we missed our plane. Fortunately, we were able to catch another flight in an hour or so.

The next time Lee was at Love Field in Dallas, he was changing planes on his way to Vancouver to see our Triple-A club play. Lee went to the same bar and started telling some people about the last time he was there when we'd missed our flight. Lee became so involved in telling the story about our missing our plane that he missed his flight again. This time he had to wait an additional four hours before he could catch another flight.

The trip Lee and I made to Arizona was the first time we'd ever had a chance to spend much time together. We had a couple of days to talk and share ideas and formed a great friendship that has lasted to this day. Lee eventually left the Orioles, became general manager of the Yankees, and then president of the American League. He and Bette and I still get together whenever we can.

• • •

By 1959 I'd become a full-time scout. The organization had a farm director named Jim McLaughlin, who didn't like the way Paul Richards ran things. As a result, we had a good deal of turmoil in the organization, since Jim had hired most of the minor league managers and scouts, creating two factions. It was not a good situation, but eventually McLaughlin was convinced Richards knew how to run the organization as general manager, and we all got on the same page.

The Orioles moved their spring training to Miami, Florida, and trained in the big stadium there. Early on, before the pitchers' arms were in shape, Richards decided to play an intra-squad game with the Iron Mike pitching machine pitching for both teams. All we needed was someone to feed the baseballs to the machine. Iron Mike struck out Al Pilarcik, who was one of our young prospects. Al was embarrassed and couldn't live it down with all the kidding he received.

We had a left-handed pitcher in our organization named Steve Dalkowski, who could throw harder and had a better curve than Barber. He had everything it took to be a twenty or twenty-five game winner in the big leagues but for one thing—control. He could not throw the ball over the plate. He'd throw strike after strike warming up on the sidelines, but once he was in the game he'd be wild almost beyond imagination and go to pieces. Steve was very excitable, even though he'd been a great high school quarterback and had numerous college football scholarship offers.

I recall one night during spring training when our pitcher ran into trouble in an exhibition game. I was in the bullpen when the call came for Dalkowski to get ready. He was throwing strike after strike with his fastball and his curveball. Paul called Steve into the game, and after his warmups on the mound, his first pitch hit the screen. His next pitch was in the dirt, and he proceeded to walk four guys in a row. We had to bring in another pitcher to finish the inning.

Dalkowski never was able to gain control of his pitches. Because of his great arm the Orioles held on to him as long as they could, and then several other teams tried him. He just never came around. Sandy Koufax, Curt Simmons, and Steve Barber were lefties with great arms who were wild in their early days. Dalkowski never made the major leagues, but because of his incredible stuff is still remembered today.

I learned a lot just hanging around Paul Richards. It's like Yogi Berra said, "You can observe a lot by watching." Paul was innovative and was a father figure to me. I liked the way he instructed, the way he managed, in fact I liked everything he did. He never complimented you much, but if you did a good job for him you knew it. He appreciated what you did and without him saying so, you knew whether he liked you or not.

We signed eighteen-year-old Dave Nicholson in 1958 and gave him a $125,000 bonus. Many of us were appalled a kid could get that much money just to sign. Dave could hit the ball over the roof of any ballpark and had monstrous power. His first spring training with the Orioles was in 1960. One day some of the guys were taking batting practice in the batting cage down the left-field line while the game was going on. Dave got hit in the head with a batting practice pitch. While he was lying on the ground, he said, "Well, I always wondered what it would feel like to get hit in the head. Now I know." But Dave was another, despite all his strength and ability, who never became a front-line player. Nobody worked any harder than Dave, but he just couldn't consistently hit big league pitching. He eventually played seven seasons in the major leagues and retired in 1969 with sixty-one home runs and only a .212 average

Bobby Saverine was another bonus baby who ended up being a disappointment. We signed him out of high school in Connecticut in 1959 and sent him to Bluefield in the short season Class D Appalachian League, where he hit .353 and stole thirty-six bases to lead the league. He had all the tools scouts look for and showed them that first year at Bluefield, but thereafter he struggled. He finally made the Orioles in 1963 but hit only .234 and seemed to lack the desire to excel and make the most of his abilities, unlike Dave Nicholson. Bobby was finished in the big leagues at age twenty-six with a .239 average in 890 at bats with the Orioles and Senators.

By 1960 we'd gathered a pretty good group of young players, and it was beginning to show. We improved from our sixth place finishes in 1958 and 1959 to finish second with an 89–65 won-loss record, eight games behind the pennant-winning Yankees. The players were maturing, and you could see and feel the improvement. We were catching the ball better and hitting it better. The infield was knocking in a lot of runs, and our pitching staff was the best young staff in baseball.

Over the winter we'd purchased Jim Gentile from the Dodgers. Nobody knew how good Gentile would be, but we knew he had great power. He swung so hard that the bat would hit his back and bruise it. Several times he broke bats against his back and sometimes wore a back pad for protection. Marv Breeding did a nice job at second, and

Ron Hansen played a darn good shortstop. He wasn't fast, but he could cover a lot of ground. He had a good arm and was steady. We had Brooks at third.

Our pitching staff included young studs like Milt Pappas, Jerry Walker, Steve Barber, Jack Fisher, and Chuck Estrada, who had eighteen wins by himself. Veterans Hal "Skinny" Brown and Hoyt Wilhelm provided experience. Wilhelm probably had the best knuckleball of all time. Before coming to the Orioles from Cleveland in the middle of the 1958 season, he'd pitched almost solely in relief since breaking into the big leagues with the Giants in 1952 with a sparkling 15–3 record. Paul Richards, however, decided Hoyt was a starting pitcher, and after a slow start Wilhelm responded by pitching a no-hitter against the powerful Yankees on September 20. In 1959 Wilhelm won fifteen games as a starter and led the league with a 2.19 earned run average.

Wilhelm was a super guy and great to have on the club. I asked him one time how hard he could throw a knuckleball. Hoyt said, "I never throw it as hard as I can. If I threw a knuckleball as hard as I can, no one could catch it, so I have to ease off of it." Wilhelm eventually moved back to the bullpen, threw that knuckleball in the big leagues until he was forty-nine years old, and ended up in the Hall of Fame.

One of the Orioles catchers was Clint Courtney, whom Richards had reacquired from the Washington Senators before the 1960 season. Courtney stood only 5'8", but he was tough as nails, which accounted for his nickname, "Scrap Iron," and, as he got older, "Old Scrap Iron." Clint had broken in with the old St. Louis Browns in 1952 and had become the regular catcher, hitting .286 and winning the Rookie of the Year Award in the American League. He hit the first homer in Memorial Stadium in Baltimore when the Browns moved there in 1954 and became the Orioles. Scraps didn't hit for much power, but he had exceptional bat control, especially for a catcher. In 1954 with the Orioles he set a club record that stood for more than twenty years, striking out only seven times in 437 at bats.

Richards brought Courtney in to catch Hoyt Wilhelm's knuckleball. A former catcher, Richards had developed an oversized, hinged catcher's mitt to give backstops a better chance of at least knocking Hoyt's fluttering balls down. Courtney became adept at catching Wilhelm and became his personal catcher, although he looked funny behind the plate with a mitt that was almost as big as he was.

I first encountered Courtney during spring training in 1952. My White Sox were training in Pasadena, California, right across from the Rose Bowl at Brookside Park. We used to walk over to the Rose Bowl during the lunch break and sit out in the middle of the field in the stadium and imagine that the stands were full of people. In any event, the Browns were training in Burbank, and when we played them in an exhibition game, Courtney was the catcher. He was short, squarely built, feisty, and had a good arm. He was muscular but he wore thick glasses. That didn't stop him from strutting around and acting cocky. At bat, he was aggressive and swung from the heels, but he could make contact and was a good hitter.

I soon learned Scraps would do anything to beat his opponent and help his team win. He always played hard and got into more than his share of skirmishes. I'm not sure he ever won a fight, but that didn't stop him. He got into a noteworthy brawl in St. Louis against Billy Martin and a good portion of the Yankees team. He was apparently holding his own until someone knocked his glasses off. He couldn't see without them and stepped on them. The Yankees finally got him down on the ground and tore his shirt halfway off.

By the time Scraps joined the Orioles in 1960 he couldn't throw very well anymore. The story was that he'd hurt his arm Indian wrestling a teammate on the trunk of a car. They'd gotten into an argument about who was the best Indian wrestler and decided to settle it on the spot. Not only did Clint not throw to bases well, but during the season he began having trouble just throwing the ball back to the pitcher, which sometimes happens to catchers who otherwise have strong arms. It becomes a mental block we used to call "getting the monkey on your back." Courtney definitely had the monkey on his back. With runners on base, he'd be afraid he might throw the ball by the pitcher and allow the runners to advance. To build his confidence, he'd catch the pitch and walk out in front of the plate to toss the ball back to the pitcher.

Scraps also created some excitement with pop fouls. He couldn't wait until they came down, so he'd always circle under them and then jump up to catch the ball. It was his unique style, and everyone got a kick out of watching him jump.

Clint had a funny, quirky personality that kept the team loose. During that 1960 season we were playing the Athletics in Kansas City and having trouble scoring runs. Paul Richards told Courtney before he went up to hit, "I want you to go up and get hit by the pitch, so you can get on base and we can bring you around to score."

So Clint stepped up to the plate, got plunked by the pitch, and took his base. Sure enough we managed a couple of hits and drove him in. When he came to the dugout, he told Paul, "If the best offense we've got is with me getting intentionally hit, we're going to have to make some changes because that's not very good."

One day that season we were playing the Red Sox in Boston. Richards thought the Red Sox were stealing our catcher's signs when they had a runner on second base. He went out to the mound to talk to Courtney, who was catching, and to Skinny Brown, our pitcher. They were using the standard one finger for a fastball, two for a curve, and three for a change-up. Richards told Courtney to flash three signs and only the second sign would count.

The game resumed, and when Courtney flashed signs out to Brown, Skinny started laughing. When the inning was over and Brown came into the dugout, we asked what he'd been laughing about. He said, "Courtney signaled one finger, one finger, one finger."

Clint owned a farm in Coushatta, Louisiana, and had begun to raise chickens. He talked one of our young pitchers, Jack Fisher, into going into the chicken business with him, and they bought two thousand baby chicks to raise. The chicks were doing fine until one day Courtney came into the clubhouse, walked over to Fisher, and said, "Jack, we've got a real problem. Our chicks caught a disease and your half died."

While I was with the Orioles I met another unforgettable character, a former pitcher named Frank Gabler. He had been a fine prospect until he hurt his arm. He pitched in the big leagues in the 1930s and managed to win sixteen games in four years with the New York Giants, Boston Braves, and Chicago White Sox. Strange things were always happening to Frank. Paul Richards and Gabe went back a long time, and Paul had brought him to the Orioles as a scout covering California. I first met Gabler when I played for the White Sox, when he was trying to become an umpire. He had some great stories about his umpiring days. Jack Dunn III, an assistant general manager, Luman Harris, and the rest of our coaches would pitch in and pay Gabe's way to spring training in Miami just so he could entertain us. He was a delight to have around.

One of Gabler's favorite stories came from the time he was pitching for the Giants in the 1930s. He walked into a fancy bar in New York and sidled up to the crowded bar next to a good-looking blonde. Gabe was a handsome guy who got along well with women. After a minute he said to the blonde, "You are the prettiest girl in this bar and are the best dressed to boot. I'm really taken with those black pants you have on. They're the tightest pants I've ever seen. I was wondering, how do you get into those pants?"

The girl turned, looked at Gabe, and said, "Well, a couple of martinis would be a good start."

Richards was all business except when Gabler came around. Frank could always get Paul to laugh and joke with him. Paul loved to play golf. In spring training, he'd sometimes get the workout started early and head for the golf course when we took our noon break. One day at noon Paul had showered and dressed and was outside the club-house about ready to go to the golf course. Gabler thought Richards had already left and started talking about Paul. He said, "Richards has the personality of a doll, a croco-doll." The clubhouse window was open and Paul heard Frank. The next day he came in and confronted Gabler. Gabe refused to take Paul seriously, laughed, and said, "Well, Paul, it's true, and sometimes the truth hurts." Paul stalked away but had a grin on his face.

Starting in 1960, I began taking Gabler out on the town one night every spring training. I told Gabler to get ready because we were going to "do" Miami. I borrowed Jack Dunn's new Thunderbird. Frank put on a sports coat and felt "big-league" in that T-Bird. The first place we hit was the Fountainbleu, at that time the fanciest hotel in Miami Beach. We walked in the front door just to look around, but they wouldn't even let us in the lobby because we didn't have ties on. Gabler was furious. So we had to retrieve our car from the valet.

Gabler came to every spring training for as long as I worked with Paul Richards. He became part of a threesome—coach Clint Courtney, scout Frank Gabler, and minor league manager Lou Fitzgerald. They were like the Three Stooges, always doing some-thing to make us laugh, and that's how we referred to them. Gabler had a couple of favorite sayings. One was "If I had my life to live over, I'd live it over a saloon." He was a straight liquor drinker and often said, "The only thing water is good for is for fish to make love in."

Harry Dalton was a young guy who loved baseball and had desperately wanted to get into the game when he graduated from college. He managed to land a part-time pub-lic relations job with the Orioles and had to drive a taxi to supplement his income. Then an assistant farm director position opened up in the Orioles' farm department, and Harry got the job. Harry went on to become general manager of the Orioles, the California Angels, and the Milwaukee Brewers. He had a fine career that started on the bottom rung of the baseball ladder.

When Harry was working with the minor league clubs, he took a liking to Earl Weaver and brought him into the organization. My first association with Earl came when he was about twenty-five years old and managing Elmira in the New York-Penn League. The minor league managers came to spring training with us and that's how I met him. Earl's association with Paul Richards really helped him. Weaver was a bright guy in his own right. He was smart enough to observe closely and he picked everybody's brain.

Earl is of small stature and took a lot of abuse because of it. He was managing in the Southern Association when one day before the game a bunch of his players were fooling around throwing baseballs at a batting helmet that was lying on the ground. All of a sudden, Chuck Churn, one of the pitchers, jumped off the bench and yelled, "Don't throw at that helmet. Earl Weaver is under there!"

Weaver became one of the best managers I've known. Richards was the best. I'm not sure if Casey Stengel was a good manager or just a good handler of men. He seemed to be able to win and keep winning. Maybe he was just a bright tactician. Richards knew how to instruct. He knew how to handle pitchers, how to handle players. He was always ahead of the game and knew what the opposition was likely to do.

After we left Baltimore, Dalton appointed Weaver the manager of the Orioles. At that time, no one had ever heard of him. But Harry knew what he was doing, and Weaver is in the Hall of Fame to prove it.

Those first two years with the Orioles, I was the hitting instructor and worked with the hitters. I worked with the younger players like Dave Nicholson, but apparently I didn't do too good a job because Dave never really made it. I also worked with Boog Powell, Brooks Robinson, and Fred Valentine. As a hitting instructor I learned that something I told a player today might not sink in for a year or two, and after a while he'd forget who taught him. So it's hard to say if I helped anyone because I didn't see definitive results at the time. For example, I was unsuccessful in trying to get Willie Miranda to get hit by a pitched ball.

I was recently in New York to attend the baseball banquet B.A.T. (the Baseball Assistance Team) puts on every year. I ran into Tito Francona, the father of Terry Francona, the current manager of the Red Sox. I had helped instruct Tito when he was a young player with the Orioles. Tito reminded me of the time he was in a slump and came to me for help. Later Paul Richards told Tito to stay out for extra hitting and gave him some instruction. Tito laughed and said Richards told him the exact opposite of everything I'd been telling him.

When I first started playing baseball, someone told me not to crowd my arms close to my body when I was hitting. That helped me, even though I can't remember who gave me that advice. I believe I helped hitters more with theory—don't swing at what the pitcher wants you to hit and focus on getting your pitch to hit at every time at bat—than practical hitting advice.

We had a good season in 1961, winning ninety-five games and finishing in third place, fourteen games behind the famous '61 Yankees. I traveled all over and loved the transition from playing to scouting and evaluating players. I thought I had a talent for evaluating young players. I believe a scout knows after he's evaluated players for a couple of years whether he's any good or not at scouting. Some scouts get by asking questions of other scouts. We call it scouting other scouts. The best scouts tend to stay to themselves, keep their own counsel, and have confidence in their abilities. I think that's the way it should be.

## Extra Inning

When Frank Gabler pitched for the New York Giants, he had a lot of trouble getting Dolph Camilli of the Philadelphia Phillies out. Camilli hit a number of home runs off him and hit Frank like he owned him. One afternoon, Gabler was pitching against the Phillies and had a 3–0 lead in the ninth inning. The Phillies loaded the bases and Camilli came to bat. Gabler threw ball one and then ball two, with neither pitch close to the plate. Bill Terry, the Giants' manager and first baseman, called time, walked over to Gabler, and asked, "Are you trying to walk Camilli?"

Gabler said, "Yes, I am. Would you rather they have one run or four?"

Terry laughed and walked back to his position. Gabler proceeded to walk Camilli, then retired the side to win the game.

*Chapter 15*

## THE MOVE TO HOUSTON AND THE START
## OF THE EXPANSION COLT .45s

For the first time since the nineteenth century, the National League was going to expand after the 1961 season, with new franchises in New York and Houston. The Houston franchise first hired Gabe Paul from Cincinnati to serve as general manager, but after six months on the job Gabe suddenly resigned in April of 1961. The Houston group then began talking to Paul Richards, and during the 1961 season he agreed to become the Houston general manager. Paul soon asked me to go with him to Houston as assistant general manager. I still had my restaurant in Baltimore, was well thought of there, and was not sure I wanted to leave. Even though I was from Texas, my family was now settled in Baltimore. I hated to leave the Orioles and all the players we'd signed, considering all the time and effort we'd put into developing them. Those young guys were just beginning to reach the big leagues, and the Orioles were going to be very competitive because of them. I was so conflicted I went to see Lee MacPhail about it. He told me he thought, because of my close working relationship with Paul Richards, that Houston was a great opportunity for me, especially for the money Houston was offering.

So Bette and I decided to move our family to Houston, hoping someday I could become a general manager. By this time, I'd sold a percentage of the restaurant to Brooks Robinson and Joe Hamper, the Orioles' accountant. Bette and I left Baltimore with some reluctance and with many memories. Our second and third sons, Paul and Drew, were born two years apart during my tenure with the Orioles. Both were born with congenital rib cage defects that required major surgery before each one turned two years old. Fortunately, both surgeries were successful, and they've been able to live normal, healthy lives.

On September 2, 1961, Paul Richards was named general manager of the expansion Houston Colt .45s, and I was introduced as his assistant. It was the beginning of a new world for me. In the past, I'd worked mostly in a uniform-wearing capacity. Even though I worked out of the front office in Baltimore, I put on the uniform in spring training and coached. During the season I'd visit our minor league clubs and put on a uniform and work with the players. I thought like a coach and former player and had very little front office experience. I was in store for a rude awakening.

When we arrived in Houston, George Kirksey, who was largely responsible for getting the franchise for Houston, was the acting general manager. He turned the reins over to Paul. Richards immediately hit it off with Craig Cullinan, who was one of the principal investors in the team along with R.E. "Bob" Smith and Judge Roy Hofheinz. The Judge already had a number of people in the organization, including Spec Richardson, the business manager; Tal Smith, who was more or less the director of player personnel; and Grady Hatton, a former big league player and minor league manager.

But Paul brought in Luman Harris and me and soon named Harry Craft to be the Colt .45s manager. Almost instantly there was a split between the Richards people and the people Judge Hofheinz had in place. Paul's group were all former players, tried and true baseball people, while, with the exception of Grady Hatton, the Judge's folks were not. Tal Smith and I didn't get along and didn't understand each other. He had never played but had worked for the Cincinnati Reds before coming down to Houston with Gabe Paul.

Richards seemed to be friendly with Bob Smith and was cordial to the Judge, who seemed to rely more on Spec and Tal and Grady. Bob was closer to our group but didn't have an office with the team. Judge Hofheinz had an office at the team headquarters and was in charge of the stadium planning. He was there every day and was a brilliant man. I liked the Judge and am sorry I didn't get to know him better.

Our first order of business was to select our roster, along with the expansion New York Mets, from the eligibility lists of the other National League teams. I hadn't done much major league scouting so I wasn't much help. However, we had Bobby Mattick, who was one of the best scouts I've ever known, and Paul Florence, who also was outstanding. Both had scouted the major leagues.

Before Gabe Paul left he'd assembled a cadre of talented scouts including Billy Jurges, Red Murff, Earl Rapp, Dixie Howell, and Earl Harrist. They had aggressively scouted young amateur ballplayers all over the country. By September 15, 1961, the Colt .45s had signed one hundred free-agent ballplayers, more than any other major league club had ever signed in an eleven-month span. This was before the annual draft of amateur players, which began in 1965, so each team discovered and signed players in a totally open market. Earl Harrist had the biggest find, an eighteen-year-old prospect from New Orleans named Rusty Staub.

I added my former teammate Bill Wight to our scouting staff. He was selling liquor in northern California, but he was someone I thought would be a good evaluator of talent. It turned out he was because he signed Joe Morgan and Walt "No-Neck" Williams for us. Morgan was about 5'7" and Williams was about the same, with a strange build that led to his nickname. When Clint Courtney first saw them in spring training, he remarked, "That Bill Wight sure does sign some funny looking players." Williams had a solid major league career, and Morgan is in the Baseball Hall of Fame.

I flew up to Detroit to sign John Paciorek, whom we thought was going to be a fine big league player. The oldest of a large family, John, at 6'2" and a solid 200 pounds, had a perfect baseball physique. After John signed, I took him and his family out to the Chop House, a well-known Detroit steak house. John was a young man with a large appetite. He ordered a double New York strip steak, which was about thirty-two ounces. After he polished that off, I jokingly asked if he'd like another steak. He shocked me by saying, "Yes, I could eat another," and he did.

Paul Richards named Harry Craft manager on September 19, leading up to the expansion draft on October 10. Harry was a solid baseball man who'd played outfield for the Reds in the late '30s and early '40s and had managed the Kansas City A's for three years. He brought in baseball lifers Cot Deal, Bobby Bragan, Jimmy Adair, Jim Busby, and Luman Harris as coaches

Paul was unhappy about the player selection process for the expansion teams and the pool of players the existing National League teams could designate for selection. At one point he even threatened to "give back" the franchise and refocus on buying an existing team and moving it to Houston. Even before we had the list of available players, Paul was calling the pool "the biggest swindle since the Black Sox." National League president Warren Giles quickly dashed off a stern telegram telling Richards to refrain from further "ill-reasoned, uninformed, and disrespectful public comments."

Paul was undaunted. After the player pool became known he said, "All I know is I could play on any team from this list." At the time he was fifty-three years old and had played his last major league game fifteen years earlier in 1946.

The expansion draft list was loaded with veterans like Gil Hodges, Richie Ashburn, Red Schoendienst, Vinegar Bend Mizell, Robin Roberts, Johnny Antonelli (who promptly retired when he learned he was on the list), Johnny Logan, Don Zimmer, Lee Walls, Roger Craig, Gus Bell, Jim Hickman, Felix Mantilla, Ed Bouchee, Hobie Landrith, and Bobby Gene Smith. These were good, some great, ballplayers, but they were almost all well past their prime. While the Mets selected mostly veterans like Ashburn, Hodges, Craig, Mantilla, Bell, and Landrith, we tended to go with younger, less established players, with a few veterans sprinkled in.

Our second pick, Bob Aspromonte from the Dodgers, turned out to be the foundation of the franchise for many years. His career six grand slam home runs is still a club record. We also selected Bob Lillis, Roman Mejias, Merritt Ranew, Norm Larker, and pitchers like Ken Johnson, Jim Umbricht, Bobby Shantz, Dick Drott, and Jim Golden. In the so-called premium part of the draft (cost $125,000 per player rather than $75,000), we picked Dick "Turk" Farrell, the fireballing reliever who quickly became our number one starter, catcher Hal Smith, infielder Joe Amalfitano, and outfielder Al Spangler. When it was disclosed what Amalfitano cost us, he told the newspapers, "I better call my insurance agent. I'm worth more than I thought I was."

Our first spring training was held at Apache Junction, Arizona, east of Mesa near the Superstition Mountains. The community built a ballpark for us right out in the desert. It wasn't a bad ballpark for spring training purposes. We all stayed in the brand new Superstition Inn, which was very nice. For entertainment after our workouts, some of the players like Turk Farrell, who was really a free spirit, would load .22 pistols and rifles and head out into the desert to shoot rattlesnakes.

I passed on the rattlesnake hunting but began my love affair with golf that spring. Paul Richards probably loved golf more than he did baseball, and he got me started. Pretty soon I was playing every day at the small course in Apache Junction, and I haven't stopped since. I'm eighty-nine years old as we write this, and I still play golf every chance I get. Paul played every chance he got, and, in fact, died of a heart attack while playing on his home course at the Waxahachie Country Club in 1986.

Over the years Paul acquired a number of golfing friends from whom he could regularly take money on the course. We called them "Paul's Pigeons." One of his favorite pigeons was Henry David, who was a Cajun from New Orleans. One day Paul beat Henry decisively and won some of Henry's money. Afterwards Henry came into Paul's hotel suite and threw a tube of KY Jelly on the bed. Henry said, "Here's your KY Jelly. You've done screwed this coon ass for the last time."

The Miner's Camp was a rustic, family-style all-you-can-eat restaurant in the mountains outside of Apache Junction. You paid one price and could have as much meat, vegetables, and bread as you could hold. John Paciorek, the kid I signed out of Detroit, could really put the grub away and ate so much at the Miner's Camp that they told him he wasn't welcome back. The next year John was in the minor league camp in Moultrie, Georgia, where we provided lunch consisting of soup, crackers, fruit, and beverages for the ballplayers at the field. That didn't put a dent in John's appetite, so he ordered for himself, at his own expense, a dozen sandwiches to be delivered every day from a local restaurant to the ballpark during the lunch hour.

John was very strong and had a great physique, which engendered lots of teasing. To get back at his teammates he would turn the shower spigots off so hard after games that no one could turn them back on. Everyone would be in their birthday suits all lathered up and unable to get the water back on. His teammates would have to beg John to come back and turn the water on.

John worked out hard. When he ran his laps with the team he would add five pound weights to each ankle. His teammates all thought he was nuts.

John's major league career turned out to be very brief but notable. Late in the 1963 season he appeared in one game for the Colt .45s and had a perfect day at the plate, getting three hits in three official at bats, with two walks, three runs batted in, and two runs scored. Pretty hard to top that, but Paciorek never got the chance because he developed a chronic back problem and never again made a major league roster. It was John's only big league game; he remains the only major leaguer to end his career with a 1.000 batting average from going 3 for 3.

John's younger brother is Tom Paciorek, who attended the University of Houston and had a solid eighteen-year big league career with the Dodgers, Braves, Mariners, White Sox, and Rangers. Tom announced the White Sox games for many years on WGN with Ken Harrelson.

Near the end of that first spring training I decided to visit our minor league camp in Moultrie, Georgia, which was at a closed Air Force base. Tal Smith, our farm director, was there directing our lower minor league operation. Our Triple-A club was training in Chandler, Arizona, in an inadequate facility. When I visited Moultrie it was quickly apparent to me that it wasn't going to work with Tal as farm director. It wasn't that Tal was always wrong or that Richards's people were always right. They just had different ideas about how to run a farm system, and a rift quickly developed, which seemed to be growing wider all the time. Both sides were pretty abrasive, which did not help matters.

I had a long talk with Richards, and he told me he was going to make a change and name me farm director. So right after spring training, when we were all back in Houston, Paul relieved Tal of his duties as farm director and put me in charge.

I came into the office early the next day to find that Tal had left a neat pile of papers in the middle of his desk to be filled out for the assignment of our minor leaguers to their different minor league teams. I didn't know anything about assignment papers, other than that it was something that had to be done. Tal's secretary, Jane Woods, left with Tal, leaving me without a secretary. I needed a secretary, but most of the staff predated Paul and me and were loyal to Spec Richardson and Tal. They weren't happy Tal had been let go, and none of the secretaries wanted to work for me. Finally a woman in the organization named Jean Lutrey came by and said, "Eddie, I'll work for you and we'll get the job done."

I appreciated her offer and said, "You're on; let's get started." We each pulled out bluebooks, which was the rule book published by the National Association of Minor League Baseball. We called the National Association whenever we had a question and started the process of assigning our minor leaguers to their respective teams. Jean was a jewel who was very bright and didn't mind working long hours. We had a great working relationship. Bette and I soon became good friends with Jean and her husband Frank.

After two years Jean resigned to take a higher paying job, and I again needed a secretary. Jim Campbell, the general manager of the Detroit Tigers, happened to call and told me that his secretary, Allene Mutter, had just moved to Houston and might be someone I should consider. The timing was perfect and I hired Allene. She became a fixture with Paul Richards and me. She knew all of the baseball rules and seemed never to make a mistake. She also kept me from making mistakes. She eventually followed Richards and me to Atlanta, and I brought her to the Rangers when I later became GM there. Allene was like one of the family.

Lynwood Stallings was the assistant farm director for the first year I was with Houston. He was an able guy but not really a baseball person, so I wanted to make a change. I had my eye on Pat Gillick, who was a pitcher in the Orioles organization. He had the well-deserved nickname "Yellow Pages" when he was a player because of his knowledge of baseball statistics and his ability to answer his teammates' questions about virtually anything. A good memory is a prerequisite for a farm director, and Pat had one. I called him and convinced him he'd probably topped out as a player at Triple A, but told him I thought he'd have a promising future in a baseball front office. I asked him to come work for me as assistant farm director for the Colt .45s.

Pat remained with Houston for several years before moving to the Yankees as their director of player personnel. He became one of the most successful and well respected general managers in the game. He won a World Series ring in 1993 as general manager of the Toronto Blue Jays. He has also been general manager of Seattle and Baltimore and was the GM for the 2008 World Champion Philadelphia Phillies before retiring.

It was my job to follow our minor league clubs, to be in constant communication with our minor league managers, and to move players up or down the organization, depending on how well they were doing. I became comfortable in the job and enjoyed overseeing player development.

Judge Hofheinz, through the Houston Sports Authority, had promised Major League Baseball a domed stadium in order to secure the franchise, but design and legal problems early on made it clear the new stadium wouldn't be ready for our inaugural season. Something had to be done to provide a place to play. The organization hurriedly built (in only five months) a temporary or "auxiliary" ballpark called Colt Stadium on the northwest corner of the 240-acre domed stadium site. The executive offices in Colt Stadium were cramped and there was no privacy. The playing field was adequate, but the ballpark was a haven for hordes of mosquitoes since it had been built in a low-lying area. To combat them, we contracted with a firm that had a mosquito fogging machine.

Every day before the pregame workout they fogged the field, the stands, and the surrounding area. The fogging helped but did not eliminate the problem. Those mosquitoes made the planned domed stadium even more attractive to us.

Although I felt good about the progress of our minor leaguers, the '62 Colt .45s struggled to an eighth-place finish with sixty-four wins and ninety-six losses. By some measures we had a successful first year. We finished twenty-four games ahead of our expansion rivals, the New York Mets, and six games in front of the ninth-place Chicago Cubs. But we were disappointed. We thought we'd done a good job of selecting the best players in the pool, but it turned out not many had a good future in the major leagues. A few players stood out, like Bob Aspromonte at third and Turk Farrell, who pitched very well even though he ended up with twenty losses. Roman Mejias had a career year for us, batting .286 with twenty-four home runs and seventy-six runs batted in, but other than Roman we had trouble scoring runs. Our pitching was solid, but we didn't catch the ball very well. Poor defense, coupled with our lack of hitting, ended up making for a long year. Our expectations were probably higher than they should have been. But at least we knew where we stood competitively. We had decisions to make about which players to keep under contract, and we knew we had to go out and sign more young talent to become a force in the National League down the road.

After the season we headed back to Arizona for the fall instructional league. We had signed so many young players that we had two teams in the instructional league, the Colt .45s and the Colt .22s. By now I was serving both as the scouting director and the farm director and enjoying both roles immensely. I was in charge of player procurement and development. I loved working with the scouts and deciding which prospects to try to sign, and I enjoyed working with the managers and coaches in developing the players we signed. Paul Richards was very involved and was a tremendous mentor to me. He was at his best working with pitchers, probably as good as anyone has ever been.

Richards and I also played golf almost every day during the two months of the instructional league. We had hired Clint Courtney, my old buddy from the Orioles, and Dave Philley, as coaches, and they, along with Paul and me, became a regular foursome. The instructional league games started at noon and were over by about two o'clock or two thirty. We'd work the players out for a while after the game and then hit the nice little Apache Junction golf course by three or three thirty. Paul was a good golfer with a low handicap. He'd give Dave Philley and me a stroke a hole, since we were beginners. Courtney was a worse player than Philley and I were, so Paul would give him a stroke and a free throw every hole. Yes, Clint got to throw the ball once a hole.

We had a lot of laughs and didn't take ourselves too seriously. One day I was playing with Courtney and hit a great drive right down the middle of the fairway. Clint sliced his tee shot, and I could tell it was out of bounds. Clint drove me in our cart to my ball and then drove over towards his ball. I saw him drop a ball out of his pocket in bounds. I hit my fairway shot and yelled over, "Scraps, that's not your ball."

Clint said, "What do you mean, that's not my ball?"

There's not a lot of high rough or weeds to hide a ball in the Arizona desert, and I said, "I can see your ball over there, in the rough and out of bounds."

Courtney got a sheepish grin on his face and reached down and grabbed the ball he'd dropped and said, "Well, you caught me fair and square. Let's play the next hole."

One day Dave Philley hit a big slice that went through the plate glass window of one of the homes along the fairway. He drove over to the house in the golf cart, and the owner came out and said, "You broke my window."

Dave said, "Yeah, well I'm sorry."

The man said in a belligerent tone, "Well, what are you going to do about it?"

Dave, who was known to have a quick temper, said, "I'm not going to do anything about it. All I want is my ball back." Believe it or not, he got his ball back, and we went on and finished the round

Later, after we moved into the Astrodome, Courtney became our bullpen catcher. He warmed up relief pitchers in the Astrodome bullpen, which was down the right field line. He still had a problem throwing the ball back to the pitcher. Many times he'd throw the ball wild, and it would go onto the field, stopping the game while someone retrieved it. One night after throwing a couple of balls away, he was so embarrassed that he went into the clubhouse in the middle of the game, took his uniform off, and said, "I quit. That's the last time I'll put on a major league uniform." And it was, although I later hired him to manage for the Astros and then the Braves in the minor leagues.

The minor league players all loved Scraps. He managed the Durham Bulls in the

Carolina League, and one night he was coaching third base against Winston-Salem. The opposition was really riding him from their dugout on the third base side. Courtney finally got so mad he charged the dugout from the coaching box and took on the entire bench. Suddenly he yelled, "Time out. I broke my arm." That ended the fight because his arm was indeed broken.

When Richards and I went to Atlanta, we hired Scraps to manage the Shreveport Sports in the Texas League. He did a fine job, helping to develop players. We then moved him up to manage our Triple-A club in Richmond, Virginia. He managed there until June 15, 1975. On that date, the Richmond Braves were playing in Rochester against the Red Wings. They'd played a Sunday afternoon game, and that evening Scraps and some of the players were playing ping-pong in the hotel lobby. Scraps said he was tired and went up to his room to take a shower. He came back down, and the players were still playing ping-pong, so he sat down to watch. He suddenly had a heart attack and died in the chair in the lobby.

Roger Bartoff, the general manager of Richmond, called me at midnight and said, "I've got some bad news. Courtney is dead."

I was greatly saddened but almost immediately thought Clint had been in a fight and gotten knifed. I asked Bartoff, "What happened to him?" I was relieved to learn he had died of a heart attack rather than in a brawl.

The entire Braves staff attended Courtney's funeral in Coushatta, Louisiana. The night before, many of us were sitting around talking to his wife Dorothy. She told the story about one of their children who was born at home without a doctor or midwife. Clint had tried to assist but Dorothy said he didn't do much. Afterwards, he was very proud of himself and his wife. He told her, "Dorothy, you are a bull of a woman."

Courtney's sudden death was a blow to the organization, and I lost a good friend much too early.

Altogether I was with Houston for five years. The club announced on December 1, 1964, that our new name would be the Houston Astros. Bill Giles, the head of community relations for the club, was a quick wit. He happened to be at the stadium on the day of the name change announcement. The phone rang and Bill answered it, "Houston Astros. Head Ass speaking."

The Astrodome opened in 1965. We immediately faced two major problems. First, the grass that had been developed specifically for the dome would not grow in there.

Second, infielders and outfielders couldn't see fly balls or pop-ups against the background of the translucent roof. The solutions were to paint the roof blue, look for an artificial playing surface, and give up on the idea of growing grass inside the dome. We ended up with Astroturf, an artificial turf developed for us by the Monsanto Company.

During the time I was with the organization, Richards and I developed a talented young ballclub. We had good young catchers: Jerry Grote, John Bateman, Ron Brand, Dave Adlesh, and John Hoffman. Rusty Staub came into his own in right field, as did Joe Morgan at second. Our shortstop was Sonny Jackson, whom I scouted and signed out of Silver Spring, Maryland. I went to see Sonny play while he was in high school and took George Adams, one of my best restaurant customers from Baltimore, with me. George asked me who I was looking at, and I pointed Sonny out to him. George was wearing a straw hat, and after the game was over, he said, "Eddie, if Jackson ever makes the big leagues, I'll eat my straw hat." Sonny ended playing in the big leagues for twelve years and is still a big league coach. I didn't make George eat his hat, though I probably should have.

After Sonny's high school season was over, Paul Richards and I went back up to try to sign Sonny. Paul asked how much of a bonus Sonny wanted and I told him, "Twelve thousand." Paul said, "That's too much. Offer him six."

So I made my pitch to Sonny and his parents and said we could only offer a $6,000 bonus. The family was disappointed and started telling us why Sonny should get $12,000. After listening to them a while, Paul said, "Eddie, go ahead and give him twelve thousand." I about fell out of my chair. Paul had made himself seem like the generous one and me like the cheapskate.

Doug Rader was a highly regarded minor league prospect at third. We had drafted Jimmy Wynn from Cincinnati, and he became a power-hitting All-Star center fielder. Bob Watson became an outstanding Astros outfielder and is today baseball's disciplinary czar in the commissioner's office, meting out suspensions for players' and managers' on-field misbehavior. Our pitching was young, but we had a lot of good arms, including Larry Dierker, whom we signed as an eighteen-year-old bonus baby, Dave Giusti, Bob Bruce, Don Wilson, and Jim Ray. Turk Farrell from the original expansion draft was still productive.

Near the end of the 1965 season, Judge Hofheinz bought out R.E. "Bob" Smith's interest and became the sole owner of the Astros. That was not good news for Paul Richards because Smith had been Paul's biggest supporter. Soon after the World Series, the Judge called Paul in and told him he was going to make a change. He relieved Paul of his duties and named Spec Richardson as the new general manager. Paul immediately called me and told me the bad news. I knew with Spec Richardson and Tal Smith in charge of baseball operations, the Richards people were all short-timers. I began calling the scouts to tell them they should probably start looking for another job. When I called Frank Gabler, who was one of our West Coast scouts, his first response was, "What's Paul going to do with all his dependents?" I told him his dependents would just have to wait until Paul got another job.

I called my old friend and nemesis Eddie Lopat, who had just become the general manager of the Kansas City Athletics. He was the toughest pitcher I ever faced, but we'd become friends barnstorming together in Hawaii and Japan. (Eddie was also on Ted Williams's list of hardest-to-hit pitchers.) The Athletics job was Eddie's first as GM, and I thought Eddie might be in need of an assistant who knew all of baseball's technical rules and regulations. He was receptive to the idea and said he would speak to Charlie Finley, the owner of the Athletics. Charlie agreed and Lopat offered me a position as his assistant.

So in December of 1965 I resigned from the Astros and joined the Athletics' organization. Of course, I had to move to Kansas City and leave Bette and the kids again. We decided the boys would finish the school year in Houston and then the family would join me in Kansas City.

My five years with Houston were busy and necessitated my being away from home a great deal. I was in my early forties and had sons aged five, three, and one when we moved there. Marc had been born in June 1957 while I was still playing. Paul was born in March of 1959 when I was coaching with Baltimore. Then we had Drew in March of 1961, while I was still with the Orioles. Looking back makes me appreciate the job Bette did raising our children almost single-handedly. The boys have turned out to be fine, upstanding men, and all the credit goes to Bette.

Bette always found time to be involved with the other ballplayers' wives. In Houston, she organized the first baseball wives' club in professional baseball. The club sponsored charity events for worthy causes. She later did the same thing when we moved to Atlanta. Today virtually every big league team has an active wives' club.

## Extra Inning

Jackie Burke and Jimmy Demaret, two prominent professional golfers with wins in many top tournaments, had developed the Champions Course, which had opened just prior to our going to Houston. They were very proud of the course and kept it in immaculate condition. Paul Richards had become friends with Jackie, who allowed us to play for free, so we played the course a lot. Paul had a habit of driving his golf cart up very close to the greens, which really bothered Burke. One day after Paul and I had played we walked into the pro shop and Jackie said, "Dammit, Richards, you are the only guy out here we have any problem with driving his cart up to the green."

Without hesitation, Paul replied, "Jackie, if I'm the only one doing it, it isn't going to hurt anything."

*Chapter 16*
## ON TO KANSAS CITY AND CHARLIE FINLEY

Kansas City was a big change from Houston, where the team had a large front office and people assigned for every job you could imagine. In contrast, Charlie Finley must've had the smallest front office in baseball. He had Carl Finley, his cousin, overseeing just about everything, including tickets. Gertrude McClure was the ticket manager and Myrna Peterson was the bookkeeper. Eddie Lopat was the general manager, Ray Swallow was the farm director, and Art Perrick was Ray's assistant. Tom Ferrick, a fine major league scout, was director of scouting, and that was the whole front office. Charlie soon hired Paul Bryant Jr. to help in the tickets department. Paul, a nice, talented young man, was the son of Bear Bryant, the famous Alabama football coach. Paul later did very well owning and managing greyhound race tracks.

The A's trained in Bradenton, Florida, and held their minor league camp in Daytona Beach. The camp was housed at an old Army base with abandoned barracks. It was dilapidated, and the way it was arranged didn't give us enough control over the players. They could wander hither and yon, and it was difficult to get them to eat together, get enough rest, and make sure they were ready to play when they reported to the field.

We had a lot of talent in the minor league camp, including Sal Bando; Dave Duncan, the present-day pitching coach for the Cardinals; and Blue Moon Odom, then a young pitching prospect. The major league club had finished in the cellar for the last two seasons, losing 105 and 103 games in 1964 and 1965 respectively, but it was starting to develop a solid nucleus. In the major league camp we had Catfish Hunter, who had won eight games as a rookie in '65, Ken Harrelson at first base, and a terrific double play combination of Campy Campaneris and Dick Green.

Near the end of spring training we had the annual meeting with the managers and all the coaches to determine which players were going to be released and where the ones we were keeping were going to play. We were in a big board room, and when the name Gene Tenace, a young catcher, came up, everyone around the room wanted to release him. He'd struck out a lot during spring training and didn't hit much. But I liked him anyway. He had a good physique and could catch and play the outfield. I thought if this kid ever loosens up and starts making contact, he'd be a good player. I said, "I think we should hold onto him for at least part of the season and see if he'll start hitting because I think he will."

The A's followed what I thought was an excellent policy about player retention. If anyone thought he saw something in a player, the player was retained until it was unanimous that he be released. So we kept Gene Tenace, and he began to improve. Within a couple of years he was on the major league club, and he became a key player in the A's championship teams in the 1970s. He later won the Most Valuable Player Award for the 1972 World Series.

We had a big crowd for Opening Day at the old Kansas City Municipal Stadium. Before the game I happened to look outside, and there was Charlie Finley on the street directing traffic with the police and really enjoying himself. The fans were yelling and waving at him and having a great time, too.

Charlie had a mule named Charlie O, who grazed during the ball games in a grassy area between the left-field line and the stands. He was a big black mule, and Charlie outfitted him with a large blanket with a big A on it, for Kansas City A's. He was a beautiful mule, but why Charlie wanted him around mystified me. Later on when the Oakland A's got into their first World Series, Charlie made quite a scene when he appeared in the media tent with his famous mule in tow. Bowie Kuhn, the commissioner, was very unhappy about the mule in the tent. I knew firsthand Charlie and Bowie Kuhn were sworn enemies. Charlie would do just about anything to get under Bowie's skin, and I'm sure bringing the mule to the media tent was a calculated move.

Bette and the boys joined me in Kansas City in June 1966 after school was out.

Charlie Finley let us live rent free in a little house in Mission Hills that his cousin Carl had moved out of. It wasn't long before we began to enjoy Kansas City. We were close to the Plaza, one of the finest shopping areas in the Midwest, and Bette and I thought Kansas City was a well designed, very livable city.

Alvin Dark was the manager, and the team was on its way to becoming a dynasty. Sometimes the team progressed in spite of Charlie Finley. Charlie was hard-headed and sometimes acted impulsively. He would listen to advice, but that didn't mean he would follow it. He was no dummy, having made millions in the insurance business, and he had studied and thought about baseball for a long time. He had a good feel for putting a baseball team together.

During the winter I was put in charge of all the minor leagues, but I was still Eddie Lopat's assistant. In June, we sat down for the amateur player draft. We had the second pick, and so it was an important draft for us. Reggie Jackson at Arizona State had caught my eye, as had Tom Grieve, who after his playing career became general manager of the Texas Rangers. Grieve was a high schooler from Pittsfield, Massachusetts, and Cot Deal and I flew up to work him out. Cot pitched to him, and we thought he was an outstanding prospect, a catcher with a strong arm and solid gap power. I scouted Jackson at Arizona State and thought he had great potential as a power hitter.

The New York Mets had the first pick, and we thought they'd take Jackson. If that happened I was going to pick Grieve. The Mets surprised everyone by taking a catcher named Steve Chilcott, whom we weren't very high on. That gave us the unexpected choice between Jackson and Grieve, and we took Reggie. Tom Grieve had a solid big league career, but Reggie Jackson is in the Hall of Fame, so we struck gold thanks to the Mets.

In the draft the following year we selected Vida Blue, a young, hard-throwing southpaw pitcher out of rural Louisiana. At the time, everyone laughed and accused me of looking for a roommate for Blue Moon Odom, a highly regarded young pitcher who was black, as was Vida Blue. Apparently not many clubs knew about Vida, but I did because Connie Ryan, who scouted for us out of New Orleans, was recommending him highly. So I drafted Blue, but he wanted $25,000 to sign, and I couldn't get Charlie Finley to give him that kind of money. Vida was going to LSU to play football if we didn't come up with the money, and we were going to lose him. Finally near the end of the summer, Charlie relented and said, "All right, if you really want to sign him, go ahead and give him the money."

I immediately called Connie Ryan and told him to sign Blue, who would win the Cy Young Award in 1971 after a 24–8 year. He became the ace of the great Oakland A's teams in the early '70s, along with Catfish Hunter, Odom, and Rollie Fingers.

Fingers was with the Birmingham Barons, our Double-A farm club in the Southern Association, in 1967. I went down to see Rollie start the Barons' opening game. In the first inning, one of the opposing players hit a line drive right back at him. He got his glove up to deflect the ball and it careened right into his nose. His nose was broken and an ambulance carted him off to the hospital. That club also had Joe Rudi, who went on to star as the Athletics' left fielder, as well as Tony La Russa, whose chronic back problems limited him as a player. As a manager, however, he is probably headed to the Hall of Fame.

The Barons also had a highly touted nineteen-year-old pitcher named George Lauzerique. John McNamara, the Barons' manager, was under my orders to keep George under one hundred pitches. During the year Lauzerique had a no-hitter going into the eighth inning but had already thrown 110 pitches. McNamara took him out of the game to protect his arm, blowing his chance at a no-hitter. The irony was that George later did hurt his arm, ruining what should've been a good major league career. Instead, he finished with a 4–8 lifetime big league career spread over four seasons.

Late in the season, I received an urgent call from McNamara telling me both his catchers were injured and, with a doubleheader the next day, he had no one to catch. I said, "John, you do have a catcher."

He said, "What do you mean?"

I said, "You were a catcher. Put yourself on the active list because I don't think I can get you a catcher by tomorrow."

John said, "You've got to be kidding."

I said, "No, you can do it." And he did. He was then about thirty-six years old, but he put himself on the active list, caught the doubleheader, and did a good job while he was at it.

## Extra Inning

Two of our scouts, Napoleon Reyes and Felix Delgado, were helping coach during our minor league spring training in Waycross, Georgia. During their playing days, they had both been fast runners. They started arguing about who could run from home plate to first base the fastest. The argument got heated and they challenged each other to a race. Then betting by the players and other coaches got hot and heavy. The day came for the race with all the players and coaches as eager spectators. The race started when someone dropped a cap in front of them. They both took off, but neither one ever made it to first base. They both collapsed with pulled muscles and neither was able to work for a couple of days.

*Chapter 17*

## BACK TO THE NATIONAL LEAGUE WITH THE ATLANTA BRAVES

N ear the end of the 1967 season, it began to look like the A's were moving to Oakland, and so I had a decision to make. Paul Richards had become the general manager in Atlanta and asked me if I'd be interested in becoming the Braves' farm director. I was. It turned out that Charlie and the rest of the A's went to California, where Charlie ran the club on a shoestring but had a lot of success on the field. I went to Atlanta, and I'm glad I did because things eventually fell apart in Oakland, and I had a good experience with the Braves.

Once again I had to leave Bette and the kids behind while I started a new job. Fortunately, we soon found a great old house in Oxford, Georgia, about forty miles east of Atlanta. Bette loved the house, which was over a hundred years old and had a fascinating history. During the Civil War a Confederate spy named Zora Fair lived in the house. She would dress up as a black mammy and hang around Union troops, picking up information for the Confederacy. The house even had a secret room where Zora hid when Union soldiers came looking for her.

Atlanta was quite a change from the Athletics, where we'd had a very small staff and an old ballpark. The Braves had a brand new ballpark with beautiful offices. I had a big picture window in my office. All I had to do was turn around in my chair to look out on the field. I could watch the ballgames from my office, and in the fall and winter, I could sit there and watch the Atlanta Falcons play football. The stadium had a large tunnel around its perimeter, underneath the stands where we parked our cars. It was nifty—we drove in, parked our cars, rode an elevator up to the office level, and walked right into our offices. In addition, there was a beautiful stadium club, which in those days was unique. We could go over for lunch, and I could take Bette there for a nice dinner before our home games. Then, if we wanted to, we could sit in the club or go to my private box and watch the game.

I inherited some good people with the Braves, foremost among them a young man named Bill Lucas. Bill had played in the minor leagues, had served as an officer in the Army, and was a talented young man. He was one of the first blacks in a front office, and he was a forward thinker. Bill started working for the Braves in the mail room and moved into public relations before he got into the baseball operations department of the front office. He was the assistant farm director to Jim Fanning when I came aboard. Paul Richards made Jim a coach and before long he was hired away by John McHale in Montreal.

The Braves were owned by a group consisting of ten owners. Since most of them were based in Chicago, they were known as the Chicago Ten. They had purchased the Braves when the team was still in Milwaukee and moved them to Atlanta in 1965, two years prior to my coming over. Bill Bartholomay was the chairman of the board and the owner we had the most contact with.

The Braves had a great new spring training facility in West Palm Beach, Florida. It had a fine new stadium that seated about ten thousand, great clubhouses, and everything a team needed. The minor league facility was just down from the right-field foul line. It contained six diamonds, a beautiful minor league clubhouse, and offices. Since I was farm director, I headquartered there. I was in charge of all the minor league players, managers, coaches, and scouts. I had responsibility for player procurement and player development, both of which were demanding jobs. We had farm clubs in Richmond, Virginia; Shreveport, Louisiana; and Greenwood, South Carolina. Our rookie team was in West Palm Beach.

The prior year, in 1967, the Braves had finished in seventh place with a 77–85 record, twenty-four and a half games out of first place. Paul Richards fired the manager, Billy Hitchcock, at the end of the season and replaced him with Luman Harris. We had a veteran club with Joe Torre at catcher; Hank Aaron, Felipe Alou, and Rico Carty in the outfield; Felix Millan at second base; Clete Boyer at third; and Denis Menke at shortstop most of the time. It was a potent lineup but aging, and if we didn't win soon, we'd be faced with a major rebuilding job. We had Dusty Baker and Ralph Garr as top minor league prospects, but they weren't quite ready. Our pitching was suspect, even though we had Phil Niekro to anchor the staff. Pat Jarvis and Ron Reed were good, but after them the staff was made up of journeymen like Ken Johnson, Denny Lemaster, and Wade Blasingame.

In the June draft we made some monumental mistakes, drafting Curtis Moore out of Denison, Texas, with our first pick and Danny Landis from Columbus, Ohio, with our second. Even baseball aficionados have likely not heard of either. I had wanted to take Bobby Valentine with our first pick, but Paul Richards liked Moore, and so the Dodgers snapped up Valentine. The Dodgers had one of the finest drafts ever that year, one that was responsible for the Dodgers' pennants in the 1970s. They selected Davey Lopes and Geoff Zahn in the January phase and then picked Valentine first and Bill Buckner with their second pick in June. They also selected future All-Stars Steve Garvey and Ron Cey, plus Joe Ferguson, who caught for them for years; Tom Paciorek, a fine outfielder; and future big league pitcher Doyle Alexander. Suffice it to say, no club has yet topped the quality of the Dodgers' draft that year.

In contrast, the best we did that year was select three pitchers, Mike McQueen; Mike Beard, out of the University of Texas; and Clint Compton, who at least made the big leagues. On the field we were so-so as well, improving to .500 with an 81–81 won-loss record to finish in fifth place, sixteen games behind the pennant-winning Cardinals. We suffered a blow coming out of spring training when Rico Carty, one of the top hitters in the league, was diagnosed with tuberculosis, putting him out for the year. In that year of the pitcher, we had strong starting pitching from Phil Niekro, Pat Jarvis, Ron Reed, and, after we acquired him in a trade with the Reds, Milt Pappas. Cecil Upshaw emerged as one of the top relievers in baseball. We were tied for first as late as June 1, but plagued by injuries to Clete Boyer, Felix Millan, and Joe Torre, we played sub-.500 ball the rest of the way.

Our backup catcher was Bob Uecker, who had a tough time catching Niekro's knuckleball. Uecker was quick with a quip, and one day he announced that the secret to catching the knuckleball was to wait until it stopped rolling and pick it up.

In August, we added more pitching depth, sixty-two-year-old Satchel Paige, my old Cleveland Indians teammate. It wasn't just a publicity stunt, although Satch wasn't on the active roster. We signed him as a coach so that he could qualify for his big league pension.

Our performance didn't leave us overly optimistic for 1969, but going into spring training we thought we had a pretty good ballclub. During spring training Paul Richards traded Joe Torre, with whom he couldn't come to contract terms, to the Cardinals for Orlando Cepeda. That gave us an even more potent lineup, with Hank Aaron, Felipe Alou, Cepeda, and Rico Carty. We were excited to have Carty back after he sat out the 1968 season with tuberculosis. He came back strong, and despite separating his shoulder three different times, hit a rousing .342 in about three hundred at bats. Rico was one darn good hitter and an incredible two-strike hitter. He was big and strong and used the whole field to hit. When he'd get two strikes on him he'd wait on the ball and powder it to right field like no one I've ever seen. Later Julio Franco, who played for the Texas Rangers and many other clubs, had the same ability.

Our pitching was pretty much the same as in 1968 with Phil Niekro, Pat Jarvis, Ron Reed, George Stone, and Milt Pappas, with Cecil Upshaw as our top man out of the bullpen. The '69 season was the first year the two leagues were split into divisions with divisional playoffs. The divisional playoff winners then met in the World Series. We quickly contended for the National League West Division title. Phil Niekro and Ron Reed were on their way to career years (twenty-three and eighteen wins respectively), and Upshaw was lights out in relief. They enabled us to hang at or near the top of the division all summer. In June we picked up veteran outfielder Tony Gonzalez from San Diego for three minor leaguers. Tony did a great job for us, batting almost .300 the rest of the year, filling in when Rico Carty and Felipe Alou were sidelined with injuries.

Although Joe Torre would eventually win a batting title and a Most Valuable Player Award with the Cardinals, the trade for Cepeda had much to do with our success that year. Although "Cha Cha," playing on a gimpy leg, didn't put up great numbers for us, his enthusiasm was infectious. He'd already played for three pennant winners, and he knew how to keep it light in the clubhouse. Felix Millan was solid as a rock at second, and Sonny Jackson and Gil Garrido handled shortstop together. Clete Boyer was outstanding defensively at third and came through with timely hitting. Twenty-year-old rookie Bob Didier stepped into Torre's spot behind the plate and had a knack for handling the knuckle-balling Niekro and, later, Wilhelm. He batted a respectable (especially for a twenty year old) .256. Sadly, after that year, Bob could never hit enough to catch regularly, and by the age of twenty-five he was through as a big leaguer.

After our strong start we faltered in August, hitting rock bottom on August 19 when Ken Holtzman of the Cubs pitched a no-hitter against us, despite not striking out a single batter. The loss dropped us to fifth place in our tight six-team division and made thoughts of a division title seem remote. But we quickly climbed back into the race, and after beating Houston 4–3 on September 12, regained first place. After jostling with the Giants and Reds for first place for another week, we forged a ten-game winning streak to open up some breathing room.

That spring we'd drafted Mickey Rivers, a lightning-fast young outfielder whom we had assigned to Magic Valley in the Pioneer League for his first year of organized ball. In early September Paul Richards learned that the California Angels were willing to trade us Hoyt Wilhelm for Rivers. Paul believed that adding Wilhelm to Upshaw in the bullpen would put us over the top, and he made the deal, Rivers and pitcher Clint Compton for Wilhelm and Bob Priddy, another pitcher. It turned out he was correct; Hoyt made eight appearances for us, recorded four saves and a 0.73 ERA in the last three weeks of the season.

We finally clinched the division on September 30 by beating Cincinnati 3–2 behind our two knuckleballers, Niekro and Wilhelm, before over forty-six thousand fans in Atlanta Stadium. The victory set off a raucous celebration in Atlanta, and legendary *Atlanta Journal* sportswriter Furman Bisher wrote that "it was the first time the South has ever won the West."

Unfortunately, our euphoria was short-lived. That was the year of the Amazin' Mets. Bob Scheffing was the Mets' general manager, and about a month before the season was over the Mets were in Atlanta to play the Braves. We beat them in the first game of the series, and afterwards Bob, Paul Richards, and I were all talking in Paul's box. The Cubs had a big lead in the East and Bob said, "Well, I think we're out of it."

The rest is history. The Mets started and kept winning, and the Cubs collapsed. By the end of the season the Mets had one hundred victories and had won the East by eight games. That meant we faced the Mets in the first National League Championship Series, which in those days was only a best of five. The Mets stayed hot, behind Tom Seaver, Jerry Koosman, Gary Gentry, and Nolan Ryan, and beat us three straight. That set up a World Series match-up against the powerful Baltimore Orioles, who had won 109 games while winning the American League East by nineteen games and then sweeping the Minnesota Twins three straight in the ALCS. The Orioles, however, had no answer for the streaking Mets, who won the Series in five games.

During those years in Atlanta our traveling secretary was Donald Davidson, who had started with the franchise as a clubhouse boy for the old Boston Bees in the late 1930s. He had worked himself up to the front office in 1948, and spent most of his career as the traveling secretary. Donald was only forty-eight inches tall due to a childhood illness that stunted his growth. That, coupled with his sassy, outgoing personality, made him well known throughout baseball. Not surprisingly, he was the constant butt of jokes. Lew Burdette once hung him on a coat rack when the club was still in Milwaukee. One of the players' favorite tricks was to race onto an elevator with Donald, punch all the top floors, and then leave him there. Donald would be stuck stopping at each floor on the way down.

We knew we had a veteran club going into 1970. We had some outstanding prospects in the minor leagues, such as Dusty Baker, Ralph Garr, and Darrell Evans, whom I'd drafted from the Oakland A's organization when they left him unprotected. But they weren't quite ready for prime time. In the off-season we'd traded Felipe Alou to the A's for Jim Nash to bolster our starting pitching. But, as it turned out, the season was doomed before it began. Phil Niekro had an emergency appendectomy right before spring training and ended up 12–18 with an earned run average of over 4.00. During spring training Ron Reed tripped over first base and broke his collarbone, causing him to miss the first nine weeks of the season. He dipped from eighteen to seven wins. Even worse, Cecil Upshaw severely cut his right ring finger in a freak accident and missed the entire year. Cecil was walking down the street in San Diego with a couple of teammates. He was 6'6" and had been a good basketball player. He decided to demonstrate his dunk shot and jumped up and slapped an awning. Unfortunately he caught his ring on a nail that ripped the flesh off his finger. Cecil had several operations on his finger, but he was never again a productive pitcher.

Tragically, Jim Breazeale, a first baseman, and Mike McQueen, a left-handed pitcher, both of whom we considered sure-fire major league prospects, were seriously injured in an automobile accident returning from a hunting trip over the winter. The accident ended both of their careers.

We finished fifth out of six in the West with a 76–86 record, twenty-six games out of first. The only highlights were Hank Aaron's three thousandth hit on May 17 off Wayne Granger in Cincinnati's Crosley Field and the wonderful year Rico Carty put together. Orlando Cepeda, Aaron, and Carty all drove in more than one hundred runs, but Rico put together a thirty-one-game hitting streak early in the year and on May 31 was hitting .436. He finished with a league-leading .366.

We improved to 82–80 in 1971, finishing in third place in the West, only eight games out. Hank Aaron had a monster year with 47 homers, 118 runs batted in, and a .327 average. Earl Williams, whom we'd signed and developed, broke in with a bang, clubbing 33 home runs and earning National League Rookie of the Year honors. Ralph Garr batted .343, second only to Joe Torre in the batting race.

Early in the 1972 season, Bill Bartholomay was growing increasingly unhappy with Paul Richards as general manager. Apparently Bill thought Paul was spending too much time playing golf and not enough being GM. In June he approached me with a plan. He asked if I would like to become the general manager. He said Paul would remain with the team as special consultant to me as GM. I told Bill I'd always wanted to become a general manager.

When Bill talked to Paul about his plan, Paul became angry and refused to accept a position as special consultant. The next day Bartholomay named me as general manager and Paul was out. He left town in a huff. I had nothing to do with Bill Bartholomay's decision to make a change, but I know Paul didn't view it that way. It bothered me tremendously that he felt the way he did. I was very loyal to Paul after working for him all those years and had never said anything negative about him to anyone. But the opportunity to become a general manager was what I'd worked for since I retired as a player, and I didn't see how I could turn it down. I was disappointed that Paul wasn't happy to see me get the opportunity to become general manager since the Braves were going to make a change anyway. It also disappointed me that he didn't want to stay involved with the Braves and help me.

Shortly after I took over, Paul Richards asked to meet with me in Cincinnati where the Braves were playing. We met in the team hotel, and he asked me what I thought Bartholomay wanted him to do. I told him I thought Bill wanted him to do some scouting, be available, and help me with difficult decisions. Paul wasn't receptive to that idea and decided to part ways with the Braves and with me. Our relationship was definitely still strained, and I didn't know what to do to mend it.

During our meeting he said, "You know, this means when the time comes you're going to have to fire Luman." Luman Harris was one of the closest friends Paul and I had, and the prospect of having to fire him one day was an unhappy thought.

I think Luman knew his days were numbered when Richards was fired. It seemed to me Luman's interest was waning. He and some of the coaches were avid hunters. Luman had an elaborate setup in his office in the clubhouse for reloading and testing different kinds of shotgun shells. I never said anything to him about it, but it was obvious to me that he wasn't focusing solely on the ballclub.

In early August 1972 the club was struggling along, ten games under .500, and I approached Bill Bartholomay about making a change. His first choice to succeed Luman was Eddie Mathews, who'd never managed but was one of our coaches. I was willing to go along with Bill because of Eddie's stature with the Braves organization and his rapport with the players. Eddie was a proven winner and he and I had a good relationship. We decided to make the change in Cincinnati. Bartholomay came down from his home in Chicago so we could make the change together. I met with Luman in the morning in my hotel suite, and told him we were going to make a change. Since Luman and I had been such close friends from our days in Baltimore and Houston, it was tough duty for me. He made it easier by accepting the news graciously, and we decided to go down to the hotel bar and have a farewell drink before he left to return to Atlanta.

We parted on good terms, and I thought everything was fine between us. Later, however, I got word Luman was terribly upset with me. I called him; his wife answered and told me Luman had nothing to say to me. I immediately wrote Luman a long letter revisiting our friendship over the years and telling him I didn't understand why he was so upset, but that I would do anything within my power to restore our friendship. I told him there were several positions within the Braves' organization he could have. These were positions in which he could have been of real help to me.

Luman never answered my letter. One of the sad things in my life is that I never saw or talked to Luman again before he passed away in 1996.

The only concern Bartholomay and I had about Eddie Mathews was his drinking. We voiced our concern to him in my hotel suite the same afternoon I fired Luman, prior to offering Eddie the job. Eddie promised that his drinking would not be a problem, and that he would not drink any hard liquor, only beer occasionally. With that promise, we signed him to a contract for the rest of the 1972 season and the 1973 season. Eddie took over as manager that night and won his first game. He was readily accepted by the team and did a commendable job for the remainder of the season. We finished fourteen games under .500, but the club's record improved once he took over.

I had inherited an old ballclub when I took over as the Braves' GM. We still had veterans like Hoyt Wilhelm, Pat Jarvis, Ron Reed, Orlando Cepeda, and Rico Carty, who were all past their prime. We also had some talented young players we'd signed and were developing the previous three years like Jim Nash, who had won thirteen games the year before, Phil Niekro, Cecil Upshaw, Darrell Evans, Earl Williams, Ralph Garr, and Dusty Baker.

Heading into the winter, it was clear we needed to trade to try to strengthen our pitching. Our team earned run average for 1972 was 4.27, by far the worst in the National League, and our relief pitching was particularly shoddy. In November at the general managers' meetings in New Orleans, I traded Felix Millan, our second baseman, to the New York Mets for Danny Frisella, a right-handed relief pitcher, and Gary Gentry, a starter coming off an off year. Unfortunately, both came up with sore arms in 1973 and were not much help to us. That trade has to go down not only as my first trade, but as one of my worst.

In December at the winter meetings in Honolulu, Earl Weaver and Frank Cashen, the Orioles' manager and general manager, respectively, pursued me relentlessly about acquiring Earl Williams, our young catcher who'd hit twenty-eight homers in 1972. The Dodgers were also interested in Williams, and Weaver was scared to death I was going to make a deal with the Dodgers. Weaver and I met a number of times at the outdoor bar under the kapok tree at the Moana Hotel in Honolulu trying to work out a deal. I wanted front-line pitching, and so we finally pulled off the biggest trade of the meetings, swapping Earl Williams and Taylor Duncan, a minor league infielder, to the Baltimore Orioles for Davey Johnson, their regular second baseman; Pat Dobson, a front-line starting pitcher; Johnny Oates, a good left-handed hitting catcher; and Roric Harrison, a young pitching prospect.

Earl Williams quickly got into Weaver's doghouse and never emerged. He didn't hit for as much power, didn't hit for average, and didn't live up to Weaver's expectations as a catcher. Two years later I got Williams back from the Orioles for Jimmy Lee Freeman, a southpaw pitching prospect. Pat Dobson couldn't seem to win in the National League, and I traded him to the Yankees in the middle of the 1973 season for five minor league prospects. Davey Johnson had a career year for us in 1973, hitting forty-three home runs, the most ever for a second baseman.

Early in spring training, I continued to revamp the club by trading Pat Jarvis, a fan favorite in Atlanta who was past his prime, for Carl Morton, a twenty-nine-year-old starter for the Montreal Expos. I'd seen Morton pitch for the Expos and liked him, even though he had an off year in 1972. When Montreal showed an interest in Jarvis, I jumped at the chance to swap him for Morton even up. Jarvis was ineffective in a relief role for the Expos and was out of the major leagues within a year, while Morton became our top winner for '73, going 15–10. He was our bellwether starter for several years in the mid-seventies, winning fifteen games in 1973, sixteen games in 1974, and seventeen games in 1975.

In early August, I purchased Joe Niekro from the Detroit Tigers. Joe had been struggling with the Tigers, and Jim Campbell, Detroit's GM, called me and asked me to take him. Jim thought he could help us, and since Joe was Phil's brother, I thought I'd take a chance.

Dan Donohue became president of the Braves during the winter, replacing Bill Bartholomay, who'd always officed in Chicago. Dan had worked with the Braves' ownership group in a number of capacities and moved to Atlanta to oversee the Braves. Bartholomay and I had gotten along fine, but it was nice to have someone representing ownership on the scene. Dan and I quickly formed a good working relationship, and we've remained friends over the years. He was an understanding boss who knew baseball. Bette and I still visit him and his wife Marilyn every year in Carefree, Arizona.

After our winter trades, we believed we'd be much improved in 1973. We showed some progress, finishing 76–85, but we were still disappointed with our season. I thought Eddie Mathews was learning and becoming a very good manager. His drinking, however, was still a problem, so I only extended him for one year. Dan Donahue, a sympathetic guy who loved Mathews, and I met with Eddie several times about Eddie's drinking. On one occasion Eddie said, "I guess you guys think I'm an alcoholic. Well, I'm not. I've just got to find a better place to drink so you guys don't know about it."

Our hitting carried us as far as we were able to go. We led the league in hits, RBIs, batting average, on-base percentage, slugging percentage, and home runs with 206, one shy of the franchise record. We became the only team in major league history to have three players hit forty or more home runs. In addition to Davey Johnson's forty-three,

Hank Aaron hit forty, and Darrell Evans slugged forty-one. I'd made all kinds of trades to help bolster our pitching staff, and we ended up a ferocious hitting team that led the league in just about everything.

Our pitching was still sour, especially our bullpen. We lost thirty games in which we had the lead or were tied after seven innings. The 1973 Braves were a classic example of how you can't win without good pitching, especially competent relief pitching, no matter how strong your hitting is.

I first saw Mike Thompson throw as a young pitcher for the Montreal Expos. He had a great arm but no control. The Cardinals had acquired him from the Expos, but they couldn't solve his control problem either. After the 1973 season I decided to acquire Thompson and gave up Barry Lersch, a minor league pitcher, for him. I'd read in the newspaper about how a hypnotist had helped Maury Wills overcome his fear of stealing bases. Maury had become afraid he was going to break a leg sliding, and this guy had helped him, according to the article. I called Maury and asked for the name of the hypnotist, and then called the hypnotist and asked if he would come to spring training to work with Thompson.

I intended to keep it quiet that we were using a hypnotist. I flew him down to Palm Beach, Florida, our spring training headquarters, and he started to work with Thompson. After the hypnotist had been with us a few days, I went looking for him one morning. I knocked on the door to his hotel room and found six of my players, including Thompson, sitting in chairs with their legs and arms stretched out in front of them, all in a hypnotic trance. Clearly the word was out, and I decided I'd better show the hypnotist the door. Mike never solved his control problem that spring, and we soon had to release him, too.

That winter I decided to move the fences in Fulton County Stadium back five feet to try to help our pitching staff. I never dreamed that decision would affect Davey Johnson's hitting so drastically. As it turned out, he dipped to fifteen home runs in 1974. The home runs he hit in 1973 became warning track outs in 1974.

I spent the off-season trying to improve our pitching. I purchased Buzz Capra on waivers from the Mets. Bob Scheffing, the Mets' general manager, called me and said Capra wasn't going to make their team, but he thought Buzz could help us. Bob and I were friends, and I think Bob felt badly that Frisella and Gentry had come up with sore arms and not helped us in 1973. Capra had only gone 2–7 for the Mets, but Bob thought he was a better pitcher than that. Bob may have come to regret being so generous. Capra had a career year for us in 1974, winning sixteen games and losing only eight while leading the National League with a 2.28 earned run average.

Hank Aaron stood at 713 home runs to start the 1974 season, one shy of Babe Ruth's lifetime home run record of 714. We were scheduled to open the season with two games in Cincinnati. Eddie Mathews and I had decided we weren't going to play Aaron in those two games so that he could tie and set the record at home. Commissioner Bowie Kuhn must have surmised what we had in mind. He called me and told me we had to play Aaron because we were obligated to put our best team on the field. I thanked him and said we would consider his wishes.

I traveled to Cincinnati with the team and, the night before the season was to begin, got a call from Johnny Johnson of the Commissioner's Office. Johnson told me Bowie Kuhn had sent him to make sure we put Hank Aaron in the Opening Day lineup. I felt obligated to play Aaron, but Eddie Mathews wanted to sit him out anyway. Eddie and I met at the ballpark early before he made out the lineup, and I prevailed upon him to put Hank in it. Aaron had never before hit a home run on Opening Day, but this day he hit a home run on his first swing against the Reds' Jack Billingham to tie Ruth.

We didn't, however, play Aaron in the second game, so that he could break the record at home. It didn't take long. In his second at bat against Al Downing of the Dodgers in our home opener, Hank swung and deposited the ball in our bullpen behind the left field fence for one of the most famous home runs in major league history. Tom House, one of our pitchers, caught the historic ball on the fly in the bullpen.

In spite of all the excitement over Aaron's home run record, the club was shuffling along at about .500 for much of the first half of the season. Eddie had improved as a manager and was doing a good job on the field, but his drinking was a continuing problem. In late July we played an exhibition game in Richmond against our farm club, and Eddie and Connie Ryan showed up at the ballpark intoxicated. After the game, Eddie got into a heated argument with our traveling secretary Donald Davidson on the bus in front of the entire team. They were arguing about money, and at one point Eddie told Donald, "You've got all your money in your backyard buried in tin cans."

We'd met with Mathews several times, telling him to stay off the hard stuff and reminding him of his promise to drink only beer. But after the Richmond incident I knew it was time to make a managerial change. I called Dan Donohue and he agreed. I met with Eddie and told him of our decision. I also told him I wanted him to remain with the Braves' organization and offered him the lucrative job of head scout for the Braves in California, which meant he could operate out of his home in Santa Barbara.

Eddie was surprised, but I think he knew why we were making a change. He accepted our decision gracefully, and was grateful he was going to remain with the organization and go back to California.

Dan and I decided to name Clyde King the manager for the remainder of the season. Clyde was my special assistant and had managed in the minors and in the majors with the Giants. He knew the team and had the necessary experience. The team played well under his leadership and won thirty-eight and lost only twenty-five to put us solidly in third place for the year.

Our improvement in 1974 was largely due to improved pitching. After two years of having the worst pitching in the league, we improved from a 4.25 to a 3.05 earned run average, second best in the division. We threw twenty-one shutouts, tying a Braves' franchise record set in 1916. In addition to Capra's great year, Phil Niekro won twenty games for the second time, Carl Morton won sixteen, and Ron Reed was an effective starter. I'm not sure if the improvement was due to my moving the fences back five feet in the power alleys or my astute trading. I do know that we hit 120 home runs for the year, down from the league-leading 206 the year before, but the team still played much better. The 1974 team proved that if you can pitch, you've got a chance to win.

After the 1974 season at the general managers' meeting in November in Kansas City, Lee MacPhail and Chub Feeney, the league presidents, appointed me chairman of baseball's salary commission. I'd been active in proposing a players' salary structure based on performance. Because of the extensive record keeping in baseball, it was easy to ascertain the average offensive and defensive production of players by position. I wanted to pay players handsomely for above-average performances. My thought was that the teams would have the discretion to cut salaries for below-average performances. Bob Howsam of the Reds and Harry Dalton of the Orioles were in favor of my plan. I'd mentioned it to Marvin Miller, the executive director of the Players' Association, in spring training in Florida in 1975, and he had shown interest, suggesting the use of the median rather than average performances.

Initially, the owners locked the players out of spring training since there was no collective bargaining agreement. However, Bowie Kuhn surprised everyone by opening spring training on his own, still without an agreement with the Players' Association. Bowie's decision was a colossal error because the players were showing definite signs of capitulating rather than sitting out spring training and the start of the season. Walter O'Malley of the Dodgers and some of the other owners, however, didn't want to miss any gate revenue and convinced Bowie to open spring training. That decision gave the Players' Association the clout and momentum they've never relinquished.

Most of the owners were reluctant to put my plan on the bargaining table because they were afraid it would lessen the chances for an agreement. At first I thought my plan was on the table because Bowie Kuhn called me to New York. He sent Frank Cashen of his office to see me at the Roosevelt Hotel. Frank informed me that the owners thought my plan would just make Marvin Miller angry. I told Frank I'd already run it by Marvin and that he'd been receptive, but Frank was not to be convinced. The plan was never presented, and I still believe that was the second huge mistake of that year.

Many years later, in 1989, the owners' Players' Relations Committee approached me, asking me for details about my player compensation plan. I told them I thought it was much too late for my plan to work. Its day had passed, but I think it would have worked beautifully at the time I proposed it.

The winter after the 1974 season was the first time I was involved in a salary arbitration with a player. Ralph Garr had led the league in hitting with a .353 batting average and wanted $100,000 to sign for 1975. I was offering him $75,000. It sounds silly today, but we went to arbitration over $25,000. Ralph won, and all the owners and general managers threw up their hands, saying there was no way baseball could withstand $100,000 salaries. Of course, today the minimum salary is $400,000 and the average big league salary is over $2 million.

The arbitration of player salary disputes initially had some appeal to the owners. What no one realized, however, was that the arbitrators from the American Arbitration Association who would preside often had no understanding or knowledge about baseball. As a result, they were poorly prepared to assess a player's value even after both sides had presented their arguments. I was involved in an arbitration with Frank Tepedino, a utility player on the Braves, and the arbitrator asked what an RBI was.

When a club goes to arbitration with a player, the club presents a figure it believes is an appropriate salary, and the player presents the salary he believes he is worth. The arbitrator cannot split the difference, but must select between the two submitted figures. The idea is to force each side to submit a reasonable figure, rather than an outlandish one secure in the knowledge that the arbitrator will compromise. Under the system, the arbitrator cannot compromise.

Players are eligible for arbitration after three years in the major leagues and can become free agents after six. Even though a player may have had mediocre statistics, if he has one good year he can compare himself to players who have had several productive seasons. In many cases, the player wins the arbitration, encouraging future players to arbitrate. The arbitration awards keep growing and growing, with no end in sight. As a result, today teams often feel compelled to buy out a player's arbitration years by awarding long-term contracts early in a career, such as the Tampa Bay Rays did a couple of years ago with Evan Longoria shortly after he was called up to the majors.

Long-term contracts shift much of the risk to the owners because, under the collective bargaining agreement, the contracts are guaranteed. Thus, if a player is injured, even if it's a career-ending injury, he is paid in full. Similarly, if a player doesn't perform well, he still gets paid in full, no matter what. The Los Angeles Dodgers signed Andruw Jones to a two-year $36 million contract in 2008 and then released him after the 2008 season. Jones made the Rangers in 2009, and they paid him $500,000, while the Dodgers remained stuck for the balance of Jones's contract. It is a bizarre system, especially for someone who played when I did, under the reserve clause, with no agents and no bargaining power. I would've liked to try my luck under the current system with Frank Lane, the old penny-pinching general manager of the White Sox.

The point is that the pendulum has swung too far. I've often wondered what would happen if the players' union, with all its resources, one day considered taking over a struggling franchise. I'm quite sure one look at the long-term contracts it would inherit would queer the deal.

Although the owners regret agreeing to the arbitration system, I liked to arbitrate when I was general manager. Perhaps it's just my perverse nature, but it's a way I could resist agreeing to a player's excessive contract demands. I thought the general managers who didn't arbitrate often settled for a figure well in excess of what the player deserved.

Overall, I participated in ten arbitrations, won seven and lost three. So I suppose I saved the club some money.

Hank Aaron was still on our club in 1974 and, at age 40, had slipped to 20 home runs and a .268 batting average. I'd talked to Hank, who told me that he wanted to play another year, although he understood that we wanted to give younger players an opportunity. Hank commanded a sizeable salary. I'd called Bud Selig, then the owner of the Brewers, to see if he had any interest in bringing Aaron back to Milwaukee. Bud said he was indeed interested. Dan Donohue, Bill Bartholomay, and I visited with Hank, and he indicated he wouldn't mind a trade back to Milwaukee to finish his career.

We quickly reached an agreement, and on November 2, 1974, we traded Aaron to the Brewers for Dave May, an outfielder, and Roger Alexander, a minor league pitcher. After the announcement of the trade, there wasn't any hostility in the press, probably because Hank didn't make an issue of it. I've always admired the way Hank graciously accepted the trade. I also admired the manner in which Hank handled Barry Bonds's breaking his lifetime home run record, refusing to comment on the steroid issue.

At the winter meetings, Roland Hemond, the general manager of the White Sox, came to me about trading Dick Allen, who'd been a great hitter and run producer for Chicago. Dick was at odds with the White Sox management, and Roland felt obligated to trade him. I was reluctant at first to make a deal for Allen since I'd heard he didn't want to play in Atlanta. After Roland and I talked for a while, we agreed that if Allen refused to play in Atlanta, the White Sox wouldn't get anyone in return, but if he did, Chicago would get a front-line player comparable to Ron Reed. We announced the deal at the winter meetings on December 3.

My hole card was that if Dick refused to play for the Braves, I could turn around and deal him to Philadelphia. Paul Owens, the Phillies' general manager, had told me he had an interest in Allen because Dick was such a good hitter and lived near Philadelphia.

After the trade with the White Sox was announced, I called Dick, who said he wasn't interested in playing for the Braves. I asked if I could come up and visit him and he said okay. In January I flew to Philadelphia, rented a car, and drove out to Dick's horse farm in Bucks County. Dick's greeting was less than cordial and, in retrospect, somewhat comical. It was bitter cold and he was out feeding his horses. I just followed him around, trying to convince him to play baseball that year.

He still didn't want to play for the Braves. When I asked him if he'd accept a trade to the Phillies, he was noncommittal, but he didn't say no. I found that I liked Dick. He was a no-nonsense guy and was straight with me. He eventually took me into his house and introduced me to his wife, and by the time I left we were on good terms.

I returned to Atlanta, and after a few days, contacted Paul Owens, who really wanted Dick if he would play for the Phillies. We even agreed on the deal—Johnny Oates and Allen to Philadelphia for Barry Bonnell, a highly touted outfield prospect; Jim Essian, a catcher; and $150,000. I called Dick and, after a lengthy conversation, he agreed to accept the trade.

Since Allen didn't play for the Braves, we didn't owe the White Sox a player. Roland Hemond was going to be left high and dry for trading a player of Allen's caliber and receiving nothing in return. I didn't feel right about that, so I called Roland and told him I'd send him Essian and $50,000 as compensation for Allen. I considered Roland a friend, and I didn't think it was fair to not reimburse him for Allen.

We went into the 1975 season with high hopes but floundered from the start. I had tried to trade Davey Johnson over the winter, but only the Red Sox showed any interest. I was looking for pitching, but the Red Sox wanted Roric Harrison, one of our young pitchers, and Johnson in return. I didn't want to give up any pitching, but in retrospect I wish I had. The Red Sox were willing to give us two pitchers and throw in Cecil Cooper, a young minor league first baseman. Cooper, the recent manager of the Houston Astros, went on to become an All-Star for Boston and the Milwaukee Brewers. I was a dummy not to make that deal.

During spring training, Cappy Harata, the U.S. scout for the Tokyo Giants who also had a relationship with the Dodgers, called me and offered $150,000 for Davey Johnson. I knew Davey wanted to go to Japan, but before spring training was over, Charlie Finley of the A's called and offered me $100,000 for Johnson. I told Finley that if he'd match the Tokyo Giants' offer I'd sell him Johnson. Charlie refused to up the ante. We opened the season in San Francisco, which was where Cappy was located, and we agreed to finalize the deal then. Davey pinch hit in our opener, hit a double, and drove in a run.

All the while Davey had been emphatic that he wanted to play in Japan. In San Francisco I met with Davey; Harata; Peter O'Malley, the son of Walter O'Malley, who was owner of the Dodgers; and Bob Nieman, one of the Dodgers' scouts. The Dodgers had a working relationship with the Tokyo Giants and were trying to help convince me to sell Johnson to the Giants. I knew once I asked irrevocable waivers on Johnson, I would lose control over him because I would have to release him if no big league club claimed him. I told Davey at the meeting he could take advantage of the situation by refusing to go to Japan and then signing with another club, leaving me without any compensation for him. Everyone, including Johnson, assured me that would never happen. Davey was emphatic that he'd never do such a thing.

We all shook hands and agreed I would place him on waivers and agree to sell him to the Tokyo Giants. It took five days for Davey to clear waivers, and by then I was back in Atlanta. Davey then called and told me he'd decided not to go to Japan unless I agreed to give him half of the $150,000 sale price. I couldn't believe what I was hearing from a guy who'd begged me to go to Japan. Now he was turning around and trying to steal money from the Braves. But I knew he had me because I couldn't rescind the irrevocable waivers I'd placed on him.

I told Davey I couldn't believe what he was pulling and that I'd always thought he was an honorable guy, but that this was not honorable. He remained firm that he wouldn't go to Japan unless I gave him the money. I immediately called Bowie Kuhn, the commissioner, and asked him to bar Davey from signing with any other major league team. Bowie said he couldn't do that, because once I put Johnson on irrevocable waivers he could sign with any team. So I had to give the money to Davey, who proved not a man of his word.

As I thought about it, I decided Charlie Finley had probably told Davey to take his free agency, and then Davey could sign with the A's for the remainder of the year. Charlie would then release him, and Davey could then cut his own deal with the Tokyo Giants for the following year. But I had no proof, just a suspicion. In any event, I gave Johnson the money, and he went to Japan and hit a resounding .197 for the Tokyo Giants.

The 1975 season was a forgettable one. We suffered through a lot of injuries, and both our hitting and pitching struggled. The ballclub just did not play well. In late

August I decided we needed to make a managerial change. Donohue and Bartholomay agreed, and on August 30 in Chicago, I let Clyde King go and named Connie Ryan, one of our coaches, as interim manager. I had the feeling Clyde was relieved, and he returned to serving as my special assistant. I didn't want to name a permanent replacement that late in the season, but wanted to take my time searching for a new manager. I knew I could work with Connie, who had previous managerial experience.

I appreciated the fact that, even with as bad as we played in 1975, neither Donohue nor Bartholomay put any pressure on me or interfered with my search for a new manager. We continued to flounder and finished fifth in our division. After the season I interviewed a number of managerial candidates and settled on Dave Bristol. I was impressed with his knowledge of the game. He had big league managerial experience with the Cincinnati Reds and Milwaukee Brewers. I'd spent time with Dave at minor league meetings, and liked the fact that he was always trying to get better at his job and gain additional baseball knowledge. I hired him at the winter meetings in Boston in early December.

I suspect the dismal 1975 season had something to do with the Braves' owners' decision to sell the franchise. I'm not sure when they began serious negotiations with Ted Turner about selling the team, but the first Bill Lucas and I heard about it was in early January, when Dan Donohue told us a sale was imminent. We were surprised by the news, which led me to believe the deal must have been struck quickly.

## Extra Inning

While Clint ("Scraps") Courtney was managing the Richmond Braves, he had a young right-handed pitcher whom I wanted to see start and pitch a complete game. I called Scraps to find out when the kid was scheduled to pitch. He gave me the date and I told him I was going to fly up to watch. I saw Scraps before the game and he said, "Yeah, I'm pitching your boy."

I went up in the stands and sat with Whitey Herzog, who was there scouting. Whitey and Scraps had played together in the Yankee chain, and Herzog was a big Courtney fan. The game started and "my boy" got into trouble in the first inning, walking two or three batters and giving up a couple of runs. The next thing I knew Courtney went out to the mound and took the kid out of the game, in the first inning.

After the game, I confronted Scraps in the locker room and asked why he took my boy out. Clint said, "I'm trying to win. If he can't get the ball over the plate, he can't pitch for me."

Every time I see Whitey Herzog he reminds me of the time I flew to Richmond to evaluate a pitcher, only to have Courtney pull him in the first inning.

With my son Robby, who was not yet two years old.

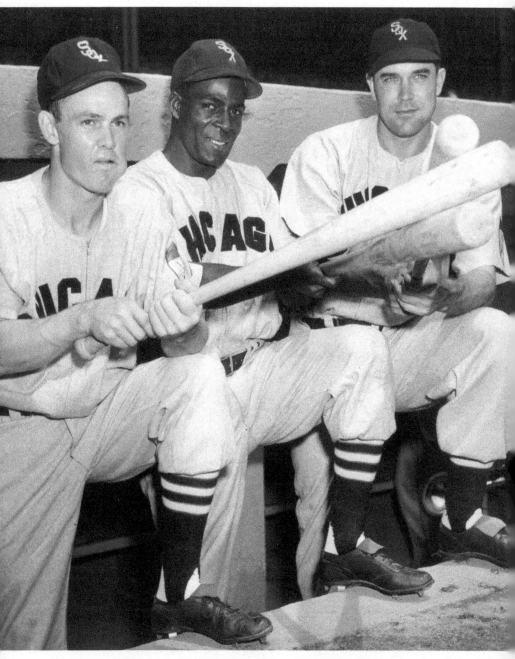

With Nellie Fox and Minnie Minoso after my trade to the White Sox.
Both were very talented ballplayers who became great friends.

I'm safe at second in the 1952 All-Star game. That is Jackie Robinson covering.

Posing with Vern Stephens and Ted Williams of the Red Sox. Ted always paid me the nicest compliments on my hitting.

Although I wasn't too crazy about the city of Philadelphia, I did enjoy my teammates with the A's. Here I am with two fine ballplayers, Bobby Shantz and Cass Michaels.

The 1953 Eddie Lopat All-Stars. After a stay in Hawaii, we toured Japan, Okinawa, and the Philippines and only lost one game. With that group, I wonder how we lost one. Front row, from left: Curt Simmons, Gus Niarhos, Jackie Jensen, Nellie Fox, Mike Garcia, and Yogi Berra. Back row, from left: Frank Scott (promoter), Hank Sauer, Eddie Lopat, Bob Lemon, Robin Roberts, Harvey Kuenn, Eddie Mathews, yours truly, and Billy Martin.

December 16, 1953, one of the happiest days of my life. I've just been traded from the Philadelphia A's to the New York Yankees.

Patti Page was my favorite singer.

Celebrating clinching the 1955
pennant in Boston with Whitey Ford
and Yogi Berra. Happy Days!

Bette and I at the 1955 World Series, just before our wedding and around-the-world honeymoon trip

We arrive in Tokyo for the Yankees exhibition tour of Japan immediately after the 1955 World Series. Johnny Kucks, Andy Carey, and I were all on our respective honeymoons with our brides.

Bette and I at dinner with Yogi and Carmen Berra at the Dai Iti Hotel in Tokyo, October 22, 1955.

Talk about a glut at first base! And all these guys could play. Left to right, Frank Leja, Moose Skowron, me, and Joe Collins.

The original Houston Colt .45s assembled some fine minor and major league coaching talent. Clockwise from the top left are Chuck Churn, my buddies Clint Courtney and Frank Gabler, Pat Gillick (later the very successful general manager with Seattle, Baltimore, Toronto, and Philadelphia), me, my mentor Paul Richards, Lou Fitzgerald, and Billy Goodman.

Watching the Atlanta Braves take batting practice with Braves president Dan Donohue, a great boss.

Bette and I in Cincinnati the day Hank Aaron hit home run number 714 to tie Babe Ruth's record. I'm the proud general manager of the Braves.

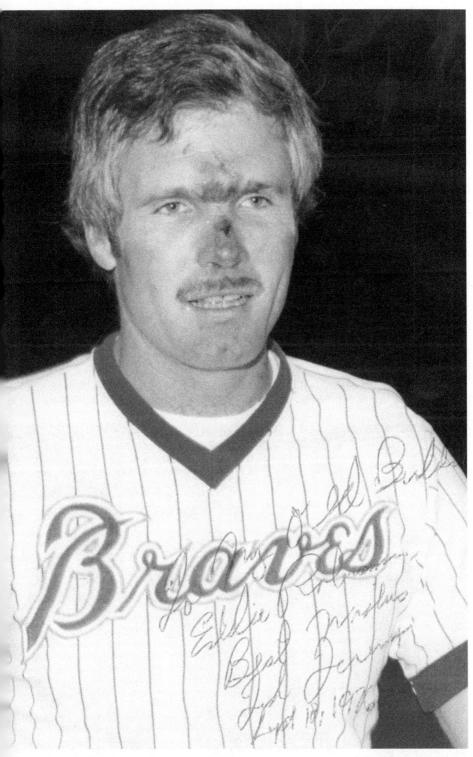

My boss Ted Turner after he lost a contest against Tug McGraw pushing a baseball
with his nose from third base to home.

Brad Corbett was my favorite owner after my playing career. Brad is on the right with my old friend Bobby Brown on the left.

Hanging out with some old ballplayers and buddies at the Baseball Assistance Team (B.A.T.) dinner in New York City. Clockwise from top left are Jerry Coleman, Carl Warwick, Charlie Silvera, me, and Bobby Brown.

Bette and I and our three sons, Marc, Drew, and Paul at our golden wedding anniversary celebration.

Four generations of Eddie Robinsons.

This photo says it all.
It really has been "Lucky Me."

*Chapter 18*
## FUN AND GAMES WITH TED TURNER

**B**rad Corbett bought the Texas Rangers from Bob Short in 1974 and appointed Dr. Bobby Brown president of the club. Bobby came to visit me in Atlanta to see what type of situation I had there. At that time I was happy in Atlanta. Dan Donohue was my boss, and I loved working for him. In addition to running the club, I had a lot of perks, including travel for Bette paid for by the team, a Cadillac, and suites on the road. We had the nucleus of a good team with pitchers Phil Niekro, Buzz Capra, Mickey Mahler, and Ron Reed; catchers Johnny Oates and Biff Pocoroba; and outfielders Claudell Washington and Clarence "Cito" Gaston, with Dale Murphy up and coming at Richmond.

That off-season, Bobby Brown introduced me to Brad Corbett at an owners' meeting at the Plaza Hotel in New York. Brad told me he would like me to come to Texas and run the Rangers. He offered me a three-year evergreen contract, meaning that I would always have three years remaining on my contract. Even as attractive as that offer was, I told Brad I wasn't ready to make a change.

When Ted Turner bought the Atlanta club before the 1976 season from the investors who had brought the Braves to Atlanta from Milwaukee, my job security became less certain. Ted is an eccentric guy who came in with a bang. He had purchased the Braves on a shoestring, and it looked to me like he was scraping to make ends meet. Ted drove a Toyota, and I was driving a Cadillac, which the club furnished for me. We parked in a tunnel under the stadium, and my parking space was in front of Ted's. He made it clear that he wasn't thrilled about my driving a company Cadillac when he drove a Toyota.

Before we went to spring training, Ted invited Bette and me to have dinner with him and his wife so we could get to know each other. After dinner, Ted said, "Robinson, I don't know if I like you or not."

I said, "Well, Ted, I don't know if I like you or not either."

The following week Ted invited me out to his home one afternoon. We took a long walk and discussed the team and its prospects and a lot of things that had to do with the organization. After this extended time together, I understood him better, and I think he understood me better. From then on we got along well, although I was aware he knew very little about baseball. Spring training was just around the corner, and I went about preparing for the 1976 season.

Early during spring training, I joined Ted and his wife in Palm Beach, Florida, for dinner. Ted had learned that Donald Davidson, our traveling secretary, had a suite when the team was on the road. During dinner, Ted asked, "Eddie, can you tell me why a goddamn midget needs a suite on the road?"

I explained that was one of the perks each hotel gave the traveling secretary in appreciation of our staying there, and that it didn't cost us anything. Ted was satisfied with my answer, but I knew he didn't like Donald Davidson. Furthermore, Donald knew it.

That spring Ted had a guest who was a beautiful, wealthy French woman he knew through sailing circles. One day she was sunbathing topless by the hotel pool. The manager of the hotel called Donald and said, "Hey, Turner's friend is sunbathing without a top on, and you've got to do something about it."

Donald, not wanting to incur Ted's wrath, said, "I'm sure as hell not going to say anything to her. If you want her to put a top on, tell her yourself."

By the end of spring training, Ted and I were becoming friends. He was a man's man and was direct with his thoughts. I appreciated that. Soon after the season opened, Ted hired a young man named Terry McGuirk, a crewman on Turner's winning America's Cup sailing crew. He was hired as an executive-in-training, but I thought from the beginning he was there as a spy for Ted. That didn't bother me, because I thought it appropriate Ted should have someone working for him who could report on the Braves. Terry spent a lot of his time with Turner Broadcasting, but also hung around the ballpark quite a bit. I liked Terry and we became friends and golfing buddies. Terry went on to become Ted's most valued associate and is today vice chairman of the Turner Broadcasting empire.

During the middle of the 1976 season, Ted complained to me about all the free food the press consumed in the press room at the stadium. He told me he was going to put a stop to it and called a press conference to announce to the press that from then on they would have to pay five dollars to eat in the press room. At that time every club gave the press free food, but today most, if not all, clubs charge the press for food.

Ted was a competitor and a promoter. He agreed to compete in a pregame promotion side-by-side against Tug McGraw of the Phillies, by pushing a baseball with his nose from third base to home plate. Tug won the race and they both ended up with skinned, bloody noses for their efforts.

Ted's dislike for Donald Davidson never lessened, and in August I got a call from Ted while we were in Philadelphia to play the Phillies. I don't know what brought this on, but Ted said, "I'm firing Donald Davidson and I want him out of town by sundown."

I tried to talk him out of it, but he was adamant. Of course, I had to be the messenger and tell Donald that he was fired.

The Braves didn't have a good year in 1976, finishing 70–92, in last place in the West Division, thirty-two games out of first place, but as I will explain, I wasn't around at the end of the year. Near the end of the season, after a Sunday day game, Ted invited the entire team and their wives to his house for a party. Everyone showed up, and Ted proceeded to show us the video of his winning the America's Cup. Afterwards, he made a speech, telling the players he was used to winning and that he was going to make the Braves a winning team. He pointed to a large sea chest and said, "We're going to win the World Series and take all the money we get, put it in that sea chest, have a big party, and divide it up."

In the spring of 1976 the rumor had been that Ted was going to make Johnny Alevizos the general manager. Alevizos had been a competitor of Ted's in buying the Braves. The word was that Ted told Alevizos if he dropped out of trying to buy the Braves, Ted would make him GM. I first heard about this from one of the team directors after the start of spring training in West Palm Beach, Florida.

That spring the owners locked the players out of spring training because no new collective bargaining agreement had been reached and the old one had expired. The commissioner's office issued an edict telling the clubs not to furnish equipment or facilities to the striking players. Ted Turner wanted to supply the players with equipment to work out with, but I told him I didn't want to be involved in going against the commissioner's directive. I subsequently attended an owners' meeting with the Braves' officials in New York City. Bob Scheffing and I were the only two former ballplayers at the meeting, and I stood up and probably overstepped my bounds, but pleaded with the owners not to give in to the players. I believed many of the players wanted to get started with spring training and would be willing to enter into an agreement. When we left the meeting, the owners were all in favor of holding firm against the players.

It was thus a shock to me to pick up the morning paper and read that Bowie Kuhn had opened spring training sites without an agreement. As I mentioned, that was the turning point in player-owner labor relations. From then on it seems the players have prevailed in every labor dispute. Marvin Miller, head of the Players' Association, was in the driver's seat forevermore.

The players opened the season without a labor agreement. Early in the season, Ted Turner called me to his office to tell me he was making Alevizos general manager. Ted said he didn't want me to leave. I was in the last year of my contract with the Braves and needed that year to complete ten years with the organization, which vested my pension plan with the team. I told Ted, "I'll stay, but I'm not going to help you train the general manager."

So all of a sudden, I was in limbo with the Braves. I had a feeling Ted wasn't going to renew my contract at the end of the year. Toronto had been awarded a new American League franchise, and so I applied for the general manager's job there. I interviewed for the job, but they hired Peter Bavasi instead. I also called Brad Corbett and told him I'd like to come to Texas if the job was still open. Brad said he'd call me back. He did call me back and told me the evergreen contract was waiting for me.

I immediately told Ted Turner I was going to Texas. Ted surprised me by saying he didn't want me to go. He said, "I'll get rid of Alevizos and you can take over as GM. I'll give you a five-year contract and you can even keep your Cadillac." I thought that was a most generous offer, considering his earlier posture with my Cadillac. I told Ted I appreciated the offer, but the lure of going back to Texas was too great and I was going.

Then Ted took me to the Stadium Club for lunch. On the walk over, he asked me not to make up my mind for two weeks. He told me if I'd wait two weeks, he thought I'd change my mind. He said, "Let me tell you a story." Ted proceeded to tell me a little about himself. His father had committed suicide. When Ted was a young man living in Nashville, he was madly in love with a girl who threw him over for another guy. He was so despondent he decided he'd do like his father and kill himself. He rented a room on the top floor of the tallest hotel in Nashville. He planned to jump out the window and do himself in. He got up in the window, ready to jump, when he thought to himself, wait a minute, you don't have to do this today; you can do it tomorrow.

He got up in the window again the next day, and again said to himself, wait a minute; you don't have to do this today; you can do this tomorrow. The third day, he got up in the window and told himself, wait a minute; you don't have to do this at all. So Ted told me if I would just wait two weeks, he was sure I'd do as he'd done and change my mind and stay in Atlanta.

By this time we'd arrived at the Stadium Club, and Ted asked me whom I'd recommend to be GM if I ended up going to Texas. I told him Bill Lucas, my assistant and the director of minor league player personnel and procurement, would be my first choice. If he decided to go outside the organization, I told him Cedric Tallis, the assistant GM of the Yankees, would be my recommendation.

My mind was made up. The idea of going back to my home state as general manager of a major league ball club was too appealing for me to pass up. It was a dream job for a kid from Paris, Texas.

Ted Turner named Bill Lucas to succeed me. Bill was the first black general manager, and I think Ted deserves a lot of credit for making that move. Bob Watson is often thought to be the first black general manager from his time with the Houston Astros. Bill Lucas, however, was without question the first black general manager.

*Chapter 19*
## HOME TO TEXAS

T he move back to Texas was particularly rough on my family. We'd lived near Atlanta for ten years and our boys had grown up there. Marc had graduated from high school but Paul was heading into his senior year and Drew would be a junior. We enrolled the boys in Nolan Catholic High School on the east side of Fort Worth, and Paul and Drew adjusted well. In fact, Paul got to play on a state championship basketball team his senior year, the only one in the school's history.

When I arrived in Texas the fun began. Brad Corbett and Nick Martin, one of Brad's major partners in the Rangers, met me at the airport. Brad and I hit it off immediately. He was a young, successful, and energetic businessman. He was always on the go and ready and eager to make deals. He loved having a good time and had a burning desire to make the Rangers a winning team.

Soon after I joined the Rangers, Brad had a private dinner at the ballpark to introduce me to the club's directors and their wives. Brad and I were both big cigar smokers. We were both puffing away when Brad got up to introduce me. I took one last puff from my cigar before getting up to speak. The next thing I heard was a big pop as the cigar blew up in my face. It turns out my kids had loaded my cigar in Atlanta and put it in my cigar box. I just happened to pick that one out of the box to smoke at the wrong time. It was embarrassing for me, but everyone else enjoyed it.

Dan Donahue and Bill Bartholomay had pretty much let me run the show in Atlanta. I soon learned that Brad Corbett was going to be a hands-on owner in Texas. But this arrangement worked because neither of us would make a move without consulting the other. Brad loved making a deal, and he hired the right GM to make deals when he hired me. Many nights, more than I can count, the phone would ring at 2:00 a.m. and Brad's first words would be, "Would you trade so-and-so for so-and-so?" I would put him off until morning when I was fully awake.

Brad was friends with Gabe Paul, the general manager for Cleveland. One evening Gabe, Brad, and I were having dinner at the Carriage House Restaurant in Fort Worth. We were discussing a trade when Gabe and Brad excused themselves and followed each other to the men's room. When they came back to the table, they informed me they'd made the trade in the men's room.

Brad was a practical joker as well. Earlier, when Gabe Paul was general manager of the Yankees before he returned to Cleveland, he was having a tough time dealing with George Steinbrenner. George was rough on his employees, as I would later find out, and Gabe was about ready to have a nervous breakdown. In fact, Gabe was admitted to a hospital in New York to rest and recuperate. While he was there, Brad hired a prostitute to dress up like a nun and visit to cheer him up. Brad didn't count on the fact that Gabe's wife Mary would be visiting when "the nun" arrived. Fortunately, Mary was downstairs when the woman showed up in Gabe's room. The fake nun said, "How are you today, my son?" Gabe was telling her he was feeling better when the woman stepped back into the center of the room and opened her habit, revealing that she had nothing on underneath. Gabe almost fainted, but recovered in time to tell the woman to get the hell out because his wife was due back any moment.

Even with the high jinks, I never lost sight of the fact that Brad had invested his money in the team. He was the boss, and I respected that.

The Rangers had finished in a tie for fourth place in 1976, ten games under .500 and fourteen games out of the division lead. Free agency was a new phenomenon, and Brad was eager to spend money on free agents to improve the team immediately. As a result, we signed Campy Campaneris and Doyle Alexander the winter after the '76 season.

We needed some pop in the outfield after we'd traded Jeff Burroughs to the Braves for outfielders Ken Henderson and Dave May, pitcher Adrian Devine, plus cash or a player to be named later. The market for Burroughs was not strong because his numbers had declined every year since his MVP year in 1974, so I wasn't able to get what

I considered to be his true value. I believed that the prevailing wind in from left field had gotten into Jeff's head, and that he wasn't going to be a productive player for us any longer. He'd hit too many high fly balls the wind knocked down.

I made the deal with Bill Lucas, my old assistant, and felt Burroughs had a chance to be productive with Atlanta. I bet Ted Turner a Hart Schaffner & Marx suit that Burroughs would hit over thirty home runs for the Braves and he did, slugging forty-one in 1977. Ted still owes me a suit.

Brad and I had some trying times together. Spring training 1977 was the first time I got to know the players on our roster. Lenny Randle had been our second baseman for the past five years. He had batted .302 in 1974 but had slumped to .224 in 1976. During the early part of spring training he came to me to express his concern about the amount of playing time he was getting. Bump Wills was a rookie second baseman with the club and Frank Lucchesi, our manager, had been playing Bump in most of the spring training games. I tried to assure Lenny that he'd get an ample chance to retain his job, but that we needed to play Bump to see what he could do.

Lenny's coming in to me to ask about playing time wasn't new to me; it's a common occurrence when players think they aren't playing enough. But on March 28, Lenny crossed the line and, without provocation, physically assaulted Lucchesi behind the batting cage before a spring training game in Orlando, Florida. He walked up to Frank, punched him in the face, and when Frank dropped to the ground, continued to rain lefts and rights until his teammates could pull him off. Frank was taken straight to the hospital with a broken cheekbone, lacerated lip, a concussion, and bruises to his back and kidney. He needed plastic surgery on his face and remained in the hospital for a week.

I had just arrived in St. Petersburg, where the Rangers were to play the next day, from our minor league camp in Haines City, when I received word of the attack from Bert Hawkins, our traveling secretary. I told Bert to tell Randle that he was suspended and off the team. Then I called the commissioner, Bowie Kuhn, to advise him of the situation. I knew Randle was not going to play for the Rangers again. Kuhn suspended Randle from baseball indefinitely. Eventually, after depositions and a hearing, Randle was fined $10,000. Lenny was also arrested for assault and paid a fine with probation and an agreement to pay Lucchesi's medical bills.

Lenny never wore a Rangers uniform again. On April 27 we traded him to the Mets for cash and a player to be named later. To his credit, he became the Mets regular third baseman and led the team with a .304 batting average. Later he had stints with the Giants, Pirates, Yankees, and Mariners. With the Mariners, he's remembered for getting down on all fours to blow a fair ball foul over the third base line, which prompted a rule change.

The assault was a tragic event for all of baseball. And I'm not sure Frank Lucchesi ever fully recovered emotionally from the attack.

Still we had a season to play and had to try to move on. We won on opening day in Baltimore 2–1 behind Bert Blyleven and started the season with four straight wins. On April 13 we purchased veteran Willie Horton from the Tigers to bolster our offense, but even so we muddled along below .500 after our quick start. Attendance began to lag and Brad Corbett became impatient with the team's performance.

By mid-June, Brad and his partners believed a managerial change was necessary. Brad asked me to compile a list of prospective managers, and we were discussing my list in Brad's box with some of the directors of the team before a game. Although Eddie Stanky was an afterthought and the last name on my list, his name caught everyone's attention. Being a man of action, Brad suggested I get Stanky on the phone to see if he'd be interested. Stanky was then coaching at the University of South Alabama.

Our switchboard and reception area was out in front of the offices by the elevator and easily accessible to everyone. I walked out and asked the telephone operator to see if she could get Eddie Stanky on the telephone and then returned to Brad's box. It wasn't ten minutes until there was a knock on the door. We opened the door and there stood Jim Reeves, sportswriter for the *Fort Worth Star-Telegram*. He asked, "Are you hiring Eddie Stanky to replace Lucchesi as manager?" Reeves had been walking down the hall to the press box and had overheard the telephone operator trying to get Stanky's phone number. We said we hadn't even talked to Stanky, which of course was true.

I talked to Stanky the next day, and he was interested. That day the papers printed the story that we were changing managers and hiring Stanky. The situation was unfair to Frank Lucchesi and not the way we planned it. I flew over to Mobile to meet with Stanky in director Bill Seay's private plane. Stanky wanted the job and agreed to take it, but couldn't start for four days because of prior commitments. I agreed, but it created a problem because it meant Lucchesi had to suffer through four more days of speculation about his job. The newspapers were running stories every day, but we couldn't confirm anything.

Stanky was going to join us in Minneapolis. I accompanied the team up there, and after our game, scheduled a press conference for the next morning, June 21. There I announced Stanky was replacing Lucchesi. I was relieved, and I'm sure Frank was, when I could finally end the suspense. He took it like a man, and I will always respect him for the way he handled a tough situation.

The Rangers were 31–31 when Stanky took over. Stanky was enthusiastic at the press conference and promptly went out to manage his first game that night, which we won. The coaches told me that on the bus back to the hotel, Eddie was planning for the next game and seemed very happy. The next morning at eight o'clock I was getting ready to go down for breakfast when the phone rang. It was Stanky. I asked him to join me for breakfast. He said, "Eddie, I apologize, but I can't take the job."

I said, "What do you mean, you can't take the job?"

He said, "I'm unhappy. I miss my family. I'm at the airport, talking on a pay phone. My plane is boarding, and you can't talk me out of it."

I said, "Well, if you feel that way, good luck." And I hung up.

I was in a daze. Five minutes later the phone rang again. The voice on the phone said, "Eddie?" I immediately recognized that it was Yogi Berra.

I said, "What in the hell are you doing calling me at eight o'clock in the morning?"

He said, "Who is this?"

I said, "This is Eddie Robinson."

He said, "Oh. I didn't want you. I wanted Eddie Stanky. I was going to congratulate him on getting the job."

I said, "Yogi, you're not going to believe this, but Stanky just quit."

Yogi said, "You're shittin' me?"

I said, "Yogi, I'm looking for a manager. Do you want the job?" He was then coaching for the Yankees.

He said, "Hell no, but I wish you luck."

Then I went down to breakfast, trying to decide what to do. What I should have done but didn't, was make myself interim manager. If I'd ever managed for any length of time I would have done that. Instead I decided to ask Connie Ryan, one of our coaches who had served as interim manager in Atlanta when I replaced Eddie Mathews, if he would take over until we could name a permanent replacement. Connie joined me in the coffee shop and accepted the job.

I called Brad Corbett and filled him in, along with my recommendation that Connie Ryan take over on an interim basis, and Brad agreed. Then I called the sportswriters traveling with the team and told them what had transpired. They were shocked, but had their story for the next day. I next went to Metropolitan Stadium to meet with the team and tell them what Stanky had done and that Connie Ryan would be taking over.

The Rangers traveled next to the West Coast to play the California Angels. I stayed with the team and met Brad Corbett and Danny O'Brien in Los Angeles at the Beverly Hills Hotel. Brad wanted my recommendation, and I immediately said Billy Hunter, who was in his fourteenth year as the third base coach of the Baltimore Orioles, mostly under Earl Weaver. Billy was number one on my list. He'd been my roommate when we were both with the Yankees, and he was highly regarded as a baseball man. I asked Brad if he had any ideas. He wanted to talk to Harmon Killebrew. Killebrew was a great player who'd never managed at any level.

Brad asked Killebrew to meet us in Los Angeles, and I called Billy Hunter to see if he was interested in the job. Brad had rented a three-bedroom bungalow connected to the classy Beverly Hills Hotel, and Brad, Danny O'Brien, and I met Harmon there. Harmon made it clear he would only consider the job if Cal Ermer, a respected baseball man, could be his coach. To me, that meant Ermer would be the manager until Killebrew got his feet on the ground. The next day, Killebrew called and graciously withdrew from consideration. That left us with a choice between Billy Hunter and Connie Ryan, who very much wanted the permanent job. We decided on Billy Hunter.

Billy accepted the job and joined the team in Oakland on June 28. Billy immediately emphasized fundamentals. He got everyone's attention and instituted early workouts prior to the day's game. He instilled a more aggressive approach, urging the team to take the extra base, sacrifice, and run. The team was 33–35 when Hunter took over, and promptly lost five of the first nine under him. But then the club caught fire, and beginning July 6 won seven in a row and thirty-one of our next forty games to become the hottest team in baseball.

On August 17 in Arlington Stadium, Jim Sundberg hit a tenth-inning single to drive in Toby Harrah with the winning run against the Blue Jays. The win pushed us into first place, a half-game ahead of the Royals. Dock Ellis shut out the Blue Jays the next day to keep us in first place. Unfortunately, the Yankees followed the Blue Jays to town and swept a three-game series to knock us out of the lead. We still played well down the stretch, going 26–15, but finished eight games behind the Royals, who won 102 games that year. But Billy Hunter had effectively lit a fire under the team. We were 60–33 after he took over, the best record in the league over that span, and August 18 was the latest the franchise had ever held first place.

Several unusual events happened in 1977. On May 15, one day after Jim Colburn of the Royals threw the first no-hitter ever against us, Willie Horton slammed three homers against the Royals, the first Ranger to slug three home runs in a game. We pulled the first triple play in franchise history on August 8, and on August 27 in Yankee Stadium Toby Harrah and Bump Wills hit back-to-back inside-the-park home runs for only the second time in baseball history. On September 23 in Anaheim, Bert Blyleven no-hit the Angels 6–0 for the second no-hitter in our history.

Quality starting pitching by Doyle Alexander (17–11), Gaylord Perry (15–12), Bert Blyleven (14–12), and Dock Ellis (10–6) kept us in almost every game. Our defense was improved as Juan Beniquez and Jim Sundberg both won Gold Gloves, and five players stole more than twenty bases.

Over the winter, we believed if we could pick up a power-hitting outfielder and a quality left-handed starting pitcher, we could win our division. Toby Harrah had led us in 1977 with 27 homers and 87 runs batted in, but no one else topped 20 home runs or 75 RBIs.

Don Baylor and Richie Zisk were our two options from the free-agent market. Brad Corbett and I both thought highly of Baylor. I talked Brad into signing Zisk, but it didn't work out well. In fact, signing Richie Zisk was one of my two biggest mistakes with the Rangers. I'd seen a lot of Zisk when he played for the Pirates in the National League. He was more of a line-drive power hitter, and I thought he'd be a real force in our lineup. The previous year with the White Sox, Richie had hit thirty homers and driven in 101 runs. But in retrospect, Baylor would've been a better choice. He was great in the clubhouse and turned out to be an outstanding hitter. Richie, on the other hand, was never able to regain his National League form and struggled with us.

At the winter meetings Brad engineered a blockbuster four-team trade with the

Mets, Pirates, and Braves, obtaining southpaw starter Jon Matlack from the Mets, line-drive hitting outfielder Al Oliver from the Pirates, and Nelson Norman, a highly touted shortstop prospect. We gave up Blyleven, Tom Grieve, and Adrian Devine, who had fifteen saves for us in 1977. Oliver hit over .300 every year in the National League and was a great gap hitter. Earlier we'd signed Doc Medich from the free-agent market to give us another quality starting pitcher.

The week after the meetings, Haywood Sullivan, the GM of the Red Sox, called to ask me if I was interested in bringing Fergie Jenkins back to Texas, and I jumped at the chance. That's one acquisition I take pride in. The Red Sox had a number of young pitchers and were looking to move Fergie, so I was able to snag him for $10,000 and a minor leaguer. Jenkins definitely had something left in the tank, as he would lead us with an 18–8 record in 1978.

We thought we'd improved a good club going into the 1978 season with the addition of Oliver, Zisk, Jenkins, Medich, and Matlack. Opening Day, at least, made it look like we were right. We opened against Billy Martin's New York Yankees before an overflow crowd of more than 41,000 in the expanded Arlington Stadium. Matlack hooked up in a terrific 1 to 1 pitching duel with Ron Guidry. In the bottom of the ninth, Richie Zisk belted an 0-2 slider over the wall in the left-field corner off flame-throwing Goose Gossage to send us home winners. We took two of three in that opening series, with Al Oliver the hitting star, before heading out on our first road trip.

It was a disaster. We lost eight in a row as our bullpen performed poorly and our infield defense proved to be shaky. We'd had to include Adrian Devine in the Matlack and Oliver trade, and no one stepped up to close effectively. We then purchased veteran starter Reggie Cleveland early on and put him in the closer role, where he was fairly effective. Our offense was sputtering, and on May sixteenth I traded Claudell Washington, who was off to a slow start, to the White Sox for veteran Bobby Bonds, who had speed and power.

Roger Moret was coming back from some arm trouble and was pitching pretty well for us in the early part of 1978. We were hoping he'd return to the dominating form he'd displayed with the Red Sox earlier in his career. In those days, I'd sometimes come home for dinner and then head back to the ballpark for the game. One night I was eating dinner at home when I got a call from Bill Zeigler, our trainer. He said, "Eddie, there's something wrong with Roger Moret. He's standing in front of his locker naked and stiff as a board. He won't talk and won't acknowledge anyone. He's been that way for thirty minutes."

I told Zig I'd come right out. When I arrived at the clubhouse, Roger was still standing in front of his locker in his birthday suit, in some sort of trance. He still wasn't communicating. Roger had played for me in Atlanta, and we'd developed a friendship. I thought if he wouldn't talk to me, something was seriously wrong. We decided to pick him up and carry him into the manager's office, where there was a big leather lounge chair. We put him in the chair. At first he remained stiff, but he gradually relaxed to a sitting position. As I continued to talk to him, he began to acknowledge some of the things I said.

In the meantime, we'd called the team doctors and a psychiatrist from a local psychiatric hospital. The players were in and out of the clubhouse while all this was going on, and peeking into the room to check on Roger. Mark "the Bird" Fidrych was pitching for Detroit against us that night. I'd never seen him pitch, and it didn't look like I was going to see him pitch that night. I finally talked Roger into coming into a private examination room off the training room. He lay down on the table while I continued to talk to him. He was relaxing a little. The room had a bright light in it, and I thought that if I turned it off it would help him relax. When I did, he sat straight up and got stiff again.

I turned the light on and he lay back down, the opposite of what I expected. The only thing he said to me, over and over, was that he wanted to see his sister. I kept asking him where his sister was, and he finally said, "New York."

I asked him how I could get in touch with her. I told Roger if he'd give me her phone number, we'd fly her down from New York right away. Finally he told me that his sister's phone number was in his billfold in his locker. I asked him to go get it, hoping that would get him to move around a little. He got up from the examining table and started hopping like a rabbit backwards. He hopped out of the room and back down the hallway to the clubhouse, jumped up backwards onto the valuables trunk, hopped backwards across a large table used for autographing baseballs, hopped down on the floor and back to his locker, reached in backwards and retrieved his billfold, and walked normally back into the examining room where I was.

He gave me his sister's number, and we called to have her fly down as soon as possible. The psychiatrist had by now arrived, and Roger allowed us to give him a shot to help him relax. The shot, however, had no effect. Dr. Bobby Brown, who had also come to see Fidrych pitch, was also now on the scene, and wanted to give Roger another shot to sedate him further. Roger, still naked, objected, and Bobby followed him around with a syringe. Roger retreated into the trainer's room, followed by Bobby and the rest of us. By then an ambulance had arrived, and we were pleading with Roger to let us give him the shot and to get into the ambulance.

Roger finally said, "I'll go in the ambulance if you'll give me my release."

I said, "Roger, I'll give you your release if you'll take a shot and get into the ambulance."

He then walked back into the clubhouse, with Bobby Brown still following him, still refusing the shot. I got some stationery and wrote in big letters that I, as general manager of the Texas Rangers, would give Roger Moret his release provided he took the sedative and got into the ambulance. I signed it and Roger asked the doctors to sign it. Then he asked the trainer to sign it. Then he wanted the clubhouse boy to sign it. We all signed it, and Roger took the shot from Dr. Brown and climbed into the ambulance.

By this time the game was over, and Bobby Brown and I had missed seeing the Bird pitch. Roger responded to medication and treatment quickly. In two days, he was throwing to a catcher behind the hospital. In a few more days he was back with the team. His first game back, he was greeted by a standing ovation from the Texas fans. He pitched very little for us afterwards, but was generally all right as long as he was on his medication. The doctors told us he'd had a catatonic seizure.

We thought Roger could help us in 1979, and he came to spring training in good shape. Then one day Bill Zeigler came and told me that Roger was refusing to take his medication. I called Roger into my office and told him he had to take his medication. Roger said he wasn't going to take it anymore. I told him in that case I'd have to release him, and, when he continued to refuse his medication, I did. He returned to his native Puerto Rico and pitched well in the league down there. The next year he had a brief tryout with the Cleveland Indians, but was again released.

I was distressed about Roger. He was a good guy and we'd had a good relationship. But he had a problem, and it wasn't in our power to handle it effectively.

With Bonds, Oliver, and Zisk in the middle of the order and solid starting pitching, we righted ourselves and played well in June. Spurred by Jim Sundberg's club record twenty-two-game hitting streak, we shot into first place for a few days in early July. How-

ever, Billy Hunter's boot camp approach was wearing thin on some of the players, nota-
bly Dock Ellis and Bert Campaneris, among others. After the All-Star break we went
into another tailspin, losing fifteen of twenty, to fall out of the division race by the end
of August. We then got hot again in September and won eighteen of our last twenty-two
games to finish 87–75. It was good enough to tie California for second place, five games
behind the Royals, but it was well below our expectations heading into the season.

I knew we had to make a managerial change for next season, and we decided to let
Billy Hunter go right at the end of the season and promote Pat Corrales, one of Billy's
coaches, to manager. Pat had been a solid big league catcher who was well respected by
our players. He became the first Mexican American manager in the big leagues.

Al Oliver had batted .324 in 1978 to finish second to Rod Carew for the batting title
and our starting pitching had been solid, led by Fergie Jenkins, who finished 18–8, and
Jon Matlack, who was 15–13 with a sparkling 2.30 earned run average. Rookie Steve
Comer was a pleasant surprise at 11–5.

Relief pitching had been our undoing, however, and we had a hole at third base.
We thought we could win our division if we could solve those two problem areas. Two
days after the season, we acquired flame-throwing bullpen ace Jim Kern from the Cleveland Indians for Bobby Bonds and Len Barker, a young pitcher with lots of unfulfilled
potential. Then in November we made a blockbuster ten-player trade with the Yankees.
Our key acquisition was Sparky Lyle, who'd won the 1977 Cy Young Award before losing his closer's job in 1978 to Goose Gossage. We gave up Dave Righetti, our top minor
league pitching prospect. Hindsight is always 20–20, but that deal is one we ultimately
would have liked back. Sparky was a disappointment, saving only twenty-one games in
two years, while Righetti had an All-Star career as the Yankees' closer in the 1980s.

Much more positive was our deal with the Indians to obtain Buddy Bell to play
third in exchange for original Ranger Toby Harrah. Toby had been one of our stalwarts,
but we thought he was expendable with Nelson Norman at shortstop. In Bell we were
gaining a great glove at third and some bona fide gap power. Buddy went on to hold
down the hot corner for seven years and become one of the most popular Rangers in
the history of the franchise.

Occasionally I've been asked if the fact that I was traded so often as a player
had anything to do with my rather prolific trading record as a general manager. The
answer is that I really don't think so. Of course, I understood from my playing career

that baseball is a business and that as part of that business, players could be swapped any time. As general manager, I made trades to improve my team, frequently obtaining younger players to replace older veterans. It was an important part of my job and I took it seriously.

Brad Corbett was a trader extraordinaire, both in business and with the Rangers. It was a passion for him, and since we talked trades day and night, I'm sure he was an influence, although I had a pretty active record as a trader while I was the general manager of the Braves.

The 1979 club won its first six games out of the gate, the best start in our history, but by mid-June we were in fourth place. Jon Matlack tried to pitch despite bone chips in his left elbow but was only able to make thirteen starts before undergoing surgery and missing the rest of the year. We got hot and ripped off an eight-game winning streak right before the All-Star break, to bring us within two games of the division lead.

Unfortunately, we lost ten of twelve after the All-Star game, leading to a trade for Mickey Rivers from the Yankees for outfielder Oscar Gamble, whom we'd acquired from San Diego in the off-season, and three minor leaguers. "Mick the Quick" had great speed and hit an even .300 for us but could not turn us around single-handedly. By late August we were nine games out of the division lead before winning nineteen and losing only eight games in September. We finished 83–79, in third place, five games behind the division-winning California Angels.

We'd had a lot of bright spots in our up-and-down year. Buddy Bell had become the first Rangers player to play in all 162 games, to amass 200 hits, and to win a Gold Glove. His 101 runs batted in were the second highest in team history. Jim Kern, dubbed "Emu" after the large, gangly, nonflying bird, was named Rolaids Relief Pitcher of the Year. He had a year for the ages with a 13–5 record in 143 innings and a club record 29 saves. He posted a glittering 1.57 ERA and held opposing batters to a .199 average. Off the field, Emu's practical jokes and clubhouse agitation kept everyone entertained. Pat Putnam took over at first base from Mike Hargrove, whom we'd traded to the Padres for Oscar Gamble, slugged eighteen home runs, and was named *The Sporting News* American League Rookie of the Year.

Given those performances, we thought the club had underperformed in 1979, finishing only four games over .500. Surely with a little tweaking and a healthy Jon Matlack, we would win our division in 1980.

## Extra Inning

During the 1977 season while the team was in first place, I'd played golf at the Shady Oaks Country Club. I was showering in the men's shower room when Ben Hogan came in. I said, "Ben, our team is in first place and I have a nice box out at the ballpark. I'd like you to come out and watch a game with me sometime."

Ben replied in typical Hogan fashion, "Eddie, I don't like baseball."

Another time I was sitting at Hogan's table with Ben and several other golfers at the 19th hole at Shady Oaks after a round of golf. Hogan was having his usual martini. I said, "Ben, if you asked me the three most important things about hitting a baseball, I could tell you. Can you tell me the three most important things about hitting a golf ball?"

He thought for a while and said, "Eddie, there's more than that."

*Chapter 20*
## THE EDDIE CHILES ERA

E ddie Chiles bought the Rangers from Brad Corbett on April 29, 1980, ushering in a new era in Rangers history. Brad Corbett's mounting financial problems had forced him to sell, and in Chiles he found a willing buyer. Eddie was seventy years old and a self-made multimillionaire. He was already something of a celebrity in the Southwest because of his memorable radio and television commercials for his oilfield service business, the Western Company. In the ads Eddie would bark, "I'm Eddie Chiles and I'm mad" as an entree to complaining about "big government." He'd often close by saying, "If you don't own an oil well, get one."

I was sorry Brad Corbett had to sell the ballclub. I enjoyed working for him and appreciated his energy and creativeness. I also appreciated Brad's resiliency, because in the face of serious financial problems his spirit never wavered. His plastic pipe company, Robintech, which had traded on the New York Stock Exchange, struggled, and Brad had to sell a number of its plants and eventually dissolve the company. But Brad fought back and formed a new company, the S & B Manufacturing Co. He secured a patent for a rubber O–ring used in connecting plastic pipe. Today S & B ships those O–rings all over the world. Brad and I remain close friends.

Eddie came in as a high energy guy also, and I looked forward to working with him. He named me president of the team, and Pat Corrales continued as manager for 1980. Chiles was accustomed to success and intended to run the Rangers the same way he did his oil services company, by setting goals and meeting them. We had high expectations for the 1980 season, and Eddie wasn't happy when we limped in a disappointing 76–85, good for only fourth place in the West, twenty and a half games out of first place in the division. Even so, Eddie was cooperative and good to work for. He wanted to do everything he could to help the team win.

There were explanations for our poor performance, of course. Jim Kern battled injuries and went from the top relief pitcher in the league to a 3–11 won-loss record and a 4.83 ERA. Sparky Lyle was also ineffective out of the bullpen prior to our trading him to the Phillies in September. And then Fergie Jenkins, of all people, was caught going into Canada with illegal recreational drugs in his suitcase. If I were to name three or four players I was absolutely certain were not using drugs, Ferguson Jenkins would have been on that list. Fergie was nabbed on a road trip to Toronto when I happened to be with the team. Our bags did not come in with our plane, and when they arrived, the airline was going to send them to us at the hotel the next morning. At that time, the Canadian authorities searched all unaccompanied luggage. When I arrived at the ballpark the next day, I learned the police had already come, arrested Fergie, and hauled him off to jail.

Needless to say, it was a huge story. Jenkins was born and raised in Ontario, and on one of our earlier trips had been awarded the Canadian Legion of Merit as an outstanding Canadian. He was one of the highest profile and most respected Canadian athletes ever. We were able to get him out of jail on his own recognizance and bring him back to the United States with us, with a hearing scheduled later.

He was scheduled to pitch in Toronto, but Bowie Kuhn, the commissioner, advised us not to let him pitch in Canada. So I told Pat Corrales not to start him until we got to Kansas City, the next stop on our road trip. The commissioner called and was very upset because he thought he'd told us not to allow Fergie to pitch until he gave us the okay and decided what penalty to impose. Kuhn scheduled a hearing with Fergie in New York and then fined him. Fergie eventually pleaded no contest to the Canadian authorities and was given a suspended sentence and placed on probation.

One bright spot in 1980 was our acquisition of Charlie Hough. In July, Tommy Lasorda, the manager of the Los Angeles Dodgers, called me and told me they were going to move Hough. Tommy knew I liked knuckleballers and wanted me to have first crack at him. He said Charlie was a good guy to have on the team, and they'd sell him to us for the waiver price of $20,000. I decided to take a chance on Charlie and made the deal.

I'd known Charlie from back in 1964 when I was with the Houston Astros. I'd gone to Miami to scout Charlie's brother Dick Hough, who was then one of the top first base prospects in the country. I wanted to watch Dick work out and hit in batting practice, and Charlie, who was a sophomore in high school, agreed to pitch to his brother. Charlie laid them in there, and Dick was slugging them out of the ballpark. After a little while they needed a rest, and I was standing near the water fountain when Charlie came over to get a drink. I said, "Boy, your brother can really hit you."

Charlie said, "Not when I put something on it."

I said, "When you go back out there, put something on it," and he said he would.

Charlie was true to his word. When he started putting something on it, his brother stopped hitting them out of the ballpark, and I stopped being interested in signing him. The Red Sox signed Dick to a $25,000 bonus, a large sum in those days, but he was never successful in professional baseball.

Charlie went on to pitch for more than ten years with the Rangers and holds the club record for most victories as a Ranger, with 139.

Although 1980 was a disappointing season, Eddie Chiles and I met all summer and put together a plan to improve the team for 1981. I was happy with Pat Corrales, and Eddie and I were operating on the assumption that Pat would be back as manager. Then, just before the season concluded, we had a board meeting. It turned out even though Chiles was committed to continuing with Corrales, most of the board members were opposed to his coming back. Even though Pat had done a fine job, Eddie and the board ultimately decided to make a change. Chiles allowed me to keep Pat as my assistant at a nice salary, so for the following year Pat did a lot of specialized and advance scouting for us.

Eddie Chiles operated on the reasonable premise that as owner of the club, he had the final say. I was the chief operating officer with the dual responsibility to run both the business and baseball parts of the team. I ran the player personnel side and made trades, but Eddie reserved the right to intercede at any time. If Eddie wanted something to be done, it was up to me to do it or see that it was accomplished. That's what happened with Pat Corrales. As time went on, Eddie interjected himself more and more into the everyday running of the ball club. As chief operating officer, I had the authority to make decisions—except when Eddie thought otherwise.

We went into the winter after the 1980 season looking for a manager. I had a lot of names, but good managers are difficult to find. It's a tough job and not many people can do it well. Don Zimmer, who'd been fired by the Red Sox, was available, and I wanted to talk to Ralph Houk, the former manager of the Yankees and Tigers, who was retired from baseball and living in Florida. Dick Howser was on my list as well. George Steinbrenner had fired him as the Yankees' manager, even though he'd led the team to the American League East Division title with 103 wins. The Kansas City Royals had swept the Yankees three straight in the American League Championship Series, and Steinbrenner had pulled the plug on Dick.

I had to ask Steinbrenner for permission to talk to Howser since George was still paying Dick under their contract. For some reason George was reluctant to give me permission, and it was a long time coming. During the World Series I visited with Don Zimmer and was impressed. He was a baseball man, and had managed the Red Sox for four and a half years and the San Diego Padres for a couple of years before that. I called Haywood Sullivan, the president of the Red Sox, who told me Zimmer had done a good job for Boston. Zim had them contending for their division every year, but they felt they needed to make a change since they hadn't been able to break through and win the American League East.

I was still interested in talking to Ralph Houk, who'd been a general manager and had managed for many years. We were teammates when I was with the Yankees and Ralph was a backup catcher. We'd always gotten along well, and I respected him as a baseball man. He'd been out of the game for just two years, and when I called him about the Rangers job, he told me he was getting itchy feet and would like to come back and manage the Rangers and work for me. The general managers' meetings were at the Turnberry Isle Resort in Florida, near where Ralph lived, so we agreed to meet there. He was going to come by after he got back from a fishing trip.

The next day I received a call from Haywood Sullivan of the Red Sox. He said, "This is going to surprise you, Eddie, but Ralph Houk asked me to call you. He had to leave on his fishing trip this morning, but he wanted me to tell you he has agreed to manage the Red Sox and so won't be available for the Rangers job."

That did shake me up. I couldn't believe Ralph would talk to me one day and tell me he wanted to manage the Rangers, and then turn around and sign a contract to manage the Red Sox the very next day. Later Ralph told me his reasons for taking the Red Sox job, and they were good ones, but I still fault him for agreeing to manage the Rangers and then signing with the Red Sox within a day without even talking to me.

That turn of events left Don Zimmer as the number one candidate. We met in Florida at the general managers' meeting, and I told Don I would get back with him in a few days. I finally was able to visit with Dick Howser and talked to Vern Rapp and a couple of others, and then flew Zim out to Texas. I picked him up at DFW Airport and took him to our house in Fort Worth, where we had a long visit about our baseball philosophies. I offered him the job, and he accepted. We agreed that he could select his own coaches, although I wanted to bring Wayne Terwilliger in to fill one coaching position. That was fine with Zim. So on November 12, 1980, we announced our new manager.

We had a productive winter, and I orchestrated an eleven-player mega-deal with the Seattle Mariners, which plugged some holes for us. We gave up Richie Zisk, four young pitchers, and a minor league shortstop for Rick Honeycutt, a quality young left-handed starting pitcher; outfielder Leon Roberts; Mario Mendoza, a slick fielder to plug our hole at shortstop; and two prospects. We also traded with the Tigers for Mark Wagner, another shortstop, and signed Bill Stein, a valuable utility man and pinch hitter.

Joe Klein continued to be the farm and scouting director. Wayne Krivsky, a bright, industrious man who did most of the research for the free-agent draft, worked with Joe. They were a good team, and they conducted the draft for us, since I was involved with the big league team and accomplishing what Eddie Chiles wanted done. I also moved Tom Grieve to an assistant position in the farm department to soak up all he could. Tom was a former number-one draft choice of the organization when it was still the Washington Senators, and had spent most of nine years in the big leagues with the Rangers. Everyone liked Tom, and I recommended to Brad Corbett that we give him a job when he retired from playing. Tom started in group sales and worked hard at it, and I brought him into our minor league operation because I thought he belonged on the baseball side. Little did I know he would be general manager of the club in a few years.

That winter I also brought Paul Richards, my old mentor, into the organization. After our meeting in Cincinnati when the Braves fired him as GM and promoted me, I hadn't had any contact with Paul until we both attended Clint Courtney's funeral in 1975. Paul had become the manager of the Chicago White Sox in 1976 after Bill Veeck bought the club for the second time. I was with the Rangers by then, and went into the White Sox clubhouse in Comiskey Park to visit with Paul one day when the

Rangers were in Chicago. We had a cordial conversation, and our relationship seemed to improve. He began inviting me each year to his golf tournament in Waxahachie, his hometown about thirty-five miles south of Arlington, and our friendship was revived.

I was still GM of the Rangers when Paul was out of baseball a couple years later. Pat Corrales had left the organization to take another job, so I approached Eddie about hiring Paul as my assistant. Paul was still a brilliant baseball man, and I believed his insight and ideas would help us. Eddie, Paul, and I had played a lot of golf together, and Eddie and Paul were good friends. Chiles thought it was a good idea, so I called Paul and offered him a job. He came up from Waxahachie to visit with me at Arlington Stadium, and I described the job I had in mind. I wanted him to work with the pitchers in the organization and assist me with deals and player evaluation. Paul was receptive but wanted to know how much I was going to pay him. I think he didn't expect much, but I offered him a lucrative contract, and he jumped right out of his chair. I think Paul was eager to get back into baseball and was very appreciative of my offer. We worked well together and our relationship was as good as ever.

Eddie Chiles had shown that he was willing to spend money to improve the team, and everyone was grateful. He was an innovative thinker, good at what people now call "thinking outside the box." Eddie had the idea that we wilted in the long hot Texas summer, and that we should do something to combat the heat. He was pretty much correct; we did seem to slump in the dog days of July and August. Eddie ordered our uniforms changed to a lighter weight material and hired a nutritionist to plan appropriate pregame meals and keep everyone hydrated during the games. He also wanted us to hire a full-time physical fitness instructor to get everyone in top shape to help withstand the heat.

I learned about a physical fitness instructor in Houston who worked for NASA, taught at the University of Houston, and worked with the Houston Astros on their conditioning. When I told Eddie about him, Eddie insisted that he, Pat Corrales, and I fly down in his private plane to talk to the man. Eddie had arranged for a rental car and he drove us to the Astrodome, where we had a meeting scheduled with the fitness instructor. It was the first time I'd gone anywhere with Eddie driving. He got behind the wheel and seemed nervous. To complicate matters, the adjustable front bench-type seat wouldn't catch. Eddie would try to adjust it, and it would slide around while he was driving. I was attempting to get the thing snapped into place on my side, and all of a sudden Eddie slammed on the brakes and threw me into the windshield. I guess that's one way to get rid of a general manager.

My head hit with such force that it shattered the windshield. Fortunately, I have a hard head, and the blow didn't knock me out or break my neck, but I did end up with a severe headache and a large bump. Pat Corrales was in the back seat laughing, and pretty soon Eddie and I were laughing as well. It wasn't any laughing matter, however, the way Eddie was driving. When we left the Astrodome, we were looking for a new ten-story building Eddie's Western Company had just completed, but he couldn't find it. Eddie was weaving in and out of traffic like a wild man, changing lanes and slamming on the brakes because he was driving so fast. It took us over an hour to find his building. Pat was scared to death in the backseat, and later told me he had never had such a ride, which was saying something since he was from Los Angeles. I was frightened, too, especially after my collision with the windshield. After that, I rarely, if ever, rode in a car with Eddie driving.

The NASA/Astros fitness instructor helped us locate a fitness instructor in Dallas. We settled on Mike Fitzsimmons, who had a degree in physical education and experience working with YMCAs.

We went into spring training in Pompano Beach with a new manager, optimism, a positive frame of mind, a nutritionist, and a full-time fitness coach. Fitzsimmons was a likeable guy, and the players quickly took to him and accepted him. He would get out and run with the players and did a fine job for us. We went 15–12 in spring training and came out the best conditioned team I'd ever seen.

Mickey Rivers, our center fielder, was less than enthusiastic with our new conditioning emphasis. He complained, "I ran two and a half miles every day and gained two pounds. My stomach got smaller, but my butt got bigger." Mickey was, to say the least, one of the more colorful guys on the team. He had hit .333 for us in 1980 as our lead-off man, with 210 hits and a twenty-four-game hitting streak. Mickey was an important part of the ballclub, but he had trouble managing money. On road trips he was always running out of cash and calling me to get some. He'd say, "Hey, Eddie, I need some walking-around money." He loved the horses, so I knew what he wanted the money for. Finally, I had to limit Rivers to cash advances of no more than $100 on road trips.

Mickey was having marital problems, which probably contributed to his never having any money. His wife once cut up all the upholstery in his car, and he must have had a poor driving record, because he couldn't get car insurance.

Even so, Mickey was a good guy to have on the team. He was funny and kept us entertained with his view of the world. One of his favorite sayings was, "There ain't no sense worrying about things you can't do nothing about because if you can't do nothing about them there ain't no sense worrying about them." Among his malapropisms was his response to a reporter who asked him his goals for the season. Mick said, "To hit .300, score 100 runs, and stay injury prone." On how the team would do, he said, "We'll do all right if we can capitalize on our mistakes." When asked about whether the Rangers had too many outfielders, he responded, "I may have to commute. You know, left field, designated hitter, whatever they want." Mick once commented on harsh weather in Milwaukee by saying, "The wind was blowing 100 degrees." His advice to youngsters learning to play center field was to first "check the wind-chill factor."

Although "Mick the Quick" was one of the fastest players in the league, he'd gotten so he was afraid to steal bases. He was afraid he was going to hurt himself and, ironically, in spring training a year or two later, he did hurt himself, sliding into second on an attempted steal. Mick must have known something the rest of us didn't, because he was never the same ballplayer after that injury.

In any event, Don Zimmer emphasized pitching, defense, and speed during spring training, and we went into the season with high hopes and optimism. Rich Honeycutt joined Jon Matlack, Fergie Jenkins, Doc Medich, and Danny Darwin in what looked like a strong rotation. Darwin, a tall, skinny, fireballing right-hander from Bonham, Texas, had made the rotation after winning eight straight games for us out of the bullpen in 1980. He might've done more, but in the middle of the streak he broke a knuckle outside Comiskey Park while punching out a fan who was abusing Mickey Rivers. For his trouble, he ended up on the disabled list for four weeks.

Out of the bullpen, we were counting on John Henry Johnson, Steve Comer, and Jim Kern, who we hoped could bounce back from injury and a sub-par year.

The 1981 season began with a dark cloud over it, as the Players' Association and the owners were at loggerheads over free-agency compensation. The players set a late May strike date. In that setting we began the year with a mediocre 6–7 record when, on April 27, Doc Medich defeated the Red Sox 10–0 in Arlington for his second shutout of the young season. That performance marked the first of four consecutive shutouts from our pitching staff to propel us into the American League West race. Fergie Jenkins, aided by Steve Comer and rookie Bob Babcock, blanked the Red Sox again the following night, followed by Danny Darwin's one-hit shutout the third night, also against Boston. Rich Honeycutt then blanked the Royals on a five-hitter.

Beginning with that stretch, we went 20–11, overtaking Oakland for first place on May 30. During May, Bill Stein, a veteran utility player whom we'd signed as a free agent in the off season, set an American League record with hits in seven consecutive pinch-hit at bats. His last hit in the string was a ninth-inning single against Doug Corbett of the Twins on May 25 to give us a dramatic come-from-behind victory.

In the meantime, the Players' Association had moved their strike date to June 12, meaning that without a settlement, no games would be played after June 11. The way the schedule worked, the A's were off on June 11 while we played at Milwaukee against the Brewers. If we won we'd be in first place on June 12, leading the A's by percentage points. We had Fergie on the mound and led early, 3–1. Former Ranger Roy Howell, however, hit a home run for the Brewers in the seventh to put them in the lead, and we ended up losing 6–3. The loss put us .017 percentage points behind the A's with a 33–22 record.

The players went on strike on June 12 and stayed out for fifty days. Don Zimmer and I used that time to visit our minor league teams and evaluate our minor leaguers. The major league players were in essence on holiday and worked out on their own.

As part of the strike settlement, the teams leading their divisions on June 12 were declared first-half winners, earning a spot in the playoffs in a miniseries against the winners of the fifty-game "second-half." Of course, there was no way for us to know that in June before the strike, but if we'd been able to beat the Brewers on June 11, we would've made it to the playoffs for the first time in our history. As it turned out, we didn't hit well in the post-strike second-half, causing us to go 24–26 to finish that segment in third place, four and a half games behind the Royals.

Overall, however, we finished 57–48 with dramatically improved pitching and defense. We'd gone from nine games under .500 to nine games over .500, an improvement of eighteen games, and seemed to be on the right track. But not making the playoffs because of that one loss to the Brewers in June was disheartening.

Don Zimmer and I thought we were only a player or two away from winning the division in 1982. I wanted to trade Jim Kern, who was struggling with arm problems. "Emu" had pitched pretty well at the end of the season, but I felt he was expendable. I also thought second base was a position we needed to improve because Bump Wills had not played well, defensively or offensively, the last couple of years. So I managed to trade Kern to the New York Mets for second baseman Doug Flynn, a decent enough hitter and a former National League Gold Glove winner. We also added a couple of free agents with Eddie Chiles's money: Lamar Johnson as a DH and Frank Tanana to give us another experienced lefty starting pitcher.

We had high expectations for 1982 but had problems from the start of spring training in Pompano Beach. Doc Medich, our top starter the previous two years, came down with hepatitis and had to be quarantined. Then early in the exhibition season Mickey Rivers came up lame and would miss most of the season. George Wright, up from Double A, hit in seventeen straight exhibition games, and looked like he'd be a solid replacement in center field. But the rest of the outfield was unsettled.

Al Oliver, who was our best bat, was unhappy with his contract and demanded to be traded. Al felt unappreciated, and, I have to say in retrospect, he was a better player than I thought he was at the time. He did an excellent job for us, batting about .320 every year. He gave 100 percent all of the time and was a good man to have on the club. He was proud of being a major league player and took care of himself. I think about Al Oliver a lot. It's too bad he never was able to play on a really good baseball team.

At the time, however, Al was disgruntled, and I thought he was being unreasonable. So on March 31, I accommodated Al and traded him to the Montreal Expos for third baseman Larry Parrish and minor league first baseman Dave Hostetler. We had Buddy Bell at third, so we planned to move Parrish to right field to take advantage of his cannon arm. It would turn out to be a good trade for both teams, as Parrish came into his own offensively for the Rangers and Oliver had a banner year for the Expos, winning the National League batting title with a .331 average and leading the league in RBIs with 109. We also got a welcome early season lift from Hostetler after his call-up from Oklahoma City. "Hoss" hammered ten home runs in June before the league caught up with him.

We still had a large hole in left field going into the '82 season, and so I pulled the switch on a trade I would just as soon forget, obtaining Lee Mazzilli from the Mets in exchange for two of our best pitching prospects, Ron Darling and Walt Terrell. It was probably the worst trade I ever made. At the time, I believed Mazzilli was the final piece of the puzzle to get the Rangers to the playoffs. It seemed like a reasonable risk to trade two prospects for a chance to win now, but it didn't turn out well. Mazzilli had just turned twenty-seven, could get on base, could run, and was just entering his prime, or so I thought. Instead, he bombed with us and never again was a big league regular.

He arrived with an attitude. First, he was a native New Yorker and loudly voiced his displeasure about being traded to "the sticks." Second, we got him to plug our hole in left field, although he had played mostly center field with the Mets. But he had a poor throwing arm, and both Rivers and George Wright were better center fielders. He popped off and called left field "an idiot's position," and he wasn't far wrong, the way he played it. He hit only .241 for us, and was such a distraction that we got rid of him in August, trading him to the Yankees for a solid shortstop, Bucky Dent.

Ron Darling and Walt Terrell both went on to successful big league pitching careers. And, in retrospect, I'm not sure Mazzilli could have put us over the top even if he'd been the second coming of Tris Speaker, which he most assuredly was not. After the first ten games of the new season, we were 6–4. We then went into a real tailspin, losing twelve games in a row to take us out of contention for good. The reasons were many, including poor starting pitching, with the exception of Charlie Hough, injuries, a slow start by Larry Parrish, poor play at shortstop, and of course, Mazzilli's disappointing performance.

The team was going in the wrong direction, and on June 10, 1982, Eddie Chiles fired me, taking over the baseball operations himself, aided by my old mentor Paul Richards. I'd gone to Chicago to watch the team play, and to speak with Paul Richards and John Ellis about moves we could make to right the ship. I'd brought John in as my assistant when Pat Corrales had left to manage the Indians. We didn't have any great ideas, and so didn't have any imminent player moves. We thought the team would be able to play its way out of its slump. When I returned home, Eddie Chiles called and asked me to meet him at his office at the top of one of the Western Company's twin towers. Although we'd been friends for several years, I suspected something was up. Eddie had been talking to too many people and getting a lot of advice. For example, John Fanning, an executive with the Western Company, helped convince Eddie that a baseball team could be successfully run the same way Chiles ran the Western Company.

When I arrived, Eddie asked me to sit down and said, "You know, you and I are like a couple of mules. We're both stubborn, and you want to do things one way, and I want to do them another. That's not a good way to run a baseball team. I think it might be better if we parted ways."

I readily agreed. I could've tried to convince Eddie that he was making a mistake by letting me go, but that would've required that I say some harsh things about people he'd brought into the organization. For instance, Eddie had hired Sam Meason as the new head of the Rangers business operations. Meason told me, "Eddie Chiles wants to spend money and I can help him do it." And that's what Meason did. He started by developing "Ranger-aid," a sports drink similar to Gatorade. It bombed and cost Chiles a lot of money.

That was the first and only time I'd ever been fired in baseball. But the truth was that Eddie's letting me go didn't make me all that unhappy. I was frustrated with Eddie's meddling and the non-baseball people he'd brought into the organization, who often replaced knowledgeable baseball people. I'd signed a new three-year guaranteed contract in spring training and had financial security. I was confident another major league club would hire me in some front office capacity.

Eddie and I drew up a statement for the press, shook hands, and parted as friends. Six weeks later, when the Rangers came home from a road trip, Don Zimmer called and asked Bette and me to drop over to visit his wife Soot and him at their apartment near the stadium in Arlington. When we arrived, Zim said, "Sit down. I've got something to tell you that you will not believe. Eddie Chiles told me he was going to fire me as manager, but asked me to stay on three days until he hired someone to replace me." Zim was correct. I couldn't believe it. But Zim said, "I guess I'll do it."

In late July, Eddie replaced Don Zimmer as manager. The Rangers were 38–58 when Darrell Johnson took over as interim manager. Darrell had managed the Red Sox and Mariners, and was a coach on Zim's staff. He couldn't right the ship either, and the Rangers finished 64–98, in sixth place (out of seven teams) in the American League West, twenty-nine games behind the California Angels, who won the division. By then, I was working as a consultant for George Steinbrenner of the New York Yankees.

*Chapter 21*
## WORKING FOR GEORGE

The news of my firing by the Rangers hit the wire about noon on June 10, 1982. Around four o'clock that afternoon I got a call from George Steinbrenner, owner of the Yankees. George told me he wanted me to come be the general manager of the Yankees. I told him I was flattered and that the job had a lot of appeal, but everything had happened so quickly and I wanted to take some time to talk with Bette to decide about our future. Brad Corbett and Steinbrenner were good friends, and I'd enjoyed the times Brad, George, and I were together when Brad owned the Rangers. On one visit to New York George, Brad, and I went to Jimmy's Restaurant and spent the whole afternoon talking trades. We wrote down proposed trades on the white tablecloth. When we'd decide one trade wouldn't work, we'd cross it out and write down another. After going back and forth for several hours, we hadn't made any trades, and we had to ask Jimmy to burn the tablecloth.

George had always been very friendly to me and often gave Bette and me theater tickets. He sometimes even loaned us his limousine to take us to the theater. I considered George one of my real friends in baseball. I'd heard from other baseball people, however, that George was difficult to work for, so I wanted to conduct a little due diligence before jumping into the job. After taking some time, I went to New York around the first of July and met with him. He wanted me to move to New York if I took the job, which would have meant either moving my family to New York or lengthy periods of separation for us. Since I was being paid by the Rangers, I asked George if he'd allow me instead just to visit his minor league clubs and evaluate the Yankee prospects for the remainder of the season.

George said okay to that, and we agreed to meet in New York at the end of the season. The plan was that I'd tell him then whether I was going to accept the general manager's job. I spent the rest of the summer extensively scouting the Yankee minor leaguers and was favorably impressed. I was in New York near the end of the major league season when Lou Saban, the Yankees president, called me aside and said he wanted to talk to me in the near future. Lou Saban was a football man who'd been a successful coach, both in college and with the Buffalo Bills. We met before a Yankees game. Lou said, "I know George really wants you to be the GM, but I want to tell you a little story. George Steinbrenner and his family and my family have been friends for years. One year I even hired him as an assistant coach under me at Northwestern University. When I was through coaching, George approached me about becoming president of the Yankees. I told him I didn't know anything about baseball, but he was insistent and finally prevailed upon me to take the job. Our relationship changed the day I took the job and has never been the same since. My office was adjacent to George's with a connecting door, and for some unknown reason about two weeks after I started, George locked that door so I couldn't get into his office from my office. My advice to you, Eddie, is don't take that general manager's job."

I told Lou I was hesitant about accepting the job because I'd seen the way George treated his employees. I heard what Lou told me, but George and I were still very friendly. Ultimately, however, I decided I didn't want to move to New York and take a chance on the situation not working out. I told George I liked the idea of working for the Yankees, but I wanted to live in Texas. I suggested that I continue to work for the Yankees as a scout and consultant. George agreed, and we settled on a three-year contract.

When we were riding in George's limo to La Guardia for my trip back to Texas, George turned around and said, "Eddie, you've got to help me find a good general manager." I said I would, but I knew I'd be reluctant to recommend a close friend for the job.

Unfortunately, it didn't take long for George and me to get crossways. In advance of my taking the scouting and consulting job with the Yankees, Bette and I had planned a trip to Europe for the end of October. The annual baseball re-entry draft was scheduled for the time we were supposed to leave. I told George about the trip and said I'd be unavailable during the draft. George wanted me to stay until the draft was over. I agreed, and so Bette went on to Europe without me. I heard nothing from George during or after the draft, and so I packed up and joined Bette in Europe. My relationship with George had cooled when Bette and I returned from Europe.

I never knew why our relationship changed. I did whatever the Yankees asked me to do, and I only heard from George one time in the remaining three years of my contract. The Yankees were playing the Rangers in Texas when George called and asked me to go to Arlington Stadium the next morning at 10:00 a.m. to see if the Yankees were working out. He said, "I told Billy [Billy Martin, then manager of the Yankees] I wanted the team to work out tomorrow morning, and I want to make sure they do."

I did what George asked and saw that the Yankees were working out. Billy Martin came over and asked, "Eddie, what are you doing here at ten o'clock in the morning?"

I said, "George called me and wanted me to come out here and make sure you were working out." Of course, Billy had already surmised what my answer would be.

*Chapter 22*

## TEAM CONSULTANT—THE LAST STAGE

I continued scouting for the Yankees until 1985. Near the end of the season I met with George in Texas. He said I could continue working for the Yankees, but he wasn't going to pay me as much as he had been.

I'd been thinking about trying something that had never before been done in base-ball—serving as a consultant for more than one team. My idea was that I would scout all the major league teams in order to offer my opinions about potential player trades or acquisitions for the teams that employed me. Since I'd been scouting both leagues for the Yankees for three years, I had a wealth of knowledge about the abilities of the players in the American and National Leagues. I knew I could evaluate specific players if a team I worked for requested me to do so. The more I thought about it, the more I thought it could work, so I decided to try it and said goodbye to George. I enjoyed evaluating major league players, prided myself in being able to do it well, and never tired of watching games.

I contacted Dick Wagner, who'd just become the general manager for the Hous-ton Astros, and he agreed to let me work for the Astros on a non-exclusive basis. I then approached Andy MacPhail, the Minnesota Twins general manager, with the same idea. He was receptive, so I went to work for the Twins as well. I continued to work for the Twins for eleven years and for the Astros for five years. At times, I also worked for the Phillies, the Giants, the Reds, the Expos, the Red Sox, the Mariners, and the Yankees again for a year. During those years I helped three teams win pennants, the Twins in 1987 and 1991, and the Reds in 1990. That made me a participant in five World Series, three as a scout and two as a player. It also gave me five World Series rings from four organizations. I ended up working for more teams (nine) as a scout, than teams I played for (seven). Altogether I either played or worked for sixteen major league clubs, including several I both played and later worked for, which has to be a major league record that won't soon be broken.

In 1987 I recommended Juan Berenguer, Jim Deshaies, George Frazier, and Dan Gladden to the Twins and they all helped the Twins to the pennant. Andy MacPhail and I had a great working relationship, as did Dick Wagner and I. The Astros picked up Danny Darwin during the 1986 season upon my recommendation. The Reds won the pennant in 1990, and I recommended Billy Hatcher, who had a great World Series, to Bob Quinn, their general manager. The Phillies acquired pitcher Terry Mulholland and Charlie Hayes, a front-line third baseman, after I recommended them. A big part of my job was to advise my teams against certain player acquisitions, and several times I steered clubs away from signing expensive free agents who, in retrospect, didn't pan out.

In 1990, Terry McGuirk, whom Ted Turner had hired when I was GM of the Braves, called me. Terry was now the Braves president. The team was performing poorly, so he asked me if I would evaluate the Braves organization from rookie ball to the big leagues. I willingly accepted, and spent several weeks traveling to evaluate the talent in the organization, including the major league club. I concluded the organization had a lot better talent than they thought. I turned in a detailed report and recommended that Bobby Cox, who was then the general manager, be hired again to manage the team and that they hire a first-class general manager to succeed Cox. I suggested a few general manager candidates I thought would be good. John Schuerholz, who was the general manager of Kansas City, was not on my list, but only because I didn't think he was ready to leave there.

Terry named Cox manager, hired Schuerholz, and, as they say, the rest is history as the Braves ripped off fourteen division titles in a row.

I started working for Dan Duquette and the Montreal Expos in 1993. In 1994 the Expos had a great team with Pedro Martinez, Larry Walker, Moises Alou, and John Wetteland. The Expos were in first place when the Players' Association struck, and the season ultimately was cancelled. I thought I might get a sixth World Series ring, but it was not to be. Duquette went on to Boston, and after working another year for the

Expos, I began scouting for the Red Sox.

When the Pirates released knuckleballer Tim Wakefield in 1995, I recommended that Duquette sign him. Wakefield had spent 1994 with Buffalo in the American Association and had won only five games, losing fifteen. I'd been associated with the best knuckleballers in the game, including Hoyt Wilhelm, Phil Niekro, and Charlie Hough, and I knew the success they could have. I told Dan I was sure Phil Niekro would work with Wakefield, since they were in spring training in Florida not too far apart. Dan asked, "Are you sure?" and I said, "Yep, sign him." He did and Wakefield responded with a 16–8 record and a 2.95 earned run average in 1995. He's still pitching for the Red Sox fifteen years later and has been an important cog in their two World Series championships.

I continued to scout for the Red Sox through the 2004 season. I was eighty-four years old, and I'd set the record for standing up for the National Anthem at baseball games. Bette and I talked it over and decided it was time to spend our summers doing something other than watching ball games. So I officially shut down my baseball career after sixty-five years in the game.

I still see an occasional ball game, and in 2008 enjoyed following the Paris Junior College Dragons, where my grandson Andrew was the starting second baseman. Bette and I now spend our days in our home by the Woodhaven Country Club golf course in Fort Worth, where I play in the noon game several days a week. Once or twice a month I travel to our pecan farm in Bastrop, Texas, about twenty-five miles east of Austin. Our farm is on the Colorado River, and I enjoy sitting on our deck looking at the river and the Pine Forest Country Club just across the river. I play in the noon game at Pine Forest whenever I'm there. I'm like the golfer who said I'm hitting the woods very well; I just can't get out of them. Bette says I'm only happy when I'm hitting or chasing some type of ball.

Every spring Bette and I travel to Phoenix, Arizona, to visit my son Robby from my first marriage and his wife Lynn. Robby was born in 1948 and wears my 1948 World Championship ring from the Cleveland Indians. He has spent his life in sports as well. He was drafted out of California Lutheran College by the Pittsburgh Steelers as a running back and field goal kicker. He was cut in training camp but had his shot at the NFL. He worked for several years as the physical fitness director for the Ping Golf Company at its state-of-the-art fitness center in Glendale. For the last twelve or so years he's found great success coaching high school football and track in the Phoenix area. He and Lynn have given me two wonderful grandsons, Shane and Robby IV. Robby IV and his wife Erin have blessed me with two great grandchildren, Bethany and Quinn, whose name is William E. Robinson V.

Bette and I have three grown sons, Marc, Paul, and Drew. Marc and Paul live in Fort Worth, so we get to see them frequently. Marc, our oldest, is a confirmed bachelor, and lives less than a mile from us. He owned a limousine business but his passion is computers. He has worked as a computer consultant and now has an interest in a small business. Every Friday night is dinner-with-Marc night for Bette, her sister Peggi, and me.

Paul and his wife Mary also live in Fort Worth with their children Andrew, Hannah, and Rachel. Paul was a good college pitcher and was drafted out of Sam Houston State by the Phillies. He hurt his arm after two years in the Phillies organization and then began scouting for the Detroit Tigers. The first player Paul signed was Hall of Famer-to-be John Smoltz. After a few years scouting for the Tigers, Paul became a cross-checker for the California Angels. He was instrumental in drafting and signing Darin Erstad and John Lackey, among others.

Paul wanted to spend more time with his family, and so when he was in his early forties, he changed careers and became a financial planner with Smith Barney. It was a risky move, but Paul has done very well and has several baseball players as clients.

Our youngest son Drew lives on our pecan farm in Bastrop, Texas, with his wife Marilue and their son Taylor. He works in the wind power energy industry in various Texas locations, commuting home to Bastrop on weekends. I see Drew and his family every month when I visit the farm.

In 2005 Bette and I celebrated our fiftieth wedding anniversary. How lucky can one guy be? We have three fine sons, Marc, Paul, and Drew, fifty-five years of happiness behind us, and I hope a few more ahead of us.

### Extra Inning

I still have the old ballplayer's yen to pull a practical joke once in a while. A few years ago our club, the Woodhaven Country Club, sponsored a chili cook-off on Super Bowl Sunday. Several of my golfing buddies were bragging to me about what great chili they could make and how they were going to win the contest. One of them spent a week cooking his. I told Bette I was going to enter the contest. She said, "How? You can't cook." I told her I was going to enter with Wolf Brand Chili. I bought four cans and put the chili in a fancy casserole dish and entered it.

The contest had six tasters, and I won first place, which was a $100 pro shop credit. Winning forced me to confess in front of all the other contestants that I had just used canned Wolf Brand. One of the judges, Mike Newbill, said, "I thought your chili had a familiar taste." Even though I disqualified myself, some of my buddies and fellow contestants were a little upset with me.

# RETROSPECTIVE

When I entered professional baseball in 1939, I didn't have any idea I was embarking on a journey that would span sixty-five years. Sixty-five wonderful years. There were many highs and lows over the years, but the highs outnumber the lows by a wide margin. I've had the privilege of witnessing and being a part of the tremendous growth and evolution of the great American game, even if the changes haven't all been good.

Through all the transitions—including corporate owners taking over from independent or family ownership, the start and growth of the Players' Association, Marvin Miller, player strikes, owner lockouts, free agency, player agents, hugely escalating salaries, the change in the role of the commissioner—the game has not only persevered, but has continued to grow. That growth can be measured in many ways, as, for example, in record attendance and fan support and the building of wonderful new stadiums in virtually every major league market. Minor league baseball is also flourishing, with new stadiums cropping up everywhere and new, independent leagues gaining a foothold in many communities. Baseball has even survived the calling off of the 1994 World Series, a move not calculated to win fans.

Today, because of the power of the Players' Association, any important change in baseball must be agreed upon by the owners and players. Perhaps that's as it should be. It's certainly a far cry from when I played fifty-plus years ago. The players have parlayed their collective bargaining successes into multi-million-dollar guaranteed salaries and too many perks to mention. I'm happy for the players, who are now rewarded so handsomely for excelling at a game that brings pleasure to so many. Collective bargaining and free agency have allowed the free market, which Americans value in our capitalistic society, to take hold. It's very different from my playing days, when, because of the reserve clause, players were stuck with one team for life and had no access to a free and open market for their services.

One can usefully question whether or not the pendulum has swung too far. Player agents now exercise great influence and frequently negotiate long-term guaranteed contracts for millions of dollars, which sometimes take away a player's desire to play to his ability. Owners don't have to give guaranteed contracts, but faced with the pressure to win and to compete in an open market, they can't seem to restrain themselves.

In my role as team consultant I first saw Jose Canseco in spring training in 1986. I was so impressed I called my old friend Bobby Brown, then president of the American League, and told him I'd just seen an amazing show by a young slugger for the Oakland Athletics during batting practice in Phoenix. Canseco hit so many balls out of the park that the A's paid some young kids to stand outside the left-field fence and chase them down because he was losing so many. I told Bobby that Canseco was the only player I'd ever seen I'd pay to watch take batting practice, and I'd seen Ted Williams and Joe DiMaggio, among others.

Of course, I had no idea Canseco was using performance-enhancing drugs, and so I was duped along with everyone else in baseball. I still don't know how you evaluate a player if you are unsure if he's on steroids or not. Happily, the Players' Association and the commissioner have finally acted to clean up baseball. Better late than never, the saying goes. But those who run baseball from both sides of the bargaining table were asleep at the switch and allowed a sad chapter in baseball history, fueled by the players' greed and unethical attempts to gain a competitive edge. It is unfortunate that statistics and records from that era mean nothing. I'd like to see baseball put asterisks by the statistics of steroid users and separate the records set in the steroid era from the true playing records of the pre-steroid days.

Although baseball observers have focused on the increase in home runs and other power statistics, I don't think enough attention has been given to the inherent unfairness of steroid use. It's unfair to those who came before and set records without cheating—players like Hank Aaron, Roger Maris, and Tom Seaver. Steroid users take unfair advantage of their teammates with whom they are competing for a job. At the minor league level, they've been able to advance at the expense of teammates who were clean, and at the major league level they've often taken away high-paying jobs from those who didn't cheat.

But whatever problems have beset our game, I still feel fortunate to have had my day in baseball, and I'm grateful for the fact that "my day" extended over sixty-five years. I'm happily retired from scouting and consulting and get to only two or three games a year now, after watching thousands in person over the years. Bette and I are able to travel, and I play a lot of golf and shoot my age almost every time I play.

A few years ago, Bette and I were attending a B.A.T. (Baseball Assistance Team) dinner at the Waldorf Astoria in New York City. We happened to get on the elevator with Robin and Mary Roberts. After we said hello, Robin said to Mary, "Do you see how good Eddie Robinson looks? Do you know why he looks so good?"

Mary said, "He sure does look good, but no, I don't know why."

Quick as a wink, Robin said, "It's because he's never had a real job."

I don't know if Robin was right or not, but I do thank God for my good fortune to have lived a life in baseball doing what I've always wanted to do.

—December 15, 2009

One of the great frustrations of any author of history or biography is what I will call "post-publication discoveries." No matter how careful and thorough a researcher or fact gatherer an author might be, he or she will always later run across great material that should have been in the book. This phenomenon may be particularly true when one takes on the writing of a memoir for an important sports figure, such as I have with Robin Roberts, Bill Werber, and most recently the remarkable Eddie Robinson. Those projects are really oral histories in which the coauthor spends an inordinate amount of time interviewing, taping, and trying to mine the memory of the subject.

After the initial publication of *Lucky Me* in 2011, Eddie and I attended something on the order of fifteen to twenty book signings in the Dallas–Fort Worth area, with audiences ranging from more than one hundred to ten or so. At the signings I would typically begin by introducing Eddie and telling the gathering some highlights of his extraordinary career, and Eddie would follow by relating stories from his time in baseball. Since Eddie spent sixty-five years in the sport, he does have a lot of stories; almost inevitably, he would tell a tale I had not earlier heard, even though we'd worked together for over seven years in writing the book. Of course, one of the great values of memoirs and oral histories is putting into print stories that will be lost if they're not recorded for posterity. In fact, one of the reasons Eddie wanted to write his memoirs was to give fans a real insight into how baseball was in the 1940s and 1950s. With that in mind, here are a few stories and anecdotes we missed the first time around.

In the book we tell the humorous story of Bill Morrell, Eddie's manager in Valdosta in the Class D Georgia-Florida League, calling Eddie in to talk about his poor performance. That conversation took place seventy-six years ago, but Eddie remembers it like it was yesterday. Eddie was hitting under .200 and was sure that he was going to be released. But Morrell, who was not about to release Eddie, told him it wasn't his hitting that concerned him, it was his fielding. In particular, Eddie was poor at catching balls thrown in the dirt to first base (which they called pick-ups in those days). Since this was Class D, there were a lot of those. So Eddie got his roommate Eddie Lukon to throw him balls in the dirt day after day until he got good at catching them. What Eddie never mentioned to me was that when he was with the Chicago White Sox later on, his manager Paul Richards told him that he was the best at catching balls in the dirt that Richards had ever seen.

Some peculiar things happen in Class D baseball. On the last day of one of Eddie's two seasons with Valdosta, the team was to play a day-night doubleheader against the Waycross Bears, with the first game in Valdosta and the nightcap in Waycross. The first game went eighteen innings, and then the teams had to pack up and drive sixty miles to play the second game. That one was also tight. Waycross had a player named Pete Thomassie, who was probably the fastest in the league. Late in the game, he was on first base with the score tied when the hitter drove a ball into the gap. As Thomassie was racing around the bases, the public address announcer got excited and blurted out, "And here comes Thomassie, hauling ass around third base, and he's going to score!" Eddie and his teammates all thought that was hilarious.

Eddie also later recalled the time Ray Brubaker, his Minor League manager in Elmira, got so upset with the team's shoddy performance in a game in Binghamton that he walked in front of the team bus from the ballpark all the way back to the team hotel, a distance of about two miles, forcing the bus to creep along. Guess he wanted the club to have time to think about the egg they had just laid. It must have had some effect since they went on to win the league championship in a league that featured three future Hall of Famers: Early Wynn, Ralph Kiner, and Bob Lemon.

In fact, one of Eddie's most embarrassing moments came against Kiner's Albany Senators in Elmira. With a runner on first base, the pitcher threw over to Eddie to try to pick the guy off. Eddie, however, didn't see it and had to chase the ball down after it sailed by him. The owner of the team, John Ogden, was in the stands and hollered out, "Robinson, we're going to have to get an alarm clock to keep you awake when the pitcher throws over!" His teammates got a big kick out of it, but Eddie didn't think it was funny at the time.

It also didn't come up until later that Eddie made the final out in Bobo Holloman's May 6, 1953, no-hitter for the St. Louis Browns against the Philadelphia Athletics. It was Holloman's first big league victory, and he would record just two more in his one-year Major League career.

We also neglected to mention that Eddie was in Havana in 1959 when Castro overthrew the Batista regime and took over Cuba. Eddie was the farm director for the Baltimore Orioles, and he and his wife Bette had gone to Puerto Rico and the Dominican Republic to scout some Winter League games. Bette was pregnant with their son Paul, so she flew home from the Dominican while Eddie flew over to Cuba to watch some more games. Immersed as he was in baseball, Eddie had not closely followed the political situation there. He stayed at the Nacionale, then the nicest hotel in Havana. One day in early January, he was sitting out by the pool when some soldiers began appearing in neatly pressed green khaki uniforms with short black boots. According to Eddie, they seemed to be just looking around, were friendly and didn't brandish any guns. He thought that the local population was calm and seemed relatively happy that the rebels were there. From his vantage, the takeover was very smooth and seemed to occur almost without incident. He recalls that people weren't cheering, but they didn't seem displeased. Eddie stayed on and flew home on his scheduled flight a few days later.

We do tell the inspiring story of Eddie's recovery from nerve damage in his leg from a botched operation during World War II. It caused foot drop, which meant that Eddie couldn't raise his foot; unless repaired, it would signal an end to his baseball career. He underwent another delicate operation at the Bethesda Naval Hospital that allowed the nerve in his leg to gradually regenerate and grow. By the time he was discharged from the navy and ready for spring training in 1946, the nerve had healed, eliminating the foot drop and allowing Eddie to resume his baseball career. What Eddie neglected to tell me, however, is that within months of his retiring from baseball as an active player in 1957 when he was thirty-six years old, his foot drop returned. And it has been with him ever since. It's as if someone above wanted Eddie to have a Major League baseball career.

*C. Paul Rogers III*
*February 17, 2015*

## ACKNOWLEDGMENTS

I'd like to thank the following people:

Brad Corbett, who brought me home to Texas.
Drew, Paul, Marc, and Robby, my sons of whom I am most proud.
Hazel, my mother, who got me started and kept me going.
Herb Castle, my best friend and confidant.
Joe Kuhel and Clyde Milan, who taught me how to hit in one easy lesson.
Mary Lou Patterson, my girl Friday who has helped me in so many ways.
My breakfast group guys, who get each day started with the news and a laugh.
Paul Richards, my mentor and positive force in my baseball life.
Teammates who had a positive effect on my life, Bob Lemon, Joe Gordon,
   Ray Scarborough, and Eddie Stewart.

### Eddie Robinson

• • •

Eddie Robinson and I began our collaboration on his memoirs in 2003. As I write this, it is 2010, and the book is scheduled for publication in early 2011, so one thing should be certain: Eddie is a patient man. And, as I have learned over these years of working with him, Eddie has many other wonderful qualities, including modesty, loyalty, humor, and a caring nature not always found in rough-and-tumble old ballplayers. At almost 6'2", Eddie is a large but gentle man whose life is centered around family and friends.

As my paying jobs frequently got in the way of progress on "Eddie's book," Eddie never wavered in wanting to see the project through with me. And I have never wavered from wanting to tell the story of his life because his is such a compelling one for at least two reasons. First, his baseball tales and recollections from his many years in the game are part of baseball's great oral tradition and should be recorded for posterity. But even more important is Eddie's amazing rags-to-riches saga—he grew up in a mostly single parent family in small town East Texas during the Great Depression and rose to the heights of professional baseball, both as a player and front office executive. His is a true American success story of tenacity, ambition, perseverance, dedication, and hard work.

As good as Eddie's stories are and as interesting as his life has been, the best part of writing his story is the friendship that my Julie and I now have with Eddie and Bette. We've had many great times together, and Bette has been a great supporter of the project, often encouraging Eddie to "open up." And, Eddie has opened up, as I hope the resulting book shows.

The manuscript itself has benefitted from careful readings by Charles C. Alexander and Lee Lowenfish, as well as several trenchant edits by Kathryn Lang of the SMU Press. I particularly want to thank Kathryn, Keith Gregory, and George Ann Ratchford of the SMU Press for laboring on and seeing the book to fruition in the face of difficult circumstances.

**Paul Rogers**

# INDEX

*The initials ER indicate Eddie Robinson.*

Aaron, Hank
  during the 1950s, 76
  during the 1960s, 164, 166
  during the 1970s, 168–69, 173, 174, 178
Abrams, Cal, 111, 112
Adair, Jerry, 132
Adair, Jimmy, 145
Adams, George, 153
Adlesh, Dave, 153
*Afoundria*, USS, 30
Aiea Heights Hospital, 30
Alabama-Florida League, 133
Albany, Georgia, 11
Albany Cardinals, 11
Alevizos, Johnny, 185, 186
Alexander, Doyle, 165, 190, 195
Alexander, Roger, 178
Allen, Dick, 178–79
All-Star players/games, 14, 45, 74–76, 77, 87,
  photo section
Aloma, Luis, 76
Alou, Felipe, 164, 166, 168
Alou, Moises, 220
Amalfitano, Joe, 146
Ameche, Alan, 118
Amoros, Sandy, 120
Anacostia Naval Air Station, 27
Antonelli, Johnny, 146
Apache Junction, Arizona, 146–47
Appalachian League, 136
arbitration of salaries, 176–78
Armed Forces Night, 41–42
Arroyo, Luis, 77
Ashburn, Richie, 146
Asia visit, ER's, 115–16
Aspromonte, Bob, 146, 150
Astrodome, 152–53
athletic director job, ER's, 39
Athletic Specialist program, U.S. Navy, 24–29
Atlanta Braves
  during the 1960s, 163–67
  during the 1970s, 168–74, 179–81, 183–86,
  190–91, 196

during the 1990s, 220
  Stengel story, 107
attendance statistics
  Atlanta Braves, 167
  Baltimore Orioles, 38
  Cleveland Indians, 53, 54, 55, 56, 57, 60,
  61–62, 67
  Texas Rangers, 196
Austria, 116

Babcock, Bob, 211
Babe, Loren, 94, 96
Bagby, Jim, 23
Baker, Dusty, 164, 168, 171
Baltimore Colts, 5, 118
Baltimore Orioles
  during the 1940 season, 14
  during the 1941 season, 15–16
  during the 1942 season, ii, 21–22, 31, photo
  section
  during the 1946 season, xv, 36, 37, 39
  during the 1947 season, 48
  during the 1950s, 127–37
  during the 1960s, 136–38, 142, 167
  during the 1970s, 171, 192
Baltimore Stadium, hitting challenges, 37
Bando, Sal, 157
Banks, Ernie, 76
Barber, Steve, 133–34, 137
Barker, Len, 199
barnstorming tours, 100–101, 111–12, 113–14
Barrett, Red, 22
Bartholomay, Bill, 164, 169, 170, 172, 178, 181
Bartoff, Roger, 152
Barton, Larry, 21–22
Baseball Assistance Team, 141–42, 227, photo
  section
Bateman, John, 153
batting averages, ER's
  Baltimore Orioles, 22
  Chicago White Sox, 80, 87
  Cleveland Indians, 39, 42, 53, 57, 70, 71
  Elmira Pioneers, 16

Kansas City Athletics, 124
Philadelphia Athletics, 94
Valdosta Trojans, 11, 14
Washington Senators, 72, 79
Bauer, Hank, 119, 121
Bavasi, Peter, 186
Baylor, Don, 195
Beard, Mike, 165
Beardon, Gene, during the 1948 season
  regular season games, 53, 56, 57, 60, 61, 62, 63
  World Series games, 66, 68, 70
Belardi, Wayne, 124
Belinsky, Bo, 133
Bell, Buddy, 199, 200, 212
Bell, Gus, 146
Beniquez, Juan, 195
Bennett, George, 31, 33, 34–35
Berardino, John, 56, 68
Berenguer, Juan, 220
Berra, Carmen, 108, photo section
Berra, Yogi
  during the 1950 season, 80
  during the 1953 season, 96–97
  during the 1954 season, 105
  during the 1955 season, 117, 120, photo
    section
  barnstorming tours, 100–101, 111, 112, 115,
    photo section
  friendship stories, 108–9, 110
  Stanky story, 193
Berry, Joe, 11
Berry, Raymond, Jr., 5
Berry, Raymond, Sr., 4–5, 118
Bethesda Naval Hospital, 32–33
Beth Thloh Community Center, 39
Beville, Red, 7
Bickford, Vern, 64, 66
Billingham, Jack, 174
Birmingham Barons, 160
Bisher, Furman, 167
Black, Don, 43, 53, 59, 60
Black, Joe, 76
Blackwell, Ewell, 22
Blasingame, Wade, 165
Blattner, Buddy, 30
Blue, Vida, 158–59
Bluefield club, Appalachian League, 136
Blyleven, Bert, 192, 195, 196
Bodie, Gary, 25–27
Bollweg, Don, 103
Bonds, Bobby, 196, 198, 199
bone tumor, ER's, 31–35
Bonnell, Barry, 179

Bonura, Zeke, 9
bonuses, 8, 42, 136, 153
Boston Braves, 45, 62, 64–68, photo section
Boston Red Sox
  during 1938 season, 8
  during the 1948 season, 58, 60, 61–64
  during the 1958 season, 128, 132
  during the 1960s, 139, 205
  during the 1970s, 179, 196
  during the 1980s, 206, 210–11, 220
  during the 1990s, 219, 220, 221
  with ER, photo section
Bouchee, Ed, 146
Bourdreau, Lou
  during the 1942 season, 23
  during the 1946 season, 38
  during the 1947 season, 48–49
  during the 1949 season, 74–75
  during the 1956 season, 124
  snake story, 42
Bourdreau, Lou, during the 1948 season
  with coaching staff, photo section
  regular season games, 45, 52–53, 55, 56, 57,
    60, 61, 62–64
  World Series games, 65, 66, 68, 69
Boyd, Bob, 88
Boyer, Clete, 164, 165, 166
Bradenton, Florida, 157
Bragan, Bobby, 145
Brand, Ron, 153
Breazeale, Jim, 168
Breeding, Marv, 136
Briggs, Walter O., xvi
Bristol, Dave, 181
Brooklyn Dodgers, 14, 36–37, 65, 76, 120
Brown, Bobby, xv–xvi, 37–38, 44, 183, 198, 226,
    photo section
Brown, Hal "Skinny," 137, 139
Brubaker, Ray, 16
Bruce, Bob, 153
Bryant, Paul, Jr., 157
Bryne, Tommy, 37
Buckner, Bill, 165
Bunning, Jim, 124
Burdette, Lew, 168
Burge, Les, 22
Burke, Jackie, 155
Burroughs, Jeff, 190–91
Burtschy, Moe, 123
Busby, Jim, 85, 131, 145
bus travel, 9–10
Byrd, Harry, 103
Byrne, Tommy, 28, 111–12, 115

Cain, Bob, 43
Caldwell, Neal, 7–8, 9
California Angels, 167, 195, 199, 200, 214, 222
Calvert, Paul, 47–48
Camilli, Dolph, 142
Campanella, Roy, 76, 101
Campaneris, Campy, 158, 190, 199
Campbell, Jim, 148, 172
Canesco, Joe, 226
Cannon, Robert, 98
Capra, Buzz, 173–74, 183
Carey, Andy, 113
Carolina League, 151–52
Carrasquel, Chico, 76, 85, 87
car stories, 86, 104, 111–12, 116, 183
Carty, Rico, 164, 165, 166, 168–69, 171
Casey, Hugh, 27
Cashen, Frank, 171, 176
Castle, Edward, 59
Castle, Herb, 88
Cepeda, Orlando, 166, 168, 171
Cerv, Bob, 115
Cey, Ron, 165
Champions Course, 155
Chandler, Happy, 77
Charlie O (mule), 158
Charlie Osborne's Cubs, 3, 4
Chase Hotel, 46
Chicago Cubs, 18, 150, 166–67
Chicago White Sox
   during the 1938 season, 44
   during the 1940s, 49, 57–58, 60
   during the 1950 season, photo section
   during the 1951 season, 52, 80–82, 84–87
   during the 1952 season, 76, 81–82, 87–90, 91, 93
   during the 1953 season, 94, 97
   during the 1954 season, 110
   during the 1957 season, 126–27
   during the 1970s, 178, 179, 196, 207–8
Chilcott, Steve, x, 159
childhood/youth, ER's, 1–5, photo section
Chiles, Eddie, 203–4, 205, 208–9, 213–14
chili cook-off, 222–23
Christopher, Russ, 53, 57, 70
Churn, Chuck, 141, photo section
Chylak, Nestor, 126
Cincinnati Reds, 14, 165, 167, 168, 174
Clark, Allie, 63
Clary, Ellis, 17, 18
Class organization, baseball, 14–15
Clearwater, Florida, 35
Cleveland, Reggie, 196

Cleveland Indians
   during the 1942 season, 21–23, photo section
   during the 1946 season, 35–36, 38–39, 43, 46
   during the 1947 season, 15, 43–44, 46–51
   during the 1948 season, 21, 44–45, 48, 52–71, 120
   during the 1949 season, 73
   during the 1950 season, 80
   during the 1951 season, 86
   during the 1954 season, 46, 104–5
   during the 1957 season, 126, 127
   during the 1958 season, 128
   during the 1980 season, 198
   Veeck's ownership style, 41–43
coaching work. *See* scouting/coaching work, ER's
Coan, Gil, 55
Coca-Cola Bottlers, 4, 7
Colburn, Jim, 195
Coleman, Jerry, 105, 110, 113, photo section
Collins, Joe, 103, 105, 118, 123, photo section
Colt Stadium, playing challenges, 149–50
Comer, Steve, 199, 210, 211
Comiskey Park, hitting challenges, 1, 79, 86, 87–88
Compton, Clint, 165, 167
Conatser, Clint, 68
consultant work, ER's, 216–17, 219–21
Cooper, Cecil, 179
Corbett, Brad
   characterized, xvi, 189–90, photo section
   club purchase/sale, 183, 203
   management decisions, x–xi, 183, 186, 192, 194
   trade activity, x, 190, 195–96, 200, 215
Corbett, Doug, 211
Corrales, Pat, 199, 203, 204, 205, 208–9
Corriden, Red, 79
Courtney, Clint "Scrap Iron," 137–39, 140, 145, 151–52, 181–82, 207, photo section
Courtney, Dorothy, 152
Cox, Bobby, 220
Craft, Harry, 144, 145
Craig, Roger, 146
Craig, Wink, 32, 33
Cramer, Doc, 85, 86
Crimian, Jack, 124
Crosetti, Frankie, 111
Cross, Jeff, 28
Culliman, Craig, 144
curveball stories
   Baltimore Orioles, 135
   Cleveland Indians, 44, 47, 70
   Detroit Tigers, 15
   Elmira Pioneers, 16

League comparisons, 77
Navy team, 24
Washington Senators, 73–74
Cy Young Award players, 160, 199

Daley, Bud, 126–27
Dalkowski, Steve, 135
Dalton, Harry, 140–41, 175
Damone, Vic, 43
Dark, Al, 64, 65, 159, photo section
Darling, Ron, 212–13
Darwin, Danny, 210, 211, 220
David, Henry, 147
Davidson, Donald, 167–68, 174, 184, 185
Daytona Beach, Florida, 157
Deal, Cot, ix–x, 145, 159
Dean, Dizzy, 129–30
deer-hunting story, 72
de Kooning, Elaine, 119
de Kooning, Willem "Bill," 119
Delgado, Felix, 161
DeMaestri, Joe, 124
Demaret, Jimmy, 155
Dent, Bucky, 213
Depression years, 1–4, 8
Deshaies, Jim, 220
Detroit Tigers
   during the 1938 season, 44
   during the 1941 season, 15
   during the 1945 season, 81
   during the 1946 season, 38
   during the 1947 season, 49
   during the 1948 season, 55, 57, 60, 61
   during the 1950s, 43, 106, 124–25, 126
   during the 1970s, 172, 192, 197
   during the 1980s, 207
   during the early 2000s, 222
Devine, Adrian, 190, 196
DeWitt, Bill, 89
Dickey, Bill, 30, 110–11
Dickson, Murry, 75
Didier, Bob, 166
Dierker, Larry, 153
Dillinger, Bob, 48, 85, 89
DiMaggio, Dom, 28, 63
DiMaggio, Joe, 38, 50, 56, 74
Disch, Billy, 8
divorce, ER's, 29, 80
Dobson, Joe, 73
Dobson, Pat, 171–72
Doby, Larry, 37, 49–50, 60, 63, 66, 70, photo
   section
Doerr, Bobby, 63

Donohue, Don, 172, 175, 178, 181, 183, 184,
   photo section
Donohue, Marilyn, 172
Donovan, Art, 118
Doppler radar training, 30
Douglas, Hal, xv
Downing, Al, 174
draft selections. *See* player selections
dream story, 121
Drott, Dick, 146
drug arrest story, 204
Drysdale, Don, 77
Duke, Willie, 17
Duncan, Dave, 157
Duncan, Taylor, 171
Dunn, Jack, III, 139
Duquette, Dan, 220–21
Duren, Ryne, 77
Durham Bulls, 151–52
Dykes, Jimmy, 94, 97

Early, Tom, 28
Eastern League, 16–17, 19, 21, 22, photo section
Eddie Lopat All-Stars, 100–101, photo section
Eddie Robinson Day, 88–89
education, ER's, 2–4, 8, 13
Edwards, Hank, 48
Elder, Eddie (son), 28–29
Elder, Ed (father), 29
Elder, Elayne (later Robinson), 28–29, 34, 51,
   68–69, 80
Elder, Mrs. Ed, 29
Elliott, Bob, 64–65, 66, 67, 68
Ellis, Dock, 195, 199
Ellis, John, 213
Elmira Pioneers, 16–17, 19, photo section
Embree, Red, 16–17
Ennis, Del, 95
Erner, Cal, 194
Erskine, Carl, 98
Erstad, Darin, 222
Essian, Jim, 179
Estrada, Chuck, 133, 137
Europe visit, 116
Evans, Darrell, 168, 171, 173

Face, Elroy, 77
Fain, Ferris, 75, 93, 94
Fair, Zora, 163
Fanning, Jim, 164
Fanning, John, 213
Farlow, Bette. *See* Robinson, Bette (earlier Farlow,
   wife of ER)

farm director job, ER's, 163–64
Farrell, Dick "Turk," 146, 150, 153
Farrell, Kerby, 126, 127
Feeney, Chub, 175
Feller, Bob
    during the 1949 season, 73
    characterized, 44–45
    museum, 55
    and Players Association, 98
Feller, Bob, during the 1948 season
    regular season games, 44–45, 53, 54, 60, 61, 63
        World Series games, 65, 66–67, 70
Ferguson, Joe, 165
Fernster, Hank, 28, 30
Ferrell, Rick, 71, 72
Ferrick, Tom, 157
Fetzer, John, xvi
Fidrych, Mark "the Bird," 197
Fingers, Rollie, 160
Finigan, Jim, 103, 124
Finley, Carl, 157
Finley, Charlie, xvi, 154, 157–60, 163, 179, 180
fire department work, ER's, 17
Fisher, Jack, 133, 137, 139
Fisher, Lloyd, 94
Fisher, Milt, 133
fitness coach, Texas Rangers, 208–9
Fitzgerald, Lou, 133, 140, photo section
Fitzsimmons, Mike, 209
Flair, Al, 16
Fleming, Les, 35, 49
Florence, Paul, 145
Florida Coastline Railroad, 14
Flynn, Doug, 212
Ford, Whitey, 104, 113, 115, 120, photo section
Foster, Dan, 100
Fox, Nellie, 80, 81, 85, 87, 100–101, 126, photo section
Foxx, Jimmy, 87
Franco, Julio, 166
Francona, Tito, 141–42
Frank, Morris, 18
Franks, Herman, 27
Frazier, George, 220
free agency, beginnings, 99, 190, 210–11
Freeman, Jimmy Lee, 171
freight line work, ER's, 3–4
Friend, Bob, 77
Frisella, Danny, 171, 173–74

Gabler, Frank, 107, 139–40, 142, 154, photo section
Gaedel, Eddie, 43

Galehouse, Denny, 62, 63
Gallick, Pat, 149
Gamble, Oscar, 88, 200
"A Game Guys' Prayer" (Stephens), 13–14
Garcia, Mike, 45, 75, 100, photo section
Garr, Ralph, 164, 168, 169, 171, 176
Garrido, Gil, 166
Garver, Ned, 124
Garvey, Steve, 165
Gaston, Clarence "Cito," 183
Gehrig, Lou, 87
Gentile, Jim, 136–37
Gentry, Gary, 167, 171, 173–74
Georgia-Florida League, 9–11
Gettel, Al, 53
Gibson, Bob, 77
Giles, Warren, 146
Gillick, Pat, photo section
Giusti, Dave, 153
Gladden, Don, 220
Gleason, Jimmy, 27
Golden, Jim, 146
Gold Glove winners, 195, 200, 212
    golf, 124, 140, 146–47, 150–51, 155, 201, 208, 221
Gonzalez, Tony, 166
Goodman, Billy, 75, photo section
Gordon, Joe
    during the 1947 season, 43, 46, 48, 49
    during the 1951 season, 81
Gordon, Joe, during the 1948 season
    and ER's father, 51
    regular season games, 53, 56, 63, 64, 72
    with teammates, photo section
    World Series games, 65, 67, 69
Gossage, Goose, 196
Governor's Cup games, Eastern League, 16–17
"Grandstand Managers" night, 43
Granger, Wayne, 168
Gray, Captain, 31, 32
Gray, John, 103
Green, Dick, 158
Greenberg, Hank, 15, 41, 52, 87, photo section
Greenwich Village, 118–19
Grieve, Tom, ix–xi, 159, 196, 207
Griffin, Pee Wee, 2, 13
Griffith, Clark, xvi, 71, photo section
Grissom, Marv, 81–82
Gromek, Steve, 53, 57, 66, 70
Grote, Jerry, 153
guard duty, ER's Navy service, 30
Guidry, Ron, 196
Gustafson, Gus, 24–25

Hall of Fame players, ER's contact
  Baltimore Orioles period, 133, 137, 141
  Chicago White Sox period, 80, 83, 85
  Cleveland Indians period, 21, 46, 69, photo
    section
  Detroit Tigers period, 124
  Houston Colt .45s period, 145
  Kansas City Athletics period, 159
  Lopat All-Stars tour, 100
  New York Yankees period, 110, 111
  retirement years, 222
  Washington Senators period, 71
Halper, Barry, 54–55
Hamper, Joe, 119–20
Hand, Rich, 78
Hansen, Ron, 137
Harata, Cappy, 179–80
Harder, Mel, 23, 38, photo section
Hargrove, Mike, 200
Harrah, Toby, 195, 199
Harrelson, Ken, 148, 158
Harridge, Will, 43
Harrington, Bill, 124
Harris, Luman
  with Atlanta Braves, 164, 169–70
  with Baltimore Orioles, 133–34
  with Chicago White Sox, 86
  and F. Gabler, 139
  with Houston Colt .45s, 144, 145
  and P. Richards, 82
  with Philadelphia Athletics, 23
Harrison, Roric, 171, 179
Harrist, Earl, 145
Hartman trunk, 17
Hatcher, Billy, 220
Hatton, Grady, 144
Hawaii, 30–32, 100–101, 112, 113
Hawkins, Bert, 191
Hayes, Charlie, 220
Haynes, Joe, 71
Heath, Jeff, 23, 65
Hegan, Jim
  drinking story, 47
  military service, 24
Hegan, Jim, during the 1948 season
  regular season games, 45, 46, 56, 63
  World Series games, 66, 67, 68
Hemond, Roland, 178, 179
Henderson, Ken, 190
Herman, Billy, 30
Herzog, Whitey, 106, 181–82
Hickman, Jim, 146
high school years, ER's, 3–5, photo section
Hiroshima, 114

Hitchcock, Billy, 64, 164
Hodges, Gil, 146
Hoeft, Billy, 126
Hoffman, John, 153
Hofheinz, Roy, 144, 149, 153–54
Hogan, Ben, 201
Hollywood, Florida, 18, 21
Holmes, Tommy, 64, 65, 68
Holzka, Joe, 119
Holtzman, Ken, 166–67
home runs, ER's
  Baltimore Orioles, 22, 37, 38
  Chicago White Sox, 80, 87–88
  Cleveland Indians, 38, 42, 56–57, 61, 71,
    126
  Kansas City Athletics, 124
  Naval World Series, photo section
  New York Yankees, 118
  Philadelphia Athletics, 94
  Valdosta Trojans, 11
  Washington Senators, 79
Honeycutt, Rick, 207, 210, 211
Hoover Hogs, 2
Hope, Bob, 41, 44
Hornsby, Rogers, 58, 72–73
Horton, Willie, 192, 195
Host, Gene, 124
Hostetler, Dave, 212
Hough, Charlie, 204–5, 213
Hough, Dick, 205
Houk, Ralph, 109, 111, 119, 206
House, Tom, 174
Houston Astros, 83, 151–53, 167, 219
Houston Colt .45s
  during the 1962 season, 150
  during the 1963 season, 147
  coach/management personnel, 143, 144, 145,
    148–49, photo section
  name change, 152
  roster development, 144–46
  spring training, 146–47
  stadium facilities, 149–50
Houtteman, Art, 55
Howard, Elston, 76, 117
Howell, Dixie, 145
Howell, Roy, 211
Howsam, Bob, 175
Howser, Dick, 206, 207
Hudson, Sid, 79
Hunter, Billy, 194–95, 199
Hunter, Catfish, 157–58, 160
hunting story, 72
Hutchinson, Freddie, 26–27, 28, 38
hypnotist story, 173

India, 115–16
infield practice, changes, 84
injuries, ER's, 10, 31–35, 50
instructional league, Houston's, 150
integration, racial, 36–37, 49–50, 55, 76, 117,
    photo section
Irvin, Monte, 76
Italy, 116

Jackson, Larry, 77
Jackson, Reggie, x, 159
Jackson, Sonny, 83, 153, 166
Japan, 101, 113–15, 179–80, photo section
Jarvis, Pat, 165, 166, 171, 172
Jenkins, Fergie, 196, 199, 204, 210, 211
Jensen, Jackie, 100–101, photo section
jewelry store work, ER's, 28
Jewish community center, 39
Johnson, Darrell, 214
Johnson, Davey, 171, 172, 173, 179–80
Johnson, John Henry, 210
Johnson, Johnny, 174
Johnson, Ken, 146, 165
Johnson, Lamar, 212
Jones, Andrew, 177
Jones, Red, 45
Joost, Eddie, 70, 95
Judnich, Walt, 60, 65
Jurges, Billy, 145

Kansas City Athletics, ix–x, 123–28, 138–39, 154,
    157–61, 163
Kansas City Royals, 195, 199, 206, 211
Katz Jewelry Store, 28
Kay, Stanley, 112
Kazak, Eddie, 14
Keane, Johnny, 11
Kell, George, 74
Keltner, Ken
    during 1942 season, 21, 23
    during 1947 season, 48
Keltner, Ken, during the 1948 season
    regular season games, 53, 56, 60, 63, 64
    with teammates, photo section
    World Series games, 65, 67, 69
Kennedy, Bob, 62–63, 66
Kennedy, John F., 119
Kern, Jim, 199, 200, 204, 210, 212
Killebrew, Harmon, 194
Kimbrel, Casey, 14
Kinder, Ellis, 63–64
King, Clyde, 175, 181
Kirksey, George, 144
Klein, Joe, 207

Klieman, Eddie, 53, 56, 57, 71
Klinger, Bob, 30
Knoxville Smokies, 7–9
knuckleball stories
    during the 1940s, 17, 66
    during the 1950s, 127, 128, 137
    during the 1960s, 138, 165
    during the 1980s 204-205, 138, 165
    during the 1990s, 221
Konstanty, Jim, 77
Koosman, Jerry, 167
Korean War, 110
Koufax, Sandy, 77
Kozar, Al, 55, 79
Kramer, Jack, 61
Kretlow, Lou, 61
Krivsky, Wayne, 207
Kubek, Tony, 104
Kucks, Johnny, 113, 124
Kuenn, Harvey, 100, photo section
Kuhel, Joe, 71, 73–74, photo section
Kuhn, Bowie, 158, 174, 176, 180, 186, 191, 204
Kuzava, Bob, 79

Lackey, John, 222
Landis, Danny, 165
Landrith, Hobie, 146
Lane, Frank, 86–87, 89, 91, 93
Larker, Norm, 146
Larsen, Don, 69, 104
La Russa, Tony, 82, 160
Lasorda, Tommy, 204
Latin American players, 76–77
Lauzerique, George, 160
leg surgeries, ER's, 31–35
Leja, Frank, photo section
Lemaster, Denny, 165
Lemon, Bob
    during the 1942 season, 21
    during the 1946 season, 36
    during the 1947 season, 46–47
    during the 1954 season, 45
    Lopat All-Stars tour, 100, photo section
    military service, 21, 24
Lemon, Bob, during the 1948 season
    regular season games, 53, 54, 55, 57–58, 61, 63
    World Series games, 65–66, 67–68, 70
Lersch, Barry, 173
Lillis, Bob, 146
Litwhiler, Danny, 83
Livingston, Dr., 32
Lockman, Whitey, 111
lockout of players, 175–76, 186
Loes, Billy, 130–31

Logan, Johnny, 146
Longoria, Evan, 177
Lopat, Eddie, 56, 100–101, 111, 154, 157, photo
    section
Lopes, Davey, 165
Los Angeles Dodgers, 136, 165, 174, 177, 179–80,
    204
Lucas, Bill, 164, 181, 187, 191
Lucchesi, Frank, 191, 192–93
Lukon, Eddie, 10, 14
Lutrey, Frank, 148
Lutrey, Jean, 148
Lyle, Sparky, 199, 204

Mack, Connie, xvi, 53–54
Macon, Max, 22, photo section
MacPhail, Andy, 219, 220
MacPhail, Lee, 134, 143, 175
Maglie, Sal, 16, photo section
Mahler, Mickey, 183
Majeski, Hank, 22
Major League Baseball Players' Alumni
    Association, 100
management positions, ER's
    Atlanta Braves, 163–64, 169–87
    Houston Astros, 152–54
    Houston Colt .45s, 143–52
    Kansas City Athletics, 154, 157–60
    Texas Rangers, 189–201, 203–14
Mantilla, Felix, 146
Mantle, Mickey, 75, 87, 109–10, 118
Marchetti, Gino, 118
Marrero, Connie, 79
marriages, ER's, 28–29, 113
Martin, Billy
    during the 1950s seasons, 110–11, 120
    during the 1978 season, 196
    during the 1980s, 217
    barnstorming tours, 100–101, 114–15, photo
        section
    brawl story, 138
    Stengel relationship, 106
Martin, Nick, 189
Martinez, Pedro, 220
Masi, Phil, 65, 68
Masterson, Walt, 27
Mathews, Eddie, 75, 100–101, 170–71, 172,
    174–75, photo section
Matlack, Jon, 196, 199, 200, 210
Mattick, Bobby, 144–45
May, Dave, 178, 190
Mays, Willie, 76
Mazzilli, Lee, 212–13
McCarthy, Joe, 62, 63

McClain, Bully, 7
McClure, Gertrude, 157
McClure, H. A., 25–26, 28
McCormick, Mike, 65, 67, 68
McCovey, Willie, 132–33
McCoy, Benny, 28, photo section
McCullough, Clyde, 18
McDermott, Mickey, 108, 124
McDougald, Gil, 105, 109, 113, 120
McGraw, Tug, 185
McGuirk, Terry, 184–85, 220
McHale, John, 124, 125, 164
McKechnie, Bill, 38, 48–49, photo section
McKinley, Bill, 75
McLaughlin, Jim, 136
McNally, Dave, 99
McNamara, John, 160
McQueen, Mike, 165, 168
Meason, Sam, 214
Medich, Doc, 196, 210–11, 212
Mejias, Roman, 146, 150
Melillo, Oscar, 38
Mendoza, Mario, 207
Menke, Denis, 164
Messersmith, Andy, 99
Michaels, Cass, 79, photo section
Milan, Clyde "Deerfoot," 7, 71–72, 73
military service, ER's, 24–28, 29–34
Millan, Felix, 164, 165, 166, 171
Miller, Marvin, 98–99, 175, 176, 186
Milwaukee Brewers, 41, 178, 211
Miner's Camp restaurant, 147
Minnesota Twins, 167, 219–20
minor league baseball, ER's
    as Atlanta farm director, 164
    as Baltimore field director/scout, 132–36
    as field director/scout, 132–36
    as Houston assistant manager, 148–49, 150–52
    as Kansas City assistant manager, 158–60
    as player, 7–11, 14–19
Minosa, Minnie, 76, 86, 126, photo section
Miranda, Willie, 131, 141
Mitchell, Dale, 43, 48, 53, 66, 67, 69
Mizell, Vinegar Bend, 146
Monroe, Marilyn, 38, 84–85, 121
Montreal Expos, 172, 212, 220–21, photo section
Montreal Royals, 22, 36–37
Moody Field, fire department work, 17
Moore, Curtis, 165
Moore, Gene, 22
Moret, Roger, 196–98
Morgan, Joe, 83, 145, 153
Morrell, Bill, 9, 10, 11, 19
Morton, Carl, 172, 175

Most Valuable Player winners, ii, 37–38, 46, 69, 81, 158, 166, 190
Moultrie, Georgia, 147, 148
mule, Finley's, 158
Mulholland, Terry, 220
Murff, Red, 145
Murphy, Dale, 183
Murray, Ray, 95, 96–97
Mutscheller, Jim, 118
Mutter, Allene, 148–49

Napp, Larry, 97, 128
Narleski, Ray, 47
Nash, Jim, 168, 171
Naval World Series, 29–30, photo section
Navy service, ER's, 24–28, 29–34
Newark Bears, 37, 38
Newbill, Mike, 223
Newcombe, Don, 76
New England Patriots, 5
Newhouser, Hal, 61, 81
Newsom, Bobo, 95–96
New York Giants, 76, 105, 132–33, 137, 142
New York Mets
    during the 1960s, x, 146, 150, 159, 167
    during the 1970s, 90–91, 171, 173–74, 192, 196
    during the 1982 season, 212–13
New York Yankees
    during the 1947 season, 43–44, 47, 50–51
    during the 1948 season, 53–54, 56–57, 58, 59–61, photo section
    during the 1950 season, 80
    during the 1953 season, 96–97
    during the 1954 season, 45, 103–6
    during the 1955 season, 76, 106, 117–18, 120–21, photo section
    during the 1956 season, 123, 124
    during the 1959 season, 136, 137
    during the 1961 season, 142
    during the 1970s, 171–72, 195, 196, 199, 200
    during the 1980s, 206, 213, 215–17, 219
    barnstorming tours, 111–12, 113–15, photo section
    brawl story, 138
    platooning practices, 78
    player/manager descriptions, 105–11
Niarhos, Gus, 100, 111, photo section
Nicholson, Dave, 136, 141
'Niekro, Joe, 172
Niekro, Phil
    during the 1960s, 165, 166, 167
    during the 1970s, 168, 171, 175, 183
    during the 1990s, 221
Nieman, Bob, 131–32, 180

Nobles, Pop, 4, 8
Norfolk Naval Air Station, 27
Norfolk Training Station, 24–28, 29–30, photo section
Norman, Nelson, 196, 199
North Carolina Preflight School, 27
Northeast Texas Motor Freight Line, 3–4

Oak Knoll Naval Hospital, 32
Oakland A's, 158, 160, 163, 168, 179, 211, 226
Oakland Oaks, 53
Oates, Johnny, 171, 179, 183
O'Brien, Danny, 194
Odom, Blue Moon, 157, 160
Oklahoma City club, Texas League, 48
Oliver, Al, 196, 198, 199, 212
O'Malley, Peter, 180
O'Malley, Walter, 176
Osborne, Charlie, 3
Ostrowski, John, 79
Owens, Paul, 178, 179
Oxford, Georgia, 163

Pacific Coast League, 36, 130
Paciorek, John, 145, 147–48
Paciorek, Tom, 147–48, 165
Padgett, Don, 28, photo section
Page, Joe, 56–57, 77
Page, Patti, 112, photo section
Paige, Satchel, 43, 55–58, 67, 165
Pappas, Milt, 133, 137, 165, 166
Paris, Texas, 1–5, 13, photo section
Paris Coca-Cola Bottlers, photo section
Paris Junior College Dragons, 13, 221
Parrish, Larry, 212, 213
Patkin, Max, 30–31, 42
Patterson, Pat, 17–18
Paul, Gabe, 143, 145, 190
Paul, Mary, 190
Pearl Harbor, 17
pecan farm, ER's, 221, 222
Peck, Hal, 46, 56, 57
Peckinpaugh, Roger, 36
Peel, Homer, 24
pension plans, 97–98, 100
performance-enhancing drugs, 99, 226–27
Perini, Lou, 66
Perrick, Art, 157
Perry, Gaylord, 195
Pesky, Johnny, 27, 63
Peterson, Myrna, 157
Pete (woman), 89–91
Philadelphia Athletics
    during the 1940s, 17, 23, 53–54, 70

during the 1950s, 87, 93–98, 103, 112, photo
section
during the 1960 season, 138–39
Philadelphia Phillies, 142, 178–79, 204, 222
Philley, Dave, 58, 87, 94–95, 151
Phoenix Giants, 133
Pickerel, Clarence, 16–17, 19
pick-off play stories, 65–66, 110, 113–14, 126–27
Pieretti, Marino, 80
Pike, Jess, 16–17
Pilarcik, Al, 135
pinch hitting, ER's
Cleveland Indians, 23, 126, 127
Detroit Tigers, 125
New York Yankees, 105–6, 118, 120, 123
Pine Forest Country Club, 221
Pittsburgh Pirates, 52, 104, 196
Pittsfield High School, ix–x
platooning practices, 77–78
Players Association, 97–100, 175–76, 186, 210,
211, 220, 225–26
player selections
Baltimore Orioles, 22–23, 36, 128, 132–33,
136, 171
Boston Red Sox, 196, 220, 221
Brooklyn Dodgers, 87
California Angels, 167
Cincinnati Reds, 165
Cleveland Indians, 21–22, 53, 71, 86, 128, 199
Detroit Tigers, 124, 192, 207
ER philosophy, 199–200
Houston Astros, 143, 153, 220
Houston Colt .45s, 145, 146
Kansas City Athletics, 123, 124, 158–59
Los Angeles Dodgers, 165
Milwaukee Brewers, 178
Montreal Expos, 172, 212
New York Mets, 171, 173, 192, 196, 212–13
Oakland A's, 168
Philadelphia Athletics, 87, 93, 103
Philadelphia Phillies, 178–79, 204, 220
Pittsburgh Pirates, 196
San Diego Padres, 166, 200
Seattle Mariners, 207
St. Louis Browns, 43
St. Louis Cardinals, 104, 166
Washington Senators, 71, 79
player selections, Atlanta Braves
during the 1960s, 165, 166, 167
during the 1970s, 168, 171–72, 173, 178–79,
190–91, 196
player selections, Chicago White Sox
during the 1940s, 71
during the 1950s, 76, 79, 86–87, 93

during the 1970s, 178, 179, 196
player selections, New York Yankees
during the 1950s, 44, 103, 104, 123
during the 1970s, 171–72, 199, 200
during the 1980s, 213
player selections, Texas Rangers
during the 1970s, 190–91, 192, 195–96,
199–200
during the 1980s, 204, 207, 212–13
Pocoroba, Biff, 183
Podres, Johnny, 120
Pohlad, Carl, xvi
Porterfield, Bob, 57
Potter, Nelson, 66–67
Powell, Boog, 141
Power, Vic, 103
Preibisch, Mel, 28
Price, Jackie, 42
Priddy, Bob, 167
Pudenz, Dr., 33, 34
purchases. *See* player selections
Putnam, Pat, 200

Quinn, Bob, 220

racial integration, 36–37, 49–50, 55, 76, 117,
photo section
radar gun, pitching speeds, 83
Radatz, Dick, 77
Rader, Doug, 153
railroad work, ER's, 14
Ramos, Pedros, 118
Randle, Lenny, 191–92
Ranew, Merritt, 146
Rapp, Earl, 145
Rapp, Vern, 207
Raschi, Vic, 56
Ray, Jim, 153
Reed, Ron, 165, 166, 168, 171, 175, 183
Reese, Pee Wee, 27, 30
Reeves, Jim, 192
relief pitchers, role changes, 77
Renna, Bill, 103, 123
reserve clause, 89, 98, 99, 226
restaurant business, ER's, 5, 54–55, 118–20, 124,
143
retirement years, ER's, 221–23
retrospective, ER's, 225–27
Reyes, Napoleon, 161
Reynolds, Allie, 42, 43–44, 50, 98
Richards, Paul
Atlanta Braves, 107, 163, 164, 165, 166, 167, 169
Baltimore Orioles, 82–83, 127, 129–35, 137,
138–39, 142

characterized, 80–84, 135–36
golf passion, 130, 140, 146–47, 150–51, 155
Houston Colt .45s/Astros, 119, 143, 144–54,
   photo section
Texas Rangers, 207–8, 213
White Sox, 80–84, 85, 88, 93
Richardson, Spec, 144, 154
Richmond Braves, 152, 181–82
Rickert, Marv, 65, 66
Riggs, Bobby, 31
Righetti, Dave, 199
Rigney, Johnny, 28, 30
Riley, Branch, 77
Rivers, Mickey, 167, 200, 209–10, 212, 213
Rizzuto, Phil, 28, 90, 105–6, 107, 110
Roberts, Leon, 207
Roberts, Mary, 227
Roberts, Robin, 77, 98, 100–101, 146, 227, photo
   section
Robertson, Al, 103
Robertson, Sherry, 74
Robinson, Aaron (not related to ER), 58
Robinson, Andrew (grandson of ER), 221, 222
Robinson, Bethany (great-granddaughter of ER),
   222
Robinson, Bette (earlier Farlow, wife of ER)
   anniversary celebration, photo section
   Atlanta Braves period, 163, 183
   Berra friendship, 108
   children of, 126, 127, 143–44, 154
   Cleveland Indians period, 126, 127
   courtship/honeymoon, 112–13, 115–16, photo
      section
   Detroit Tigers period, 124
   Houston period, 143, 148, 154
   Kansas City period, 154, 158–59
   New York Yankees period, 47, 118–19, 123–24,
      216–17
   retirement years, 221–22, 227
   Texas Rangers period, 215
Robinson, Brooks (not related to ER), 119–20,
   130, 141
Robinson, Drew (son of ER), 143–44, 154,
   158–59, 189, 222, photo section
Robinson, Eddie
   career summarized, xv–xvi
   childhood/youth, 1–5, photo section
   foreword about, ix–xi
   marriages/divorce, 28–29, 80, 113
   military service, 24–28, 29–34
   preface by, xiii–xiv
   *See also specific topics, e.g.,* batting averages,
      ER's; minor league baseball, ER's; New
      York Yankees

Robinson, Ed (father of ER), 1, 51–52
Robinson, Elayne (born Elder, first wife of ER),
   28, 34, 51, 68–69, 80
Robinson, Erin (daughter-in-law of ER), 222
Robinson, Frank (not related to ER), 76
Robinson, George (cousin of ER), 3
Robinson, Hannah (granddaughter of ER), 222
Robinson, Hazel (mother of ER), 1, 8, photo
   section
Robinson, Jackie (not related to ER), 36–37, 50,
   photo section
Robinson, Louis (uncle of ER), 3–4, 8
Robinson, Lynn (daughter-in-law of ER), 221–22
Robinson, Marc (son of ER), 124, 127, 154,
   158–59, 189, 222, photo section
Robinson, Marilue (daughter-in-law of ER), 222
Robinson, Mary (daughter-in-law of ER), 222
Robinson, Paul (son of ER), 143–44, 154, 158–
   59, 189, 222, photo section
Robinson, Rachel (granddaughter of ER), 222
Robinson, Robby Ann (daughter of ER), 28, 29
Robinson, Robby IV (grandson of ER), 222
Robinson, Shane (grandson of ER), 222
Robinson, Taylor (grandson of ER), 222
Robinson, William E., III "Robby" (son of ER),
   28, 29, 51, 80, 221–22, photo section
Robinson, William E., V "Quinn"(great-grand
   son of ER), 222
Robintech company, 203
Rochelli, Lou, 14
Rochester Red Wings, 125–26, 152
Rodriguez, Hector, 76
Rommel, Ed, 131
Rookie of the Year winners, 86, 104, 137, 169, 200
Rosen, Al, 87
Rosenberg, Aaron, 24
Rowland, June, 4
Roy Campanella All-Stars, 101
Rudi, Joe, 160
Ruel, Muddy, 38
Runyon, Paul, 30
Russell, Jack, 8–9, 35
Ruth, Babe, 54–55, 87, photo section
Ryan, Connie, 68, 159, 174, 181, 194
Ryan, Nolan, 167

Saban, Lou, 216
Sain, Johnny, 64, 65, 66
salaries
   arbitration impact, 99, 176–78
   Atlanta Braves, 126
   Chicago Cubs, 18
   Chicago White Sox, 89
   Cleveland Indians, 126

minor league baseball, 14, 15, 18
performance-based proposal, 175–76
Philadelphia Athletics, 93
Players Association impact, 225–26
Salkeld, Bill, 65, 67
Sally League, 117–18
San Diego Padres, 166, 200
Sanford, Jack, 77
Saucier, Frank, 43
Sauer, Hank, 100, photo section
Savannah Athletics, 117–18
Saverine, Bobby, 136
S & B Manufacturing Co., 203
Scarborough, Ray, 23, 56, 79, 80
Schacht, Al, 30
Schaeffer, Rudie, 42–43
Scheffing, Bob, 167, 173–74, 186
Schoendienst, Red, 146
scholarship offer, ER's, 8
Schuerholz, John, 220
Scott, Frank, 25, 100, photo section
Scottsdale, Arizona, 129–30
scouting/coaching work, ER's
    Baltimore Orioles, 132–42, 144
    Houston Colt .45s, 145, 150, 153
    as independent consultant, 216–17, 219–21
    New York Yankees, 215–17, 219
Seattle Mariners, 192, 207
Seaver, Tom, 167
Selig, Bud, 178
semi-pro baseball, ER's, 4, 7
Sepkowski, Ted, 22–23, 24, photo section
Serena Hotel, 103–4
Shady Oaks Country Club, 201
Shantz, Bobby, 95, 146, photo section
Shaughnessy, Frank, 37–38
Shavitz, Meme, 39
Shea, Frank "Spec," 56
Sheldon, Hunter, 33, 34
Shokes, Eddie, 27, 30
Short, Bob, 183
Shreveport Sports, 152
Shula, Don, 118
Siebern, Norm, 123
sign stealing, 58–59
Silvera, Charlie, 114, photo section
Silverman, Morris, 125
Simmons, Curt, 75, 77, 100, photo section
Sisti, Sibby, 68
Skizas, Lou, 123
Skowron, Bill "Moose," 103, 106, 115, 118, 121, 123, photo section
Slaughter, Enos, 75, 100–101, 104, 113, photo section

sliding pads, 10
Smith, Bobby Gene, 146
Smith, Hal, 146
Smith, R. E. "Bob," 144, 153–54
Smith, Tal, 144, 148, 154
Smith, Vinnie, 28, 30
Smoltz, John, 222
Southern Association, 7–9, 160
Southworth, Billy, 65, 66, 67
Spahn, Warren, 64, 65–66, 67, 68, 74
Spangler, Al, 146
Speaker, Tris, 52, photo section
Springfield Nationals, 16
spring training
    Atlanta Braves, 164, 165–66, 173, 185–86
    Baltimore Orioles, 15–16, 18, 129–30, 134, 135, 136, 139–40
    Chicago White Sox, 81, 84–85, 137–38
    Cleveland Indians, 35–36, 51, 72
    Detroit Tigers, 124
    Houston Colt .45s, 146–47
    Knoxville Smokies, 8–9
    lockout dispute, 175–76
    New York Yankees, 103–4, 106, 117–18
    Philadelphia Athletics, 93–94
    Texas Rangers, 191, 209, 210, 212
    Washington Senators, 72–73
St. Louis Browns
    during the 1944 season, 62
    during the 1948 season, 48, 53, 55, 59, 61
    during the 1949 season, 89
    during the 1951 season, 43
    during the 1952 season, 87, 137–38
    during the 1954 season, 127, 137
St. Louis Cardinals
    during the 1940s, 14, 62
    during the 1950s, 104
    during the 1960s, 165, 166
    during the 1970s, x, 173
St. Petersburg, Florida, 103–4
Staller, George "Stopper," 22
Stallings, Lynwood, 149
Stanky, Eddie, 65, 68, 192–94
Staub, Rusty, 145, 153
Stein, Bill, 207, 211
Steinbrenner, George, xvi, 190, 206, 215–17, 219
Stengel, Casey
    during the 1947 season, 47
    during the 1953 season, 75
    during the 1954 season, 106–8
    during the 1955 season, 106, 118, 120
    during the 1956 season, 123
    barnstorming tour, 114
    characterized, 141

drinking stories, 107–8
Europe visit, 116
housekeeper problem, 90–91
management style, 78, 105, 106–7, 141
Stengel, Edna, 91, 108, 116
Stephens, George, 13–14, photo section
Stephens, Vern, 61, 63, photo section
steroids, 99, 226–27
Stewart, Bill, 65
Stewart, Eddie, 55–56
Stockyard Inn, 88
stolen bases, ER's, 85
Stone, George, 166
strawberry injuries, 10
streaker story, Berra's, 108–9
strikes, player, 99, 211, 220
Suder, Pete, 23
suicide story, Turner's, 187
Sullivan, Haywood, 196, 206
Sundberg, Jim, 194–95, 198
Surkont, Max, 22
Susce, George, 38
Swallow, Ray, 157
swim training, military service, 25
Syracuse Chiefs, 37

Tallis, Cedric, 187
Tampa Bay Rays, 177
Tanana, Frank, 212
Tasby, Willie, 131
Taylor, Zack, 43
Tebbetts, Birdie, 64
television revenues, 97–98, 99
Tenace, Gene, 158
Tepedino, Frank, 176
Terrell, Walt, 212–13
Terry, Bill, 142
Terwilliger, Wayne, 207
Texas League, 48, 152
Texas Rangers
    during the 1976 season, 189–90
    during the 1977 season, x, 190–96
    during the 1978 season, 196–98, 199
    during the 1979 season, x–xi, 198–201
    during the 1980 season, 203–4, 209
    during the 1981 season, 205–11
    during the 1982 season, 211–14
    during the 2009 season, 177
    sale of, 183, 203
Thomas, Tommy, 15, 22, 36, 132, photo section
Thompson, Mike, 173
Tighe, Jack, 124
Tipton, Joe, 64, 71, 87
tobacco chewing, 19

Tokyo Giants, 179–80
Topping, Dan, xvi
Torgeson, Earl, 65, 66, 68, 125
Toronto Blue Jays, 145, 186, 195
Torre, Joe, 164, 165, 166, 169
trades. *See* player selections
train travel, 36, 112–13
Triandos, Gus, 131
Trout, Dizzy, 61
Trucks, Virgil, 30, 124
Truman, Bess, photo section
Truman, Harry, 79, photo section
trunk trays, 36
Tucker, Thurman, 46, 56, 60, 67, 68
Tunney, Gene, 24
Turner, Ted, xvi, 181, 183–87, 191, photo section

Uecker, Bob, 165
Umbricht, Jim, 146
Unitas, Johnny, 118
University of Texas, 8
Upshaw, Cecil, 165, 166, 167, 168, 171

Valdosta, Georgia, 8–10, 17
Valdosta Trojans, 9–11, 14–15, 19
Valentine, Bobby, 165
Valentine, Fred, 141
Valo, Elmer, 94
Vanderbilt, Alfred Gwynne, 24
Vander Meer, Johnny, 26, 28
Veeck, Bill
    characterized, xvi, 41–43
    club purchases, 41, 43, 83, 207
    management personnel, 15, 52
    night-game fundraiser, 60
    pennant win celebration, 64
    player transactions, 46–47, 53, 55
    Silverman's offer, 125–26
    World Series, 66, 68–69, photo section
Vernon, Mickey, 30, 71
Vincent, Al, 130
Virdon, Bill, 104
Voiselle, Bill, 64, 67
Volkswagen stories, 104, 116

Wagner, Charlie, 28
Wagner, Dick, 219, 220
Wagner, Mark, 207
Waitkus, Eddie, 90
Wakefield, Tim, 221
Walerus, Dr., 31–32, 33
Walker, Jerry, 133, 137
Walker, Larry, 220
Walls, Lee, 146

Warwick, Carl, photo section
Washington, Claudell, 183, 196
Washington Senators
    during the 1930s, 7
    during the 1941 season, 18
    during the 1942 season, 23
    during the 1947 season, 46–47, 71
    during the 1948 season, 55, 56, 57–58
    during the 1949 season, 72–74, 79, photo
        section
    during the 1950 season, 80
    during the 1970s, x
Watson, Bob, 153, 187
Weatherly, Roy, 23
Weaver, Earl, 82–83, 141, 171
Webb, Del, xvi
Weisman, Lefty, 44, 46, 59
Western Company, 203, 213
West Palm Beach, Florida, 164
Wetteland, John, 220
White, Hal, 38
Widmar, Al, 87
Wight, Bill, 57, 110, 126–27, 145
Wilhelm, Hoyt, 127–28, 137, 167, 171
Wilkes-Barre Barons, 16–17, 21, 22
Williams, Dick, 82
Williams, Earl, 169, 171
Williams, John Henry, 78
Williams, Ted
    during the 1941 season, 17
    during the 1948 season, 61, 63
    with ER, photo section
    female fan problem, 90
    hitting philosophy, 74
    military service, 27
    post-career, 78
Williams, Walt "No-Neck," 145
Williamsport Grays, 17
Wills, Bump, 191, 195, 212
Wills, Maury, 173

Wilson, Don, 153
Wilson, Jim, 134
Wilson, Maxie, 28
*Winchester 73*, 24
Wirek, Bill, 129–30
Wishard, Emmitt, 4
Wolf Brand chili, 223
Wolff, Roger, 17
Woodhaven Country Club, 221, 222–23
Woodling, Gene
    during the 1940s, 24, 36
    during the 1950s, 105, 119, 126, 127, 131
Woods, Jane, 148
World Series
    during the 1940s, 45, 64–69, 81, 97, photo
        section
    during the 1950s, 120
    during the 1960s, 104, 167
    during the 1970s, 158
    during the 1980s, 219–20
    during the 1990s, 99, 149, 219–20, 221
World War II period, 17–18, 23–29, 44, 45, 109,
    photo section
Wright, George, 212, 213
Wynn, Early, 16, 45, 47, 55, 71
Wynn, Jimmy, 153

Yankee Stadium, hitting challenges, 118
Yost, Eddie, 55

Zahn, Geoff, 165
Zernial, Gus
    during the 1950 season, 88
    during the 1951 season, 84–85, 86, 87
    during the 1953 season, 94, 95
    during the 1956 season, 124
Ziegler, Bill, 196–97, 198
Zimmer, Don, 146, 206–7, 210, 211–12, 214
Zisk, Richie, 195, 196, 198, 207
Zoldak, Sam, 70

Lightning Source UK Ltd.
Milton Keynes UK
UKHW042048101122
411892UK00016B/149